T0276283

Selected Liturgies

The
Book of
Common
Prayer

and Administration of the Sacraments
and Other Rites
and Ceremonies of the Church

According to the use of
The Episcopal Church

 CHURCH
PUBLISHING
INCORPORATED

Liturgias Selectas

El Libro de Oración Común

y Administración de los Sacramentos
y otros Ritos
y Ceremonias de la Iglesia

Conforme al uso de
La Iglesia Episcopal

CHURCH
PUBLISHING
INCORPORATED

The Church Pension Fund
19 East 34th Street
New York, NY 10016

ISBN 978-1-64065-611-6 (paperback)
ISBN 978-1-64065-664-2 (ebook)

Table of Contents / *Índice*

Preface to Selected Liturgies

This edition of *Selections from the Book of Common Prayer* is provided for the convenience of communities that worship regularly in both English and Spanish. The English text is from the Book of Common Prayer, 1979, and the Spanish text is from El Libro de Oratió Común, Traducción de 2022.

After consultation with users of the previous edition of *Selections*, additions have been made and some items have been omitted. Emphasis has been given to the inclusion of rites that receive regular parish use: principally Holy Baptism, Holy Eucharist, Marriage, and Burial. In addition, this volume includes Morning and Evening Prayer, as well as Compline.

The previous edition included a small selection from The Psalter that was found to be inadequate in most circumstances. The reproduction of the entire Psalter in an abbreviated bilingual volume was judged to be impractical and thus the Psalter has been eliminated altogether. In its place, this volume includes all of the prayers and thanksgivings from the Book of Common Prayer, which were abridged in previous editions.

The rubrics will sometimes refer to Prayer Book material not included in this abbreviated bilingual edition. In such cases, the reference has been judiciously eliminated or, in some cases, a cross-reference is included to the English or Spanish full-text edition. Every attempt has been made to conform the rubrics and additional directions to the respective English or Spanish full-text edition but due to the abbreviated nature of this volume some variants do occur.

Prefacio a Liturgias Seleccionadas

Esta edición de *Selecciones del Libro de Oración Común* se proporciona para la comodidad de las comunidades que adoran regularmente tanto en inglés como en español. El texto en inglés es del Book of Common Prayer, 1979, y el texto en español es de El Libro de oración común, traducción de 2022.

Después de consultar con los usuarios de la edición anterior de *Selecciones*, se han hecho adiciones y se han omitido algunos elementos. Se ha hecho énfasis en la inclusión de ritos que reciben uso parroquial regular: principalmente el Santo Bautismo, la Santa Eucaristía, el Matrimonio y el Entierro. Además, este volumen incluye la Oración Matutina y Vespertina, así como las Completas.

La edición anterior incluía una pequeña selección de The Psalter que se consideró inadecuada en la mayoría de las circunstancias. Se consideró que la reproducción del Salterio completo en un volumen bilingüe abreviado ha sido juzgado impráctico y, por lo tanto, el Salterio ha sido eliminado por completo. En su lugar, este volumen incluye todas las oraciones y acciones de gracias del Libro de oración común, que fueron resumidas en ediciones anteriores.

Las rúbricas a veces se referirán al material del Libro de Oración no incluido en esta edición bilingüe abreviada. En tales casos, la referencia ha sido juiciosamente eliminada o, en algunos casos, se incluye una referencia cruzada a la edición de texto completo en inglés o español. Se ha hecho todo lo posible para adaptar las rúbricas y las instrucciones adicionales a las respectivas ediciones de texto completo en inglés o español, pero debido a la naturaleza abreviada de este volumen, se

When questions arise, clergy and worship leaders should refer to the directives of the English or Spanish full-text editions.

J. Neil Alexander
Custodian of the Book of Common Prayer

producen algunas variantes. Cuando surjan preguntas, el clero y los líderes de adoración deben consultar las directivas de las ediciones de texto completo en inglés o español.

J. Neil Alexander
Guardián del Libro de Oración Común

Preface

It is a most invaluable part of that blessed "liberty wherewith Christ hath made us free," that in his worship different forms and usages may without offence be allowed, provided the substance of the Faith be kept entire; and that, in every Church, what cannot be clearly determined to belong to Doctrine must be referred to Discipline; and therefore, by common consent and authority, may be altered, abridged, enlarged, amended, or otherwise disposed of, as may seem most convenient for the edification of the people," according to the various exigency of times and occasions."

The Church of England, to which the Protestant Episcopal Church in these States is indebted, under God, for her first foundation and a long continuance of nursing care and protection, hath, in the Preface of her Book of Common Prayer, laid it down as a rule, that "The particular Forms of Divine Worship, and the Rites and Ceremonies appointed to be used therein, being things in their own nature indifferent, and alterable, and so acknowledged; it is but reasonable that upon weighty and important considerations, according to the various exigency of times and occasions, such changes and alterations should be made therein, as to those that are in place of Authority should, from time to time, seem either necessary or expedient."

The same Church hath not only in her Preface, but likewise in her Articles and Homilies, declared the necessity and expediency of occasional alterations and amendments in her Forms of Public Worship; and we find accordingly, that, seeking to keep the happy mean between too much stiffness in refusing, and too much easiness in admitting variations in things once advisedly established, she hath, in the reign of several Princes, since the first compiling of her Liturgy in the time of Edward the Sixth, upon just and weighty

Prefacio

Es una parte muy inestimable de la bendita «libertad con que Cristo nos hizo libres» permitir, sin ofensa alguna, diferentes formas y prácticas en su liturgia, con tal que se conserve íntegra la esencia de la Fe; y que en cada Iglesia lo que no se puede determinar claramente como parte de la Doctrina se refiere a la Disciplina; y por tanto con el consentimiento común y la autoridad, se puede modificar, abreviar, ampliar, enmendar o disponer en otra forma, si es más conveniente para la edificación del pueblo, y «de acuerdo con las distintas exigencias de los tiempos y de las ocasiones».

La Iglesia de Inglaterra, a la que gracias a Dios, debe la Iglesia Protestante Episcopal en estos Estados su primer establecimiento, y por mucho tiempo su mantenimiento, cuidado y protección, tiene como regla en el Prefacio de su Libro de Oración Común que: «Las Fórmulas particulares del Culto Divino y los Ritos y Ceremonias designados para el mismo, son cosas indiferentes y alterables por su naturaleza y, así se reconocen; por consiguiente, es razonable que, después de consideraciones graves e importantes, y de acuerdo con las diversas exigencias de los tiempos y las ocasiones, puedan hacerse tales cambios y alteraciones, si aquellos constituidos en autoridad, los juzgaren, de tiempo en tiempo, necesarios y convenientes».

Esa misma Iglesia ha declarado, no solo en su Prefacio, sino también en sus Artículos y en las Homilías, la necesidad y conveniencia de hacer alteraciones y enmiendas ocasionales en sus Fórmulas para el Culto Público; y, por consiguiente, vemos que, procurando conservar el medio feliz entre la demasiada rigidez en rehusar, y la demasiada facilidad en admitir alteraciones en las cosas ya deliberadamente establecidas, ha permitido en los reinos de varios Príncipes,

considerations her thereunto moving, yielded to make such alterations in some particulars, as in their respective times were thought convenient; yet so as that the main body and essential parts of the same (as well in the chiefest materials, as in the frame and order thereof) have still been continued firm and unshaken.

Her general aim in these different reviews and alterations hath been, as she further declares in her said Preface, to do that which, according to her best understanding, might most tend to the preservation of peace and unity in the Church; the procuring of reverence, and the exciting of piety and devotion in the worship of God; and, finally, the cutting off occasion, from them that seek occasion, of cavil or quarrel against her Liturgy. And although, according to her judgment, there be not any thing in it contrary to the Word of God, or to sound doctrine, or which a godly man may not with a good conscience use and submit unto, or which is not fairly defensible, if allowed such just and favourable construction as in common equity ought to be allowed to all human writings; yet upon the principles already laid down, it cannot but be supposed that further alterations would in time be found expedient. Accordingly, a Commission for a review was issued in the year 1689: but this great and good work miscarried at that time; and the Civil Authority has not since thought proper to revive it by any new Commission.

But when in the course of Divine Providence, these American States became independent with respect to civil government, their ecclesiastical independence was necessarily included; and the different religious denominations of Christians in these States were left at full and equal liberty to model and organize their respective Churches, and forms of worship, and discipline, in such manner as they might judge most convenient for their future prosperity; consistently with the constitution and laws of their country.

The attention of this Church was in the first place drawn to those alterations in the Liturgy which became necessary

desde la primera compilación de su Liturgia en tiempos de Eduardo Sexto, hacer alteraciones en ciertos casos, creyéndose conveniente en sus respectivas épocas, por justas y poderosas consideraciones; pero de tal manera que, el cuerpo principal y las partes esenciales de la Liturgia (tanto en las materias importantes como en su estructura y orden) han permanecido aún firmes e inmutables.

Su objeto generalmente en estas diferentes revisiones y alteraciones ha sido, como lo declara más adelante un su antedicho Prefacio, hacer lo que más tienda, según su mejor comprensión, a conservar la unidad y la paz en la Iglesia; mantener la reverencia y estimular la piedad y la devoción en el culto de Dios; y, finalmente, eliminar los motivos que den lugar a reparos y disputas sobre su Liturgia. Y aunque, según su criterio, nada hay en ello contrario a la Palabra de Dios y a la sana Doctrina, a lo que una persona piadosa no pudiese en conciencia practicar y someterse, o que no pudiese defender razonablemente, si es que tal justa y conveniente construcción es permitida, como en justicia se permite en todos los escritos humanos; sin embargo, de conformidad con las razones ya expuestas, no se deja de suponer que, en el transcurso de los tiempos, sean necesarias otras alteraciones. En efecto, en el año 1689 una comisión fue designada para hacer una revisión; pero esa labor conveniente e importante se frustró en aquel tiempo y, desde entonces, la Autoridad Civil no ha creído oportuno designar otra comisión que la lleve a efecto.

Pero cuando estos Estados Americanos en el curso de la Providencia Divina se independizaron en lo que respecta al gobierno civil, su independencia eclesiástica quedó necesariamente incluida; y las diferentes denominaciones religiosas de los Cristianos en estos Estados quedaron en igual y completa libertad para modelar y organizar sus respectivas Iglesias, sus formas de culto y disciplina, de la manera que creyeron más conveniente para su prosperidad futura, de acuerdo con la constitución y las leyes de su país.

Esta Iglesia puso su atención, en primer lugar, en las alteraciones a la Liturgia que se hacían necesarias en

in the prayers for our Civil Rulers, in consequence of the Revolution. And the principal care herein was to make them conformable to what ought to be the proper end of all such prayers, namely, that "Rulers may have grace, wisdom, and understanding to execute justice, and to maintain truth;" and that the people "may lead quiet and peaceable lives, in all godliness and honesty."

But while these alterations were in review before the Convention, they could not but, with gratitude to God, embrace the happy occasion which was offered to them (uninfluenced and unrestrained by any worldly authority whatsoever) to take a further review of the Public Service, and to establish such other alterations and amendments therein as might be deemed expedient.

It seems unnecessary to enumerate all the different alterations and amendments. They will appear, and it is to be hoped, the reasons of them also, upon a comparison of this with the Book of Common Prayer of the Church of England. In which it will also appear that this Church is far from intending to depart from the Church of England in any essential point of doctrine, discipline, or worship; or further than local circumstances require.

And now, this important work being brought to a conclusion, it is hoped the whole will be received and examined by every true member of our Church, and every sincere Christian, with a meek, candid, and charitable frame of mind; without prejudice or prepossessions; seriously considering what Christianity is, and what the truths of the Gospel are; and earnestly beseeching Almighty God to accompany with his blessing every endeavour for promulgating them to mankind in the clearest, plainest, most affecting and majestic manner, for the sake of Jesus Christ, our blessed Lord and Saviour.

Philadelphia, October, 1789.

las oraciones por nuestras Autoridades Civiles, como consecuencia de la Revolución. Y su cuidado principal consistió en conformarlas a lo que debe ser el propósito de tales oraciones, esto es, que: «Las Autoridades Civiles obtengan gracia, sabiduría y entendimiento para administrar justicia y sostener la verdad»; y que el pueblo «disfrute de una vida tranquila y pacífica en toda piedad y honestidad».

Pero mientras se revisaban estas alteraciones ante la Convención, no se pudo menos que aprovechar, con gratitud a Dios, la feliz ocasión que se les ofrecía para hacer una nueva revisión del Culto Público, sin la influencia y restricción de autoridad temporal alguna, y establecer las alteraciones y enmiendas que se estimaron convenientes.

Es innecesario enumerar todas las distintas enmiendas y alteraciones. Serán evidentes, y se espera, sus razones también, al comparar este con el Libro de Oración Común de la Iglesia de Inglaterra. Por lo que también se notará que esta Iglesia no ha intentado apartarse de la Iglesia de Inglaterra en nada de lo que es esencial a la doctrina, a la disciplina o al culto; a no ser lo que las circunstancias locales exijan.

Y ahora, concluida esta importante obra, esperamos que en su totalidad sea recibida y examinada por cada miembro verdadero de nuestra Iglesia, y por todos los Cristianos sinceros, con una disposición humilde, justa y bondadosa; sin prejuicios ni preocupaciones, considerando con seriedad lo que es el Cristianismo, y lo que son las verdades del Evangelio, rogando encarecidamente a Dios Todopoderoso que acompañe con su Bendición todos los esfuerzos que se hacen para promulgarlas a toda la humanidad, de la manera más clara, sencilla, conmovedora y majestuosa, por amor de Jesucristo, nuestro bendito Señor y Salvador.

Filadelfia, octubre de 1789.

Daily Morning Prayer: Rite Two

The Officiant begins the service with one or more of these sentences of Scripture, or with the versicle "Lord, open our lips" on page 28.

Advent

Watch, for you do not know when the master of the house will come, in the evening, or at midnight, or at cockcrow, or in the morning, lest he come suddenly and find you asleep. *Mark 13:35, 36*

In the wilderness prepare the way of the Lord, make straight in the desert a highway for our God.   *Isaiah 40:3*

The glory of the Lord shall be revealed, and all flesh shall see it together.   *Isaiah 40:5*

Christmas

Behold, I bring you good news of a great joy which will come to all the people; for to you is born this day in the city of David, a Savior, who is Christ the Lord.   *Luke 2:10, 11*

Behold, the dwelling of God is with mankind. He will dwell with them, and they shall be his people, and God himself will be with them, and be their God.   *Revelation 21:3*

Oración de la Mañana

Quien oficia comienza con uno o más de los siguientes versículos, o diciendo «Señor, ábrenos los labios» de la página 29.

Adviento

Estén alertas, pues no saben cuándo llegará el señor de la casa; si a la tarde, o a medianoche, o al canto del gallo, o en la mañana. ¡No llegue de repente y los halle *dormidos*! *Marcos 13:35, 36*

Preparen en el desierto el camino del Señor, tracen en la llanura una senda recta para nuestro Dios.   *Isaías 40:3*

Se manifestará la gloria del Señor, y todo ser viviente la verá. *Isaías 40:5*

Navidad

¡Miren! Les traigo buenas noticias de gran alegría para toda la gente: Hoy les nace en la ciudad de David un Liberador, Cristo el Señor.   *Lucas 2:10, 11*

¡Miren! La morada de Dios establecida con la humanidad. Él habitará con la gente y serán su pueblo; Dios mismo habitará con su pueblo y será su Dios.   *Apocalipsis 21:3*

Epiphany

Nations shall come to your light, and kings to the brightness of your rising.   *Isaiah 60:3*

I will give you as a light to the nations, that my salvation may reach to the end of the earth.   *Isaiah 49:6b*

From the rising of the sun to its setting my Name shall be great among the nations, and in every place incense shall be offered to my Name, and a pure offering; for my Name shall be great among the nations, says the Lord of hosts. *Malachi 1:11*

Lent

If we say we have no sin, we deceive ourselves, and the truth is not in us, but if we confess our sins, God, who is faithful and just, will forgive our sins and cleanse us from all unrighteousness.   *I John 1:8, 9*

Rend your hearts and not your garments. Return to the Lord your God, for he is gracious and merciful, slow to anger and abounding in steadfast love, and repents of evil.   *Joel 2:13*

I will arise and go to my father, and I will say to him, "Father, I have sinned against heaven and before you; I am no longer worthy to be called your son."   *Luke 15:18, 19*

To the Lord our God belong mercy and forgiveness, because we have rebelled against him and have not obeyed the voice of the Lord our God by following his laws which he set before us.   *Daniel 9:9, 10*

Jesus said, "If anyone would come after me, let him deny himself and take up his cross and follow me."   *Mark 8:34*

Epifanía

Las naciones vendrán a tu luz, y gobernantes al resplandor de tu amanecer.   *Isaías 60:3*

Te doy como luz a las naciones para que mi liberación llegue hasta los confines de la tierra.   *Isaías 49:6b*

Desde la salida del sol hasta su ocaso, grande será mi nombre entre las naciones, y en cada lugar se ofrecerá incienso a mi nombre, y una ofrenda pura; pues grande será mi nombre entre las naciones, dice el Soberano de los ejércitos del cielo. *Malaquías 1:11*

Cuaresma

Si decimos que no tenemos pecado, nos engañamos, y carecemos de la verdad; pero si confesamos nuestros pecados, Dios, fiel y justo, nos los perdonará y nos limpiará de toda injusticia.   *1 Juan 1:8, 9*

Rasguen sus corazones, no sus vestidos. Regresen a Dios, que es clemente y compasivo, lento a enojarse y de gran amor, y se arrepiente de sus castigos.   *Joel 2:13*

Me levantaré, iré a mi padre y le diré: «Padre, he pecado contra el cielo y contra ti; ya no merezco llamarme tu hijo». *Lucas 15:18, 19*

Nuestro Señor es un Dios de misericordia y perdón, aunque nos rebelamos contra él y no le prestamos atención ni obedecemos sus leyes.   *Daniel 9:9, 10*

Jesús dijo: «Si alguien quiere venir en pos de mí, niéguese a sí mismo, tome su cruz y sígame».   *Marcos 8:34*

Holy Week

All we like sheep have gone astray; we have turned every one to his own way; and the Lord has laid on him the iniquity of us all. *Isaiah 53:6*

Is it nothing to you, all you who pass by? Look and see if there is any sorrow like my sorrow which was brought upon me, whom the Lord has afflicted. *Lamentations 1:12*

Easter Season, including Ascension Day and the Day of Pentecost

Alleluia! Christ is risen.

The Lord is risen indeed. Alleluia!

On this day the Lord has acted; we will rejoice and be glad in it. *Psalm 118:24*

Thanks be to God, who gives us the victory through our Lord Jesus Christ. *1 Corinthians 15:57*

If then you have been raised with Christ, seek the things that are above, where Christ is, seated at the right hand of God. *Colossians 3:1*

Christ has entered, not into a sanctuary made with hands, a copy of the true one, but into heaven itself, now to appear in the presence of God on our behalf. *Hebrews 9:24*

You shall receive power when the Holy Spirit has come upon you; and you shall be my witnesses in Jerusalem, and in all Judea, and Samaria, and to the ends of the earth. *Acts 1:8*

Trinity Sunday

Holy, holy, holy is the Lord God Almighty, who was, and is, and is to come! *Revelation 4:8*

Semana Santa

Todos nos hemos extraviado como ovejas; cada cual se apartó por su camino; y Dios ha cargado sobre él nuestro pecado.   *Isaías 53:6*

Y ustedes que pasan de lado, ¿no se conmueven? Observen y juzguen si hay dolor como el mío o angustia como la que el Señor me ha enviado.   *Lamentaciones 1:12*

Durante el tiempo de Pascua,
incluyendo día de la Ascensión y día de Pentecostés

¡Aleluya! Cristo ha resucitado.

Es verdad: El Señor ha resucitado. ¡Aleluya!

Este es el día que hizo el Señor; gocémonos y alegrémonos en él.   *Salmo 118:24*

Demos gracias a Dios, que nos concede la victoria mediante nuestro Señor Jesucristo.   *1 Corintios 15:57*

Si han resucitado con Cristo, busquen las cosas de arriba donde está Cristo sentado a la diestra de Dios.
Colosenses 3:1

Cristo no entró en un santuario hecho por manos, imitación del verdadero, sino en el mismo cielo, para presentarse ahora ante Dios a nuestro favor.   *Hebreos 9:24*

Recibirán la fuerza del Espíritu Santo cuando venga sobre ustedes; y testificarán de mí en Jerusalén, en toda Judea, y Samaria, y hasta los confines de la tierra.   *Hechos 1:8*

Domingo de la Santísima Trinidad

¡Santo, santo, santo el Señor Dios Todopoderoso, que era, que es, y que ha de venir!   *Apocalipsis 4:8*

All Saints and other Major Saints' Days

We give thanks to the Father, who has made us worthy to share in the inheritance of the saints in light.   *Colossians 1:12*

You are no longer strangers and sojourners, but fellow citizens with the saints and members of the household of God.   *Ephesians 2:19*

Their sound has gone out into all lands, and their message to the ends of the world.   *Psalm 19:4*

Occasions of Thanksgiving

Give thanks to the Lord, and call upon his Name; make known his deeds among the peoples.   *Psalm 105:1*

At any Time

Grace to you and peace from God our Father and the Lord Jesus Christ.   *Philippians 1:2*

I was glad when they said to me, "Let us go to the house of the Lord."   *Psalm 122:1*

Let the words of my mouth and the meditation of my heart be acceptable in your sight, O Lord, my strength and my redeemer.   *Psalm 19:14*

Send out your light and your truth, that they may lead me, and bring me to your holy hill and to your dwelling.
Psalm 43:3

The Lord is in his holy temple; let all the earth keep silence before him.   *Habakkuk 2:20*

The hour is coming, and now is, when the true worshipers will worship the Father in spirit and truth, for such the Father seeks to worship him.   *John 4:23*

Thus says the high and lofty One who inhabits eternity, whose name is Holy, "I dwell in the high and holy place and

*Día de Todos los Santos y Santas,
y otras fiestas mayores de santos y santas*

Le damos gracias al Padre, que nos hizo *dignos* de compartir de la herencia de *los santos* en la luz.   *Colosenses 1:12*

Ustedes ya no son extranjeros ni migrantes: Ahora son conciudadanos con los santos y miembros de la familia de Dios.   *Efesios 2:19*

Por toda la tierra resuena su voz, y hasta los confines del mundo llega su mensaje.   *Salmo 19:4*

Para expresar agradecimiento

Den gracias al Señor, invoquen su nombre; den a conocer sus hazañas entre los pueblos.   *Salmo 105:1*

En cualquier ocasión

Gracia y paz a ustedes de parte de Dios nuestro Padre y del Señor Jesucristo.   *Filipenses 1:2*

Me alegré cuando me dijeron: «Vamos a la casa del Señor».
Salmo 122:1

Que las palabras de mi boca y la meditación de mi corazón sean de tu agrado, Dios, mi roca y mi redentor.
Salmo 19:14

Envía tu luz y tu verdad para que me guíen y me conduzcan a tu monte santo y a tu morada.   *Salmo 43:3*

Dios está en su santo templo: ¡Calle ante Dios toda la tierra!   *Habacuc 2:20*

Viene la hora, y ha llegado, en que los verdaderos fieles rendirán culto a Dios en espíritu y en verdad. Esos son los que el Padre busca para que lo adoren.   *Juan 4:23*

Así dice el alto y sublime, el que habita en la eternidad cuyo nombre es Santo: «Yo habito en santidad en las alturas;

also with the one who has a contrite and humble spirit, to revive the spirit of the humble and to revive the heart of the contrite." *Isaiah 57:15*

The following Confession of Sin may then be said; or the Office may continue at once with "Lord, open our lips."

Confession of Sin

The Officiant says to the people

Dearly beloved, we have come together in the presence of Almighty God our heavenly Father, to set forth his praise, to hear his holy Word, and to ask, for ourselves and on behalf of others, those things that are necessary for our life and our salvation. And so that we may prepare ourselves in heart and mind to worship him, let us kneel in silence, and with penitent and obedient hearts confess our sins, that we may obtain forgiveness by his infinite goodness and mercy.

or this

Let us confess our sins against God and our neighbor.

Silence may be kept.

Officiant and People together, all kneeling

Most merciful God,
we confess that we have sinned against you
in thought, word, and deed,
by what we have done,
and by what we have left undone.
We have not loved you with our whole heart;
we have not loved our neighbors as ourselves.
We are truly sorry and we humbly repent.
For the sake of your Son Jesus Christ,
have mercy on us and forgive us;
that we may delight in your will,
and walk in your ways,
to the glory of your Name. Amen.

pero siempre estoy con los de espíritu contrito y humillado, para reanimar el espíritu de los humildes y el corazón de los oprimidos». *Isaías 57:15*

Se puede continuar con la confesión de pecados; o bien, quien oficia puede pasar directamente a «Señor, ábrenos los labios.»

Confesión de pecado

Quien oficia dice:

Confesemos nuestros pecados contra Dios y nuestro prójimo.

O bien:

Amadas hermanas y hermanos: Nos hemos reunido en la presencia del Dios de todo poder, nuestro Padre celestial, para alabarlo, escuchar su santa Palabra, y pedirle por nuestras necesidades y por nuestra salvación. Preparemos la mente y el corazón para adorarlo. Confesemos nuestros pecados, arrodillándonos en silencio con corazones penitentes y obedientes para que, por la infinita bondad y misericordia de Dios, obtengamos su perdón.

Se puede guardar un periodo de silencio.

Dios de misericordia,
confesamos que hemos pecado contra ti
de pensamiento, palabra y obra,
por lo que hemos hecho
y por lo que hemos dejado sin hacer.
No te hemos amado de todo corazón;
no hemos amado al prójimo como a *nosotros mismos*.
Sincera y humildemente nos arrepentimos.
Por tu Hijo Jesucristo,
ten piedad de *nosotros* y perdónanos;
así tu voluntad será nuestra alegría
y caminaremos en tus sendas
para gloria de tu nombre. Amén.

The Priest alone stands and says

Almighty God have mercy on you, forgive you all your sins through our Lord Jesus Christ, strengthen you in all goodness, and by the power of the Holy Spirit keep you in eternal life. *Amen.*

A deacon or lay person using the preceding form remains kneeling, and substitutes "us" for "you" and "our" for "your."

The Invitatory and Psalter

All stand

Officiant	Lord, open our lips.
People	And our mouth shall proclaim your praise.

Officiant and People

Glory to the Father, and to the Son, and to the Holy Spirit: as it was in the beginning, is now, and will be for ever. Amen.

Except in Lent, add   Alleluia.

Then follows one of the Invitatory Psalms, Venite or Jubilate.

One of the following Antiphons may be sung or said with the Invitatory Psalm

Si un presbítero *está presente, declara de pie:*

Dios Todopoderoso se apiade de *ustedes*, perdone todos *sus* pecados por nuestro Señor Jesucristo, *los* fortalezca en toda virtud, y por el poder del Espíritu Santo *los* guarde en la vida eterna. **Amén.**

Un diácono o una persona laica hace la misma declaración, pero de rodillas, y sustituye «ustedes» con «nosotros», «sus» con «nuestros» y «los» con «nos».

Invitatorio y salterio

Todos de pie. Quien oficia dice:

Señor, ábrenos los labios.
Y nuestra boca proclamará tu alabanza.

Oficiante y pueblo:

Gloria al Padre, y al Hijo y al Espíritu Santo:
Como era en el principio, ahora y por los siglos de los siglos.
Amén.

Excepto en Cuaresma, se agrega:

¡Aleluya!

Sigue uno de los salmos invitatorios: el Venite *o el* Jubilate. *Con el salmo invitatorio se puede cantar o decir una de las siguientes antífonas:*

In Advent

Worship the Lord in the beauty of holiness. Come let us adore him.

On the Twelve Days of Christmas

Alleluia. To us a child is born: Come let us adore him. Alleluia.

From the Epiphany through the Baptism of Christ, and on the Feasts of the Transfiguration and Holy Cross

The Lord has shown forth his glory: Come let us adore him.

In Lent

The Lord is full of compassion and mercy: Come let us adore him.

From Easter Day until the Ascension

Alleluia. The Lord is risen indeed: Come let us adore him. Alleluia.

From Ascension Day until the Day of Pentecost

Alleluia. Christ the Lord has ascended into heaven: Come let us adore him. Alleluia.

On the Day of Pentecost

Alleluia. The Spirit of the Lord renews the face of the earth: Come let us adore him. Alleluia.

On Trinity Sunday

Father, Son, and Holy Spirit, one God: Come let us adore him.

On other Sundays and weekdays

The earth is the Lord's, for he made it: Come let us adore him.

En Adviento

Nuestro Rey y Salvador se acerca: ¡Vengan, adorémoslo!

Durante los doce días de Navidad

¡Aleluya! Nos ha nacido un niño: ¡Vengan, adorémoslo!
¡Aleluya!

*Desde Epifanía hasta el Bautismo del Señor y en las fiestas
de la Transfiguración y la Santa Cruz*

El Señor nos ha mostrado su gloria: ¡Vengan, adorémoslo!

En Cuaresma

El Señor es clemente y compasivo. ¡Vengan, adorémoslo!

Desde el Día de Pascua hasta la Ascensión

¡Aleluya! Es verdad: El Señor ha resucitado. ¡Vengan,
adorémoslo! ¡Aleluya!

De la Ascensión al Día de Pentecostés

¡Aleluya! Cristo el Señor ha subido al cielo. ¡Vengan,
adorémoslo! ¡Aleluya!

El Día de Pentecostés

¡Aleluya! El Espíritu del Señor renueva la faz de la tierra.
¡Vengan, adorémoslo! ¡Aleluya!

El Domingo de la Santísima Trinidad

Padre, Hijo y Espíritu Santo, un solo Dios. ¡Vengan,
adorémoslo!

Otros domingos y entre semana

Del Señor es la tierra, porque la hizo. ¡Vengan, adorémoslo!

or this

Worship the Lord in the beauty of holiness: Come let us adore him.

or this

The mercy of the Lord is everlasting: Come let us adore him.

The Alleluias in the following Antiphons are used only in Easter Season.

On Feasts of the Incarnation

[Alleluia.] The Word was made flesh and dwelt among us: Come let us adore him. [Alleluia.]

On All Saints and other Major Saints' Days

[Alleluia.] The Lord is glorious in his saints: Come let us adore him. [Alleluia.]

Venite   *Psalm 95:1-7*

Come, let us sing to the Lord; *
    let us shout for joy to the Rock of our salvation.
Let us come before his presence with thanksgiving *
    and raise a loud shout to him with psalms.

For the Lord is a great God, *
    and a great King above all gods.
In his hand are the caverns of the earth, *
    and the heights of the hills are his also.
The sea is his, for he made it, *
    and his hands have molded the dry land.

Come, let us bow down, and bend the knee, *
    and kneel before the Lord our Maker.
For he is our God,

Adoren al Señor en la hermosura de la santidad. ¡Vengan, adorémoslo!

La misericordia del Señor es eterna. ¡Vengan, adorémoslo!

En las antífonas que siguen, los aleluyas se usan solo en el tiempo de Pascua.

En la Fiesta de la Encarnación

[¡Aleluya!] La Palabra se hizo carne y habitó con *nosotros.* ¡Vengan, adorémoslo! [¡Aleluya!]

En Día de Todos los Santos y Santas, y otras fiestas mayores de santos y santas

[¡Aleluya!] El Señor es glorioso en sus santos y santas. ¡Vengan, adorémoslo! [¡Aleluya!]

Venite   *Salmo 95:1-7*

¡Vengan, cantémosle a Dios, *
    con gritos de alegría a la Roca que nos salva!
Acerquémonos a Dios dándole gracias; *
    cantémosle salmos con brío.

Porque el Señor es un gran Dios *
    y un gran Rey sobre todos los dioses.
En su mano están las cavernas más profundas *
    y suyas son las cumbres de los montes.
Suyo es el mar, pues Dios lo hizo *
    y sus manos formaron la tierra firme.

¡Vengan! Inclinémonos y postrémonos *
    de rodillas ante Dios que nos creó,
Porque él es nuestro Dios;

and we are the people of his pasture and the sheep of his hand. *
  Oh, that today you would hearken to his voice!

On Ash Wednesday and Fridays in Lent, continue

Harden not your hearts,
as your forebears did in the wilderness, *
    at Meribah, and on that day at Massah,
    when they tempted me.
They put me to the test, *
    though they had seen my works.
Forty years long I detested that generation and said, *
    "This people are wayward in their hearts;
    they do not know my ways."
So I swore in my wrath, *
    "They shall not enter into my rest."

Jubilate   *Psalm 100*

Be joyful in the Lord, all you lands; *
    serve the Lord with gladness
    and come before his presence with a song.

Know this: The Lord himself is God; *
    he himself has made us, and we are his;
    we are his people and the sheep of his pasture.

Enter his gates with thanksgiving;
go into his courts with praise; *
    give thanks to him and call upon his Name.

For the Lord is good;
his mercy is everlasting; *
    and his faithfulness endures from age to age.

*In Easter Week, in place of an Invitatory Psalm, the following is sung
or said. It may also be used daily until the Day of Pentecost.*

somos el pueblo que apacienta, el redil bajo su mano. *
    ¡Ojalá escuchen hoy su voz!

El Miércoles de Ceniza y los Viernes de Cuaresma, continúe

No pongan duro el corazón
como en Meriba *
    ni como en el desierto de Masá,
    cuando sus antepasados me tentaron,
cuando me pusieron a prueba, *
    aunque habían visto mis hechos.
Por cuarenta años estuve disgustado; *
    dije: «Sus corazones se desvían
    y no conocen mis caminos».
Por eso juré en mi indignación: *
    «Jamás entrarán en mi reposo».

Jubilate   *Salmo 100*

¡Cante al Señor toda la tierra! *
    Sirvan al Señor con alegría;
    vengan cantando a su presencia.

Reconozcan que el Señor es Dios; *
    Dios nos hizo y somos suyos,
    su pueblo, el rebaño que apacienta.

Entren por sus puertas dando gracias;
lleguen a sus atrios alabando; *
    denle gracias y bendigan su nombre.

Porque Dios es bueno;
su misericordia, eterna; *
    y su lealtad, por todas las generaciones.

*En tiempo de Pascua, en lugar de un salmo invitatorio, se canta
o dice lo siguiente. También se puede usar a diario hasta el día de
Pentecostés.*

Christ our Passover   *Pascha nostrum*

1 Corinthians 5:7-8; Romans 6:9-11; 1 Corinthians 15:20-22

Alleluia.
Christ our Passover has been sacrificed for us; *
    therefore let us keep the feast,
Not with the old leaven, the leaven of malice and evil, *
    but with the unleavened bread of sincerity and truth.
    Alleluia.

Christ being raised from the dead will never die again; *
    death no longer has dominion over him.
The death that he died, he died to sin, once for all; *
    but the life he lives, he lives to God.
So also consider yourselves dead to sin, *
    and alive to God in Jesus Christ our Lord. Alleluia.

Christ has been raised from the dead, *
    the first fruits of those who have fallen asleep.
For since by a man came death, *
    by a man has come also the resurrection of the dead.
For as in Adam all die, *
    so also in Christ shall all be made alive. Alleluia.

Then follows

The Psalm or Psalms Appointed

At the end of the Psalms is sung or said

Glory to the Father, and to the Son, and to the Holy Spirit: *
    as it was in the beginning, is now, and will be for ever.
    Amen.

Cristo nuestra Pascua   *Pascha nostrum*

1 Corintios 5:7-8; Romanos 6:9-11; 1 Corintios 15:20-22

¡Aleluya!
Cristo, nuestra Pascua, se ha sacrificado por *nosotros*; *
    por tanto, celebremos la fiesta.
No con la vieja levadura de malicia y maldad, *
    sino con el pan sin levadura, de sinceridad y verdad.
        ¡Aleluya!

Levantado de entre los muertos, Cristo nunca morirá; *
    la muerte ya no reina sobre él.
En su muerte, murió al pecado una vez por siempre, *
    pero en su vida, vive para Dios.
Así también ustedes, piensen que están *muertos* al pecado *
    pero viven para Dios, en Cristo Jesús nuestro Señor.
        ¡Aleluya!

Cristo ha resucitado de entre los muertos, *
    primer fruto y ofrenda de quienes se han dormido.
Así como por un hombre llegó la muerte, *
    por otro ha llegado la resurrección.
Así como en Adán toda persona muere, *
    así también en Cristo será vivificada. ¡Aleluya!

Y a continuación:

Los salmos del día

Al final del salmo (o los salmos) se canta o se dice:

Gloria al Padre, y al Hijo y al Espíritu Santo: *
    como era en el principio, ahora y siempre
    por los siglos de los siglos. Amén.

The Lessons

One or two Lessons, as appointed, are read, the Reader first saying

A Reading (Lesson) from _____.

A citation giving chapter and verse may be added.

After each Lesson the Reader may say

      The Word of the Lord.
Answer   Thanks be to God.

Or the Reader may say   Here ends the Lesson (Reading).

Silence may be kept after each Reading. One of the following Canticles, or one of those on BCP pages 47-52 (Canticles 1-7), is sung or said after each Reading. If three Lessons are used, the Lesson from the Gospel is read after the second Canticle.

8 The Song of Moses *Cantemus Domino*
Exodus 15:1-6, 11-13, 17-18

Especially suitable for use in Easter Season

I will sing to the Lord, for he is lofty and uplifted; *
    the horse and its rider has he hurled into the sea.
The Lord is my strength and my refuge; *
    the Lord has become my Savior.
This is my God and I will praise him, *
    the God of my people and I will exalt him.
The Lord is a mighty warrior; *
    Yahweh is his Name.
The chariots of Pharaoh and his army has he hurled into the sea; *
    the finest of those who bear armor have been drowned
        in the Red Sea.
The fathomless deep has overwhelmed them; *
    they sank into the depths like a stone.
Your right hand, O Lord, is glorious in might; *
    your right hand, O Lord, has overthrown the enemy.

Las lecturas

Se proclaman una o dos lecturas, según corresponda; quien lee dice:

Lectura de _____.

Se puede agregar capítulo y versículo.

Después de cada lectura, quien lee puede decir:

Palabra de Dios

Demos gracias a Dios.

O bien quien lee puede decir Aquí concluye la lectura.

Después de cada lectura puede guardarse silencio. Entonces se canta o recita uno de los cánticos que siguen. Si se proclaman tres lecturas, la del evangelio se lee después del segundo cántico.

8 El Cántico de Moisés *Cantemus Domino*
Éxodo 15:1-6, 11-13, 17-18

Especialmente apropiado para el tiempo de Pascua.

Cantaré a Dios, porque es glorioso y sublime; *
    caballos y jinetes arrojó al mar.
El Señor es mi fortaleza y mi canción; *
    fue Dios quien me salvó.
Este es mi Dios y yo lo alabaré; *
    el Dios de mi pueblo, de su grandeza cantaré.
Dios es un guerrero poderoso; *
    su nombre es el Señor.
Hundió los carros y el ejército de Faraón; *
    sus mejores tropas sepultó en el Mar Rojo.
Quedaron cubiertos por el abismo; *
    se hundieron hasta el fondo como piedras.
Tu mano, Señor, es poderosa; *
    tu diestra, Señor, ha conquistado al enemigo.
        ¿Quién como tú, Dios, entre los dioses?

Who can be compared with you, O Lord, among the gods? *
    who is like you, glorious in holiness,
    awesome in renown, and worker of wonders?
You stretched forth your right hand; *
    the earth swallowed them up.
With your constant love you led the people you redeemed; *
    with your might you brought them in safety to your
        holy dwelling.
You will bring them in and plant them *
    on the mount of your possession,
The resting-place you have made for yourself, O Lord, *
    the sanctuary, O Lord, that your hand has established.
The Lord shall reign *
    for ever and for ever.

Glory to the Father, and to the Son, and to the Holy Spirit: *
    as it was in the beginning, is now, and will be for ever.
    Amen.

9 The First Song of Isaiah *Ecce, Deus*
Isaiah 12:2-6

Surely, it is God who saves me; *
    I will trust in him and not be afraid.
For the Lord is my stronghold and my sure defense, *
    and he will be my Savior.
Therefore you shall draw water with rejoicing *
    from the springs of salvation.
And on that day you shall say, *
    Give thanks to the Lord and call upon his Name;
Make his deeds known among the peoples; *
    see that they remember that his Name is exalted.
Sing the praises of the Lord, for he has done great things, *
    and this is known in all the world.
Cry aloud, inhabitants of Zion, ring out your joy, *
    for the great one in the midst of you is the Holy One
        of Israel.

¿Quién como tú, glorioso en santidad, *
de gran renombre, autor de maravillas?
Extendiste tu diestra *
y la tierra se los tragó.
En misericordia guiaste al pueblo que liberaste; *
con poder lo protegiste y lo llevaste a tu santuario.
Tú lo traerás y lo sembrarás *
en el monte de tu herencia,
en la morada que hiciste para tu descanso, *
en el santuario que tu mano ha preparado.
El Señor reinará *
por los siglos de los siglos.

Gloria al Padre, y al Hijo y al Espíritu Santo: *
Como era en el principio, ahora y siempre por los siglos
de los siglos. Amén.

9 Primer cántico de Isaías *Ecce Deus*

Isaías 12:2-6

¡Mi salvación es Dios! *
En Dios pondré mi confianza y no temeré.
Porque el Señor es mi defensa y fortaleza; *
Dios será mi Liberador.
Y ustedes, alegres, sacarán agua *
de los manantiales de salvación.
En aquel día dirán: *
«Den gracias a Dios, invoquen su nombre;
anuncien a los pueblos sus proezas; *
recuérdenles lo grande que es su nombre.
Canten salmos al Señor por sus hazañas; *
Sus maravillas todo el mundo las conoce.
Canten fuerte, habitantes de Sion, griten de gozo, *
porque el grande entre ustedes es el Santo
de Israel».

Glory to the Father, and to the Son, and to the Holy Spirit: *
    as it was in the beginning, is now, and will be for ever.
        Amen.

10   The Second Song of Isaiah   *Quaerite Dominum*

Isaiah 55:6-11

Seek the Lord while he wills to be found; *
    call upon him when he draws near.
Let the wicked forsake their ways *
    and the evil ones their thoughts;
And let them turn to the Lord, and he will have compassion, *
    and to our God, for he will richly pardon.
For my thoughts are not your thoughts, *
    nor your ways my ways, says the Lord.
For as the heavens are higher than the earth, *
    so are my ways higher than your ways,
    and my thoughts than your thoughts.
For as rain and snow fall from the heavens *
    and return not again, but water the earth,
Bringing forth life and giving growth, *
    seed for sowing and bread for eating,
So is my word that goes forth from my mouth; *
    it will not return to me empty;
But it will accomplish that which I have purposed, *
    and prosper in that for which I sent it.

Glory to the Father, and to the Son, and to the Holy Spirit: *
    as it was in the beginning, is now, and will be for ever.
        Amen.

11   The Third Song of Isaiah   *Surge, illuminare*

Isaiah 60:1-3, 11a, 14c, 18-19

Arise, shine, for your light has come, *
    and the glory of the Lord has dawned upon you.
For behold, darkness covers the land; *
    deep gloom enshrouds the peoples.

Gloria al Padre, y al Hijo y al Espíritu Santo; *
   como era en el principio, ahora y siempre por los siglos
   de los siglos. Amén.

10 Segundo cántico de Isaías. *Quaerite Dominum*

Isaías 55:6-11

Busquen a Dios mientras se deje hallar; *
   llámenlo cuando se acerca.
Que el malvado abandone su camino, *
   y la injusta se aleje de sus planes;
que se vuelvan al Señor, y él les tendrá piedad; *
   a nuestro Dios, y él *los* perdonará.
«Porque mis pensamientos no son sus pensamientos, *
   ni mis caminos sus caminos», dice el Señor.
«Como más altos son los cielos que la tierra, *
   así son mis caminos más altos que los suyos,
   y mis pensamientos, más que los de ustedes.
Y como la lluvia y la nieve caen del cielo *
   y en vez de volver, riegan la tierra
y la hacen germinar y producir *
   semillas a sembrar y pan para comer,
así es la palabra que sale de mi boca: *
   no ha de volver a mí vacía,
sino que cumplirá mi encargo *
   y el propósito con que la envié».

Gloria al Padre, y al Hijo y al Espíritu Santo: *
   como era en el principio, ahora y siempre por los siglos
   de los siglos. Amén.

11 Tercer cántico de Isaías *Surge illuminare*

Isaías 60:1-3, 11a, 14c, 18-19

¡Levántate y brilla, que llegó tu luz, *
   y la gloria de Dios te ha iluminado!
Las tinieblas cubrirán la tierra; *
   y la oscuridad, los pueblos,

But over you the Lord will rise, *
    and his glory will appear upon you.
Nations will stream to your light, *
    and kings to the brightness of your dawning.
Your gates will always be open; *
    by day or night they will never be shut.
They will call you, The City of the Lord, *
    The Zion of the Holy One of Israel.
Violence will no more be heard in your land, *
    ruin or destruction within your borders.
You will call your walls, Salvation, *
    and all your portals, Praise.
The sun will no more be your light by day; *
    by night you will not need the brightness of the moon.
The Lord will be your everlasting light, *
    and your God will be your glory.

Glory to the Father, and to the Son, and to the Holy Spirit: *
    as it was in the beginning, is now, and will be for ever.
        Amen.

12 A Song of Creation *Benedicite, omnia opera Domini*
Song of the Three Young Men, 35-65

One or more sections of this Canticle may be used. Whatever the selection, it begins with the Invocation and concludes with the Doxology.

Invocation

Glorify the Lords, all you works of the Lord, *
    praise him and highly exalt him for ever.
In the firmament of his power, glorify the Lord, *
    praise him and highly exalt him for ever.

pero Dios amanecerá sobre ti, *
 y su gloria en ti descansará.
A tu luz andarán las naciones; *
 los gobernantes, al brillo de tu aurora.
Tus puertas estarán siempre abiertas; *
 no se cerrarán ni de día ni de noche.
Te llamarán «Ciudad del Señor, *
 Sion del Santo de Israel».
Nunca más oirás de violencia en tu tierra *
 ni de destrucción y ruina dentro de tus fronteras.
Llamarás a tus muros «Salvación», *
 y a tus puertas «Alabanza».
Ya no necesitarás la luz del sol durante el día *
 ni el brillo de la luna por la noche.
El Señor mismo será tu luz eterna; *
 Dios será tu gloria.

Gloria al Padre, y al Hijo y al Espíritu Santo: *
 como era en el principio, ahora y siempre por los siglos
 de los siglos. Amén.

12 Cántico de la creación *Benedicite omnia opera Domini*

El Cántico de los Tres Jóvenes, 35-65

*Se puede usar una o más secciones de este cántico, pero se empieza
siempre con la invocación y se concluye con la doxología.*

Invocación

¡Bendigan a Dios todas las obras del Señor! *
 Alábenlo siempre y canten su grandeza.
En la órbita de su poder, bendigan al Señor, *
 alábenlo siempre y canten su grandeza.

I   *The Cosmic Order*

Glorify the Lord, you angels and all powers of the Lord, *
    O heavens and all waters above the heavens.
Sun and moon and stars of the sky, glorify the Lord, *
    praise him and highly exalt him for ever.

Glorify the Lord, every shower of rain and fall of dew, *
    all winds and fire and heat.
Winter and summer, glorify the Lord, *
    praise him and highly exalt him for ever.

Glorify the Lord, O chill and cold, *
    drops of dew and flakes of snow.
Frost and cold, ice and sleet, glorify the Lord, *
    praise him and highly exalt him for ever.

Glorify the Lord, O nights and days, *
    O shining light and enfolding dark.
Storm clouds and thunderbolts, glorify the Lord, *
    praise him and highly exalt him for ever.

II   *The Earth and its Creatures*

Let the earth glorify the Lord, *
    praise him and highly exalt him for ever.
Glorify the Lord, O mountains and hills,
and all that grows upon the earth, *
    praise him and highly exalt him for ever.

Glorify the Lord, O springs of water, seas, and streams, *
    O whales and all that move in the waters.
All birds of the air, glorify the Lord, *
    praise him and highly exalt him for ever.

Glorify the Lord, O beasts of the wild, *
    and all you flocks and herds.
O men and women everywhere, glorify the Lord, *
    praise him and highly exalt him for ever.

I   El orden del universo

Bendigan a Dios, ángeles y poderes del Señor, *
  los cielos y las aguas de los cielos.
Sol, luna y estrellas de los cielos, bendigan al Señor. *
  Alábenlo siempre y canten su grandeza.

Bendigan a Dios, todas las lluvias y el rocío, *
  todos los vientos, el fuego y el calor.
Invierno y verano, bendigan al Señor. *
  Alábenlo siempre y canten su grandeza.

Bendigan al Señor, fríos y heladas, *
  copos de nieve y gotas de rocío.
Escarchas y hielos, bendigan al Señor, *
  Alábenlo siempre y canten su grandeza.

Que la noche y el día bendigan al Señor, *
  manto de oscuridad y luz brillante.
Nubarrones y truenos, bendigan al Señor, *
  alábenlo siempre y canten su grandeza.

II   La tierra y los seres vivientes

Bendiga al Señor la tierra entera, *
  alábelo siempre y cante su grandeza.
Bendigan a Dios, montañas, cerros,
y todo lo que brota de la tierra. *
  Alábenlo siempre y canten su grandeza.

Bendigan a Dios, ríos, arroyos, y mares, *
  ballenas y criaturas de las aguas.
Aves del cielo, bendigan al Señor, *
  alábenlo siempre y canten su grandeza.

Bendigan a Dios, bestias salvajes, *
  todos los rebaños y el ganado.
Mujeres y hombres, en todo lugar, bendigan al Señor, *
  alábenlo siempre y canten su grandeza.

III   The People of God

Let the people of God glorify the Lord, *
　　praise him and highly exalt him for ever.
Glorify the Lord, O priests and servants of the Lord, *
　　praise him and highly exalt him for ever.

Glorify the Lord, O spirits and souls of the righteous, *
　　praise him and highly exalt him for ever.
You that are holy and humble of heart, glorify the Lord, *
　　praise him and highly exalt him for ever.

Doxology

Let us glorify the Lord: Father, Son, and Holy Spirit; *
　　praise him and highly exalt him for ever.
In the firmament of his power, glorify the Lord, *
　　praise him and highly exalt him for ever.

13 A Song of Praise *Benedictus es, Domine*

Song of the Three Young Men, 29-34

Glory to you, Lord God of our fathers; *
　　you are worthy of praise; glory to you.
Glory to you for the radiance of your holy Name; *
　　we will praise you and highly exalt you for ever.

Glory to you in the splendor of your temple; *
　　on the throne of your majesty, glory to you.
Glory to you, seated between the Cherubim; *
　　we will praise you and highly exalt you for ever.

Glory to you, beholding the depths; *
　　in the high vault of heaven, glory to you.
Glory to you, Father, Son, and Holy Spirit; *
　　we will praise you and highly exalt you for ever.

III   *El pueblo de Dios*

El pueblo de Dios bendiga al Señor; *
    alábenlo siempre y canten su grandeza.
Bendigan a Dios, sacerdotes y *siervos* del Señor, *
    alábenlo siempre y canten su grandeza.

Bendigan a Dios, almas de *los justos*, *
    alábenlo siempre y canten su grandeza.
Santas, santos y gente humilde, bendigan al Señor, *
    alábenlo siempre y canten su grandeza.

Doxología

Bendigamos a Dios: Padre, Hijo y Espíritu Santo; *
    alabémoslo siempre y cantemos su grandeza.
Poderoso en el cielo, bendigamos a Dios, *
    alabémoslo siempre y cantemos su grandeza.

13   Cántico de alabanza   *Benedictus es, Domine*
Daniel 3:52-56 (parte deuterocanónica)

Bendito eres, SEÑOR, Dios de nuestros ancestros; *
    eres digno de alabanza y gloria.
Bendito y glorioso sea tu santo nombre; *
    te alabamos y exaltamos para siempre.

Bendito eres en el esplendor de tu templo; *
    en tu trono majestuoso, a ti la gloria.
Bendito sentado entre los querubines; *
    te alabamos y exaltamos para siempre.

Bendito eres al sondear los abismos; *
    en el firmamento del cielo, a ti la gloria.
Bendito eres Padre, Hijo y Espíritu Santo; *
    te alabamos y exaltamos para siempre.

14 A Song of Penitence *Kyrie Pantokrator*
Prayer of Manasseh, 1-2, 4, 6-7, 11-15

Especially suitable in Lent, and on other penitential occasions

O Lord and Ruler of the hosts of heaven, *
    God of Abraham, Isaac, and Jacob,
and of all their righteous offspring:
You made the heavens and the earth, *
    with all their vast array.
All things quake with fear at your presence; *
    they tremble because of your power.
But your merciful promise is beyond all measure; *
    it surpasses all that our minds can fathom.
O Lord, you are full of compassion, *
    long-suffering, and abounding in mercy.
You hold back your hand; *
    you do not punish as we deserve.
In your great goodness, Lord,
you have promised forgiveness to sinners, *
    that they may repent of their sin and be saved.
And now, O Lord, I bend the knee of my heart, *
    and make my appeal, sure of your gracious goodness.
I have sinned, O Lord, I have sinned, *
    and I know my wickedness only too well.
Therefore I make this prayer to you: *
    Forgive me, Lord, forgive me.
Do not let me perish in my sin, *
    nor condemn me to the depths of the earth.
For you, O Lord, are the God of those who repent, *
    and in me you will show forth your goodness.
    Unworthy as I am, you will save me,
in accordance with your great mercy, *
    and I will praise you without ceasing all the days of my life.
For all the powers of heaven sing your praises, *
    and yours is the glory to ages of ages. Amen.

14 Cántico de Penitencia *Kyrie Pantokrator*

Oración de Manasés, 1-2, 4, 6-7, 11-15

Especialmente adecuado para usarse en Cuaresma y ocasiones penitenciales.

Soberano Señor del universo, *
    Dios de Abraham, Isaac, Jacob
y de toda su justa descendencia:
Tú creaste los cielos y la tierra *
    en un gran despliegue de belleza.
Todas las cosas tiemblan ante tu presencia, *
    y se atemorizan ante tu poder.
Pero tu promesa de misericordia es tan inmensa *
    que sobrepasa todo entendimiento.
Tú, Señor, estás colmado de piedad, *
    de paciencia y de misericordia.
Refrenas el impulso de tu mano *
    y el castigo que nos merecemos.
En tu bondad, Señor, has prometido
perdonar a los que pecan *
    para que, *convertidos* del pecado, queden libres.
Y ahora, mi Dios, mi corazón se arrodilla *
    y hago mi petición confiando en tu misericordia.
He pecado, mi Dios, sí, he pecado, *
    y conozco mis iniquidades.
Y esto es lo que te suplico: *
    Perdóname, Señor, perdóname,
No dejes que me muera en mi pecado, *
    ni me condenes al fondo del abismo.
Porque tú eres el Dios de quienes se arrepienten, *
    y en mí se hará visible tu bondad.
    Aunque yo sea indigno, tú me salvarás
según tu gran misericordia, *
    y te alabaré sin pausa todos los días de mi vida.
Porque todo el universo te celebra *
    y tu gloria resplandece para siempre. Amén.

15 The Song of Mary *Magnificat*

Luke 1:46-55

My soul proclaims the greatness of the Lord,
my spirit rejoices in God my Savior; *
    for he has looked with favor on his lowly servant.
From this day all generations will call me blessed: *
    the Almighty has done great things for me,
and holy is his Name.
He has mercy on those who fear him *
    in every generation.
He has shown the strength of his arm, *
    he has scattered the proud in their conceit.
He has cast down the mighty from their thrones, *
    and has lifted up the lowly.
He has filled the hungry with good things, *
    and the rich he has sent away empty.
He has come to the help of his servant Israel, *
    for he has remembered his promise of mercy,
The promise he made to our fathers, *
    to Abraham and his children for ever.

Glory to the Father, and to the Son, and to the Holy Spirit: *
    as it was in the beginning, is now, and will be for ever.
        Amen.

16 The Song of Zechariah *Benedictus Dominus Deus*

Luke 1:68-79

Blessed be the Lord, the God of Israel; *
    he has come to his people and set them free.
He has raised up for us a mighty savior, *
    born of the house of his servant David.
Through his holy prophets he promised of old,
that he would save us from our enemies, *
    from the hands of all who hate us.
He promised to show mercy to our fathers *
    and to remember his holy covenant.

15 Cántico de María *Magníficat*

Lucas 1:46-55

Mi alma proclama la grandeza del Señor;
mi espíritu se alegra en Dios mi Salvador *
    que ha notado la humillación de su sierva.
Desde hoy, todas las generaciones me llamarán bendita: *
    Dios Poderoso me ha hecho grandes obras
y su nombre es santo.
Su misericordia alcanza a sus fieles *
    generación tras generación.
Desplegó la fuerza de su brazo *
    y dispersó a los soberbios de corazón.
Derribó a los poderosos de sus tronos*
    y levantó a la gente humilde.
Colmó de bienes al hambriento *
    y a los ricos despidió sin nada.
Ayudó a su siervo, el pueblo de Israel, *
    porque recuerda la misericordia prometida
a quienes vivieron antes que *nosotros*, *
    a Abrahán y a su descendencia por siempre.

Gloria al Padre, y al Hijo y al Espíritu Santo; *
    como era en el principio, ahora y siempre por los siglos
      de los siglos. Amén.

16 Cántico de Zacarías *Benedictus Dominus Deus*

Lucas 1:68-79

Bendito es el Señor Dios de Israel *
    que ha venido a liberar su pueblo.
Nos levantó un poderoso liberador *
    de la casa de David, su siervo,
según había prometido desde antaño *
    por boca de sus fieles profetas
para salvarnos de nuestros enemigos, *
    de la mano de los que nos odian.
A *nuestros antepasados* prometió misericordia *
    y siempre recordar su pacto santo.

This was the oath he swore to our father Abraham, *
    to set us free from the hands of our enemies,
Free to worship him without fear, *
        holy and righteous in his sight
        all the days of our life.
You, my child, shall be called the prophet of the Most High, *
        for you will go before the Lord to prepare his way,
To give his people knowledge of salvation *
        by the forgiveness of their sins.
In the tender compassion of our God *
        the dawn from on high shall break upon us,
To shine on those who dwell in darkness and
        the shadow of death, *
            and to guide our feet into the way of peace.

Glory to the Father, and to the Son, and to the Holy Spirit: *
    as it was in the beginning, is now, and will be for ever.
        Amen.

17 The Song of Simeon *Nunc dimittis*
Luke 2:29-32

Lord, you now have set your servant free *
    to go in peace as you have promised;
For these eyes of mine have seen the Savior, *
    whom you have prepared for all the world to see:
A Light to enlighten the nations, *
    and the glory of your people Israel.

Glory to the Father, and to the Son, and to the Holy Spirit: *
    as it was in the beginning, is now, and will be for ever.
        Amen.

18 A Song to the Lamb *Dignus es*
Revelation 4:11; 5:9-10, 13

Splendor and honor and kingly power *
    are yours by right, O Lord our God,
For you created everything that is, *
    and by your will they were created and have their being;

A nuestro padre Abrahán le prometió *
    que, *librados* del poder del enemigo,
podríamos adorarlo toda la vida sin temor *
    en santidad y justicia ante sus ojos.
Y a ti, niño, te llamarán profeta del Altísimo; *
    porque abrirás el camino delante del Señor
y a su pueblo le darás a conocer *
    la salvación por el perdón de sus pecados.
En la entrañable compasión de nuestro Dios, *
    la aurora romperá y brillará
para quienes viven bajo la sombra de muerte, *
    y guiará nuestros pasos por caminos de paz.

Gloria al Padre, y al Hijo y al Espíritu Santo; *
    como era en el principio, ahora y siempre por los siglos
        de los siglos. Amén.

17 Cántico de Simeón *Nunc dimittis*
    Lucas 2:29-32

Ahora deja, Señor, que me vaya en paz, *
    conforme a lo que habías prometido;
porque mis ojos han visto al Salvador *
    que has preparado ante los pueblos:
luz que ilumina a las naciones *
    y gloria de Israel, tu pueblo.

Gloria al Padre, y al Hijo y al Espíritu Santo; *
    como era en el principio, ahora y siempre por los siglos
        de los siglos. Amén.

18 Cántico del Cordero de Dios *Dignus es*
    Apocalipsis 4:11; 5:9-10, 13

Digno eres, Dios, de recibir *
    gloria, honra y toda potestad:
porque creaste todo lo que existe: *
    por tu voluntad tiene su ser y fue creado.

And yours by right, O Lamb that was slain, *
    for with your blood you have redeemed for God,
From every family, language, people, and nation, *
    a kingdom of priests to serve our God.

And so, to him who sits upon the throne, *
    and to Christ the Lamb,
Be worship and praise, dominion and splendor, *
    for ever and for evermore.

19 The Song of the Redeemed *Magna et mirabilia*

Revelation 15:3-4

O ruler of the universe, Lord God,
great deeds are they that you have done, *
    surpassing human understanding.
Your ways are ways of righteousness and truth, *
    O King of all the ages.

Who can fail to do you homage, Lord,
and sing the praises of your Name? *
    for you only are the holy One.
All nations will draw near and fall down before you, *
    because your just and holy works have been revealed.

Glory to the Father, and to the Son, and to the Holy Spirit: *
    as it was in the beginning, is now, and will be for ever.
        Amen.

20 Glory to God *Gloria in excelsis*

Glory to God in the highest,
    and peace to his people on earth.

Lord God, heavenly King,
almighty God and Father,
        we worship you, we give you thanks,
        we praise you for your glory.

Lord Jesus Christ, only Son of the Father,

Y digno eres tú, Cordero sacrificado, *
    pues, con tu sangre, redimiste para Dios
de toda lengua, nación, linaje y pueblo *
    un reino de sacerdotes para servir a nuestro Dios.

Al que está sentado en el trono, *
    y a Cristo, el Cordero,
    sean la adoración, el honor, la gloria y el poder
    por los siglos de los siglos.

19 Cántico de los Redimidos *Magna et mirabilia*

Apocalipsis 15:3-4

¡Dios, Soberano de todo el universo! *
    Has hecho hazañas y grandes maravillas.
¡Gobernante de todas las naciones! *
    Justas y verdaderas son tus sendas.

¿Quién no habría de honrarte y alabar tu nombre? *
    ¡Solo tú eres santo!
Vendrán a adorarte todas las naciones, *
    porque tu justicia y tu verdad se han revelado.

Gloria al Padre, y al Hijo y al Espíritu Santo: *
    como era en el principio, ahora y siempre por los siglos
        de los siglos. Amén.

20 Gloria a Dios *Gloria in excelsis*

Gloria a Dios en el cielo
    y en la tierra paz a quienes ama el Señor.

Señor Dios, Rey celestial,
Dios Padre todopoderoso,
    por tu inmensa gloria te alabamos, te bendecimos,
    te adoramos, te glorificamos, te damos gracias.

Señor Jesucristo, Hijo único del Padre,

Lord God, Lamb of God,
you take away the sin of the world;
    have mercy on us;
you are seated at the right hand of the Father;
    receive our prayer.

For you alone are the Holy One,
you alone are the Lord,
you alone are the Most High,
    Jesus Christ,
    with the Holy Spirit,
    in the glory of God the Father. Amen.

21 You are God *Te Deum laudamus*

You are God: we praise you;
You are the Lord: we acclaim you;
You are the eternal Father:
All creation worships you.
To you all angels, all the powers of heaven,
Cherubim and Seraphim, sing in endless praise:
    Holy, holy, holy Lord, God of power and might,
    heaven and earth are full of your glory.
The glorious company of apostles praise you.
The noble fellowship of prophets praise you.
The white-robed army of martyrs praise you.
Throughout the world the holy Church acclaims you;
    Father, of majesty unbounded,
    your true and only Son, worthy of all worship,
    and the Holy Spirit, advocate and guide.

You, Christ, are the king of glory,
the eternal Son of the Father.
When you became man to set us free
you did not shun the Virgin's womb.
You overcame the sting of death
and opened the kingdom of heaven to all believers.
You are seated at God's right hand in glory.
We believe that you will come and be our judge.
    Come then, Lord, and help your people,
    bought with the price of your own blood,

Señor Dios, Cordero de Dios,
tú que quitas el pecado del mundo:
    recibe nuestra súplica.
Tú que estás sentado a la diestra del Padre:
    ten piedad de *nosotros*.

Porque solo tú eres Santo,
solo tú Señor,
solo tú Altísimo,
    Jesucristo,
    con el Espíritu Santo,
    en la gloria de Dios Padre. Amén.

21 Tú eres Dios *Te Deum laudamus*

A ti, Dios, alabamos;
A ti, Dios, aclamamos.
A ti, Padre eterno,
toda la creación adora.
A ti todos los ángeles y todos los poderes celestiales,
los querubines y serafines te cantan sin cesar:
    «¡Santo, santo, santo Señor, Dios del universo!
    El cielo y la tierra rebosan de tu gloria».
A ti te ensalza la gloriosa multitud de apóstoles,
la hermandad ilustre de profetas,
el ejército de mártires, resplandeciente en ropa blanca.
A ti te aclama la santa Iglesia por todo el mundo:
    Padre de infinita majestad,
    Hijo único y verdadero, digno de toda adoración,
    y Espíritu Santo, defensor y guía.

Tú, Cristo, eres el Rey de gloria,
el Hijo eterno del Padre.
Cuando asumiste nuestra humanidad para salvarnos,
no desdeñaste el vientre de la Virgen.
Conquistaste el aguijón de la muerte
y abriste el reino de los cielos a quienes en ti confían.
A la diestra de Dios estás sentado en gloria.
Creemos que vendrás para juzgarnos.
    Ven, Señor, y auxilia a tu pueblo
    que compraste a costo de tu propia sangre

and bring us with your saints
to glory everlasting.

The Apostles' Creed

Officiant and People together, all standing

I believe in God, the Father almighty,
    creator of heaven and earth.
I believe in Jesus Christ, his only Son, our Lord.
    He was conceived by the power of the Holy Spirit
        and born of the Virgin Mary.
    He suffered under Pontius Pilate,
        was crucified, died, and was buried.
    He descended to the dead.
    On the third day he rose again.
    He ascended into heaven,
        and is seated at the right hand of the Father.
    He will come again to judge the living and the dead.
I believe in the Holy Spirit,
    the holy catholic Church,
    the communion of saints,
    the forgiveness of sins,
    the resurrection of the body,
    and the life everlasting. Amen.

The Prayers

The people stand or kneel

Officiant	The Lord be with you.
People	And also with you.
Officiant	Let us pray.

y llévanos con tus santas y tus santos
a la gloria sin fin.

Credo de los Apóstoles

Oficiante y pueblo, de pie, recitan:

Creo en Dios, Padre todopoderoso,
   creador del cielo y de la tierra.
Creo en Jesucristo, su único Hijo, nuestro Señor,
      que fue concebido por obra y gracia del Espíritu Santo,
         nació de la santa María Virgen,
      padeció bajo el poder de Poncio Pilato,
         fue crucificado, muerto y sepultado,
      descendió a los infiernos,
      al tercer día resucitó de entre los muertos,
      subió a los cielos
         y está sentado a la derecha de Dios, Padre todopoderoso.
      Desde allí ha de venir a juzgar a vivos y muertos.
Creo en el Espíritu Santo,
      la santa iglesia católica,
      la comunión de *los santos,*
      el perdón de los pecados,
      la resurrección de los muertos
      y la vida eterna. Amén.

Las oraciones

El pueblo, de pie o de rodillas. Quien oficia dice:

El Señor esté con ustedes.
Y también contigo.
Oremos.

Our Father, who art in heaven,	Our Father in heaven,
hallowed be thy Name,	hallowed be your Name,
thy kingdom come,	your kingdom come,
thy will be done,	your will be done,
on earth as it is in heaven.	on earth as in heaven.
Give us this day our daily bread.	Give us today our daily bread.
And forgive us our trespasses,	Forgive us our sins
as we forgive those	as we forgive those
who trespass against us.	who sin against us.
And lead us not into temptation,	Save us from the time of trial,
but deliver us from evil.	and deliver us from evil.
For thine is the kingdom,	For the kingdom, the power,
and the power, and the glory,	and the glory are yours,
for ever and ever. Amen.	now and for ever. Amen.

Then follows one of these sets of Suffrages

A

V. Show us your mercy, O Lord;
R. And grant us your salvation.
V. Clothe your ministers with righteousness;
R. Let your people sing with joy.
V. Give peace, O Lord, in all the world;
R. For only in you can we live in safety.
V. Lord, keep this nation under your care;
R. And guide us in the way of justice and truth.
V. Let your way be known upon earth;
R. Your saving health among all nations.
V. Let not the needy, O Lord, be forgotten;
R. Nor the hope of the poor be taken away.
V. Create in us clean hearts, O God;
R. And sustain us with your Holy Spirit.

Padre nuestro que estás en el cielo,
    santificado sea tu nombre;
    venga tu reino; hágase tu voluntad
        en la tierra como en el cielo.
Danos hoy nuestro pan de cada día.
Perdona nuestras ofensas,
    como también *nosotros* perdonamos
        a los que nos ofenden.
No nos dejes caer en la tentación
    y líbranos del mal.
Porque tuyo es el reino, el poder y la gloria,
    ahora y por siempre. Amén.

A continuación, se recita una de estas series de sufragios:

A

V. Muéstranos, Señor, tu gran piedad;
R. **Y concédenos tu salvación.**
V. Reviste de justicia a quienes te sirven.
R. **Que tu pueblo cante jubiloso.**
A. Danos, Señor, paz en todo el mundo;
R. **Pues solo en ti vivimos libres de peligro.**
A. Cuida y protege a esta nación;
R. **Guíanos por caminos de justicia y de verdad.**
A. Haz que tus sendas se conozcan en la tierra;
R. **Tu salud y salvación, en las naciones.**
A. No dejes que olvidemos a *los necesitados*;
R. **Ni robemos la esperanza de *los* pobres.**
A. Crea en *nosotros* corazones puros;
R. **Y que tu Espíritu Santo nos sostenga.**

B

V. Save your people, Lord, and bless your inheritance;
R. Govern and uphold them, now and always.
V. Day by day we bless you;
R. We praise your Name for ever.
V. Lord, keep us from all sin today;
R. Have mercy on us, Lord, have mercy.
V. Lord, show us your love and mercy;
R. For we put our trust in you.
V. In you, Lord, is our hope;
R. And we shall never hope in vain.

The Officiant then says one or more of the following Collects

The Collect of the Day

A Collect for Sundays

O God, you make us glad with the weekly remembrance of the glorious resurrection of your Son our Lord: Give us this day such blessing through our worship of you, that the week to come may be spent in your favor; through Jesus Christ our Lord. *Amen.*

A Collect for Fridays

Almighty God, whose most dear Son went not up to joy but first he suffered pain, and entered not into glory before he was crucified: Mercifully grant that we, walking in the way of the cross, may find it none other than the way of life and peace; through Jesus Christ your Son our Lord. *Amen.*

A Collect for Saturdays

Almighty God, who after the creation of the world rested from all your works and sanctified a day of rest for all your creatures: Grant that we, putting away all earthly anxieties, may be duly prepared for the service of your sanctuary, and

B

V. Señor, salva a tu pueblo, y bendice a tu heredad;
R. **Sostennos y guíanos ahora y siempre.**
V. Día a día te bendecimos;
R. **Y alabamos tu nombre eternamente.**
V. De todo pecado guárdanos hoy;
R. **Ten piedad de *nosotros*.**
V. Muéstranos tu amor y tu misericordia;
R. **Porque en ti ponemos la confianza.**
V. En ti, Señor, está nuestra esperanza;
R. **No dejes que esperemos en vano.**

Quien oficia dice una o más de las siguientes colectas:

La colecta del día

Colecta para los domingos

Oh Dios, cada semana nos deleitas
al recordar la gloriosa resurrección de tu Hijo nuestro
Señor: Concédenos hoy que nuestra adoración
nos inspire a servirte toda la semana;
por Jesucristo nuestro Señor. **Amén.**

Colecta para los viernes

Dios de poder, cuyo Hijo amado
no alcanzó su gozo sin haber sufrido,
ni entró en su gloria sin ser crucificado;
concédenos que, al andar por el camino de la cruz,
hallemos la senda de la vida y de la paz;
por Jesucristo nuestro Señor. **Amén.**

Colecta para los sábados

Dios de todo poder:
después de crear el mundo descansaste de tus labores
y santificaste un día de reposo para todas tus criaturas;
concédenos que, desechando toda preocupación mundana,
nos preparemos bien para adorarte en tu santuario;

that our rest here upon earth may be a preparation for the eternal rest promised to your people in heaven; through Jesus Christ our Lord. *Amen.*

A Collect for the Renewal of Life

O God, the King eternal, whose light divides the day from the night and turns the shadow of death into the morning: Drive far from us all wrong desires, incline our hearts to keep your law, and guide our feet into the way of peace; that, having done your will with cheerfulness during the day, we may, when night comes, rejoice to give you thanks; through Jesus Christ our Lord. *Amen.*

A Collect for Peace

O God, the author of peace and lover of concord, to know you is eternal life and to serve you is perfect freedom: Defend us, your humble servants, in all assaults of our enemies; that we, surely trusting in your defense, may not fear the power of any adversaries; through the might of Jesus Christ our Lord. *Amen.*

A Collect for Grace

Lord God, almighty and everlasting Father, you have brought us in safety to this new day: Preserve us with your mighty power, that we may not fall into sin, nor be overcome by adversity; and in all we do, direct us to the fulfilling of your purpose; through Jesus Christ our Lord. *Amen.*

y que nuestro descanso en la tierra nos prepare
para el reposo eterno del cielo
que has prometido a tu pueblo;
por Jesucristo nuestro Señor. **Amén.**

Colecta por la renovación de la vida

Dios, Rey eterno, cuya luz separa el día de la noche
y hace que las sombras de la muerte
broten en un nuevo amanecer:
despójanos de todo mal deseo;
inspíranos a guardar tu ley
y guíanos por la senda de la paz;
para que, habiéndote obedecido con alegría durante el día,
podamos rendirte gracias con gozo al caer la noche;
por Jesucristo nuestro Señor. **Amén**

Colecta por la paz

Dios, autor de la paz y amante de la concordia:
conocerte es vida eterna y servirte, libertad perfecta;
defiéndenos, tus humildes servidores,
de todo ataque de *nuestros enemigos*;
para que, confiando en tu defensa,
no temamos el poder de ningún adversario;
por amor de Jesucristo nuestro Señor. **Amén.**

Colecta por la gracia divina

Dios, Padre poderoso y eterno:
nos has hecho llegar *sanos* y *salvos*
a este nuevo día;
guárdanos con tu gran poder
para que no caigamos en pecado
ni nos rindamos frente a la adversidad,
y dirígenos a cumplir tu voluntad;
por Jesucristo nuestro Señor. **Amén.**

A Collect for Guidance

Heavenly Father, in you we live and move and have our being: We humbly pray you so to guide and govern us by your Holy Spirit, that in all the cares and occupations of our life we may not forget you, but may remember that we are ever walking in your sight; through Jesus Christ our Lord. *Amen.*

Then, unless the Eucharist or a form of general intercession is to follow, one of these prayers for mission is added

Almighty and everlasting God, by whose Spirit the whole body of your faithful people is governed and sanctified: Receive our supplications and prayers which we offer before you for all members of your holy Church, that in their vocation and ministry they may truly and devoutly serve you; through our Lord and Savior Jesus Christ. *Amen.*

or this

O God, you have made of one blood all the peoples of the earth, and sent your blessed Son to preach peace to those who are far off and to those who are near: Grant that people everywhere may seek after you and find you; bring the nations into your fold; pour out your Spirit upon all flesh; and hasten the coming of your kingdom; through Jesus Christ our Lord. *Amen.*

or the following

Lord Jesus Christ, you stretched out your arms of love on the hard wood of the cross that everyone might come within the reach of your saving embrace: So clothe us in your Spirit that

Colecta por la guía divina

Padre Celestial,
en quien vivimos, nos movemos y existimos:
Con humildad te rogamos
que por tu Espíritu Santo nos guíes y dirijas,
para que, en todas las responsabilidades de la vida,
no te olvidemos, sino que recordemos
que siempre observas nuestros pasos;
por Jesucristo nuestro Señor. **Amén.**

*A menos que siga la Santa Comunión o una forma de intercesión
general, se agrega una de estas oraciones por la misión de la iglesia:*

Dios poderoso y eterno,
por cuyo Espíritu el cuerpo entero de tus fieles
se gobierna y santifica:
Recibe las súplicas y plegarias que te ofrecemos
por toda la membresía de tu santa iglesia
para que en nuestras vocaciones y ministerios
podamos servirte con lealtad y devoción;
por Jesucristo nuestro Señor y Liberador. **Amén.**

O bien:

Dios Padre,
que de una sangre hiciste todas las naciones de la tierra
y enviaste a tu bendito Hijo
a predicar la paz en la cercanía y en la lejanía:
Haz que todo pueblo te busque y te encuentre;
trae a las naciones a tu redil;
derrama tu Espíritu sobre todo ser;
y apresura la venida de tu reino;
por Jesucristo nuestro Señor. **Amén.**

O bien:

Señor Jesucristo, que abriste los brazos de tu amor
sobre el rígido madero de la cruz
para que toda persona alcance a tu abrazo liberador:

we, reaching forth our hands in love, may bring those who do not know you to the knowledge and love of you; for the honor of your Name. *Amen.*

Here may be sung a hymn or anthem.

Authorized intercessions and thanksgivings may follow.

Before the close of the Office one or both of the following may be used

The General Thanksgiving

Officiant and People

Almighty God, Father of all mercies,
we your unworthy servants give you humble thanks
for all your goodness and loving-kindness
to us and to all whom you have made.
We bless you for our creation, preservation,
and all the blessings of this life;
but above all for your immeasurable love
in the redemption of the world by our Lord Jesus Christ;
for the means of grace, and for the hope of glory.
And, we pray, give us such an awareness of your mercies,
that with truly thankful hearts we may show forth your praise,
not only with our lips, but in our lives,
by giving up our selves to your service,
and by walking before you
in holiness and righteousness all our days;
through Jesus Christ our Lord,
to whom, with you and the Holy Spirit,
be honor and glory throughout all ages. Amen.

A Prayer of St. Chrysostom

Almighty God, you have given us grace at this time with one accord to make our common supplication to you; and you have promised through your well-beloved Son that when two or three are gathered together in his Name you will be in the midst of them: Fulfill now, O Lord, our desires

revístenos con tu Espíritu para que,
tendiendo una mano amiga,
llevemos a los que te desconocen a conocer y amarte;
para la honra de tu nombre. **Amén.**

Puede cantarse un himno o canto.

Se pueden agregar peticiones y acciones de gracias autorizadas.

Antes de concluir la liturgia, se puede usar una o ambas de las siguientes oraciones:

Acción de gracias de uso general

Oficiante y pueblo:

**Dios de todo poder, Padre de toda piedad,
aunque *servidores indignos*,
con humildad te agradecemos tu bondad y tu ternura
hacia *nosotros* y hacia todo lo que has creado.
Te bendecimos por crearnos, preservarnos
y por todas las bendiciones de la vida,
pero sobre todo por tu amor incalculable
al redimir al mundo por nuestro Señor Jesucristo;
por los medios de tu gracia
y la esperanza de vivir en gloria.
Te rogamos que, conscientes de tus favores
y *agradecidos* de todo corazón,
proclamemos tu alabanza no solo con los labios,
sino también con nuestras vidas,
dedicándonos a servirte
y caminando día a día en santidad y rectitud ante ti;
por Jesucristo nuestro Señor.
A él, a ti, y al Espíritu Santo
sean el honor y la gloria por siempre. Amén.**

Oración de San Juan Crisóstomo

Dios de todo poder: Por tu gracia nos has concedido
que elevemos hoy en armonía una misma súplica;
y nos has prometido por tu Hijo amado
que, cuando dos o tres se reúnan en tu nombre,
allí estarás con *nosotros*:

and petitions as may be best for us; granting us in this
world knowledge of your truth, and in the age to come life
everlasting. *Amen.*

Then may be said

Let us bless the Lord.
Thanks be to God.

*From Easter Day through the Day of Pentecost "Alleluia, alleluia" may
be added to the preceding versicle and response.*

The Officiant may then conclude with one of the following

The grace of our Lord Jesus Christ, and the love of God, and
the fellowship of the Holy Spirit, be with us all evermore.
Amen.   2 Corinthians 13:14

May the God of hope fill us with all joy and peace in
believing through the power of the Holy Spirit. *Amen.*
Romans 15:13

Glory to God whose power, working in us, can do infinitely
more than we can ask or imagine: Glory to him from
generation to generation in the Church, and in Christ Jesus
for ever and ever. *Amen.   Ephesians 3:20, 21*

Cumple ahora, Señor, nuestros deseos y peticiones
como mejor nos convenga,
y danos a conocer tu verdad en este mundo
y en el mundo venidero, vida eterna. **Amén.**

Se puede agregar:

Bendigamos al Señor.
Demos gracias a Dios.

Del día de Pascua al día de Pentecostés, al versículo anterior y a la
respuesta se les puede agregar «¡Aleluya, aleluya!».

Quien oficia puede concluir con una de las siguientes citas bíblicas:

La gracia de nuestro Señor Jesucristo, el amor de Dios y
la comunión del Espíritu Santo nos acompañen siempre.
Amén.   *2 Corintios 13:14*

El Dios de esperanza nos llene de todo gozo y paz en la fe
por virtud del Espíritu Santo. **Amén.**   *Romanos 15:13*

Gloria a Dios cuyo poder, activo en *nosotros*, puede realizar
infinitamente más de lo que podemos pedir o pensar: gloria a
él por siempre en la Iglesia, en Cristo Jesús. **Amén.**
Efesios 3:20, 21

Daily Evening Prayer: Rite Two

The Officiant begins the service with one or more of the following sentences of Scripture, or of those on pages 18-27;

or with the Service of Light on BCP pages 109-112, and continuing with the appointed Psalmody;

or with the versicle "O God, make speed to save us" on page 78

Let my prayer be set forth in your sight as incense, the lifting up of my hands as the evening sacrifice. *Psalm 141:2*

Grace to you and peace from God our Father and from the Lord Jesus Christ. *Philippians 1:2*

Worship the Lord in the beauty of holiness; let the whole earth tremble before him. *Psalm 96:9*

Yours is the day, O God, yours also the night; you established the moon and the sun. You fixed all the boundaries of the earth; you made both summer and winter. *Psalm 74:15, 16*

I will bless the Lord who gives me counsel; my heart teaches me, night after night. I have set the Lord always before me; because he is at my right hand, I shall not fall. *Psalm 16:7, 8*

Seek him who made the Pleiades and Orion, and turns deep darkness into the morning, and darkens the day into night;

Oración del Atardecer

Quien oficia comienza con uno o más de los siguientes versículos, o de aquellos de las páginas 18-27;

o se puede comenzar con el Orden de Adoración para el Atardecer en LOC en las páginas 62-66, continuando con el salmo o salmos designados;

o bien con el versículo «Apresúrate, Dios, para salvarnos» en la página 79.

Ascienda mi plegaria como incienso ante tu presencia; mis manos alzadas, como la oración del atardecer. *Salmo 141:2*

Gracia y paz a ustedes de parte de Dios nuestro Padre y del Señor Jesucristo. *Filipenses 1:2*

Adoren a Dios en la hermosura de la santidad; tiemble ante su presencia la tierra entera. *Salmo 96:9*

Tuyo es el día, tuya también la noche; la luna y el sol tú estableciste. Tú fijaste los límites del mundo; hiciste el invierno y el verano. *Salmo 74:15, 16*

Bendeciré a Dios que me aconseja; noche tras noche me instruye el corazón. A Dios he puesto siempre por delante; con Dios a mi lado, no puedo tropezar. *Salmo 16:7-8*

Busquen a quien hizo las Pléyades y Orión, al que hace nacer la mañana de las tinieblas y oscurece el día para hacer la noche; Dios recoge las aguas del mar y

who calls for the waters of the sea and pours them out upon the surface of the earth: The Lord is his name.   *Amos 5:8*

If I say, "Surely the darkness will cover me, and the light around me turn to night," darkness is not dark to you, O Lord; the night is as bright as the day; darkness and light to you are both alike.   *Psalm 139:10, 11*

Jesus said, "I am the light of the world; whoever follows me will not walk in darkness, but will have the light of life."   *John 8:12*

The following Confession of Sin may then be said; or the Office may continue at once with "O God make speed to save us."

Confession of Sin

The Officiant says to the people

Dear friends in Christ, here in the presence of Almighty God, let us kneel in silence, and with penitent and obedient hearts confess our sins, so that we may obtain forgiveness by his infinite goodness and mercy.

or this

Let us confess our sins against God and our neighbor.

Silence may be kept.

Officiant and People together, all kneeling

Most merciful God,
we confess that we have sinned against you
in thought, word, and deed,
by what we have done,
and by what we have left undone.
We have not loved you with our whole heart;
we have not loved our neighbors as ourselves.
We are truly sorry and we humbly repent.
For the sake of your Son Jesus Christ,
have mercy on us and forgive us;
that we may delight in your will,

las derrama por lo ancho de la tierra. ¡Su nombre es el
Señor!   *Amós 5:8*

Si digo: «Las tinieblas me cubrirán y me tragarán las sombras
de la noche», para ti, las sombras no ensombrecen; la noche
brilla como el día; igual te son las sombras que la luz.
Salmo 139:10,11

Jesús dijo: «Yo soy la luz del mundo; quien me sigue no caminará
en la oscuridad, sino que tendrá la luz de la vida».   *Juan 8:12*

*Se puede decir la siguiente confesión de pecados; o se puede pasar
directamente a «Apresúrate, Dios, para salvarnos».*

Confesión de pecados

Quien oficia le dice al pueblo:

Confesemos nuestros pecados contra Dios y nuestro prójimo.

O bien:

Amada familia de Dios, arrodillémonos en silencio en la
presencia del Dios de todo poder; y con corazones penitentes
y obedientes, confesemos nuestros pecados, para que, por su
infinita bondad y misericordia, obtengamos el perdón.

Se puede guardar un período de silencio.

Oficiante y el pueblo, de rodillas:

Dios de misericordia,
confesamos que hemos pecado contra ti
de pensamiento, palabra y obra,
por lo que hemos hecho
y por lo que hemos dejado sin hacer.
No te hemos amado de todo corazón;
no hemos amado al prójimo como a *nosotros mismos*.
Sincera y humildemente nos arrepentimos.
Por tu Hijo Jesucristo,
ten piedad de *nosotros* y perdónanos;
así tu voluntad será nuestra alegría

and walk in your ways,
to the glory of your Name. Amen.

The Priest alone stands and says

Almighty God have mercy on you, forgive you all your
sins through our Lord Jesus Christ, strengthen you in all
goodness, and by the power of the Holy Spirit keep you in
eternal life. *Amen.*

*A deacon or lay person using the preceding form remains kneeling, and
substitutes "us" for "you" and "our" for "your."*

The Invitatory and Psalter

All stand

Officiant	O God, make speed to save us.
People	O Lord, make haste to help us.

Officiant and People

Glory to the Father, and to the Son, and to the Holy Spirit: as
it was in the beginning, is now, and will be for ever. Amen.

Except in Lent, add   Alleluia.

*The following, or some other suitable hymn, or an Invitatory Psalm,
may be sung or said*

O Gracious Light *Phos hilaron*

O gracious Light,
pure brightness of the everliving Father in heaven,
O Jesus Christ, holy and blessed!

Now as we come to the setting of the sun,
and our eyes behold the vesper light,

y caminaremos en tus sendas
para gloria de tu nombre. Amén.

Un presbítero, de pie, declara:

Dios Todopoderoso se apiade de *ustedes*, perdone todos *sus*
pecados por nuestro Señor Jesucristo, *los* fortalezca en toda
virtud, y por el poder del Espíritu Santo *los* guarde en la vida
eterna. **Amén.**

*Un diácono o una persona laica hace la misma declaración, pero de
rodillas, y sustituye «ustedes» con «nosotros», «sus» con «nuestros» y
«los» con «nos».*

Invitatorio y salterio

De pie.

Oficiante: Apresúrate, Dios, para salvarnos.
Pueblo: Date prisa, Señor, en socorrernos.

Oficiante y pueblo:

Gloria al Padre, y al Hijo y al Espíritu Santo:
Como era en el principio, ahora y siempre
por los siglos de los siglos. Amén. ¡Aleluya!

Se omite el Aleluya en Cuaresma.

Se puede cantar o decir el himno que sigue, o un salmo invitatorio.

Himno de la luz gozosa

Luz gozosa, gloria clara
del Padre inmortal del cielo,
santo y alegre consuelo.
¡Cristo bendito, Luz santa!

Al elevar este canto,
al ponerse el sol, *reunidos*

we sing your praises, O God:
Father, Son, and Holy Spirit.

You are worthy at all times to be praised by happy voices,
O Son of God, O Giver of life,
and to be glorified through all the worlds.

Then follows

The Psalm or Psalms Appointed

At the end of the Psalms is sung or said

Glory to the Father, and to the Son, and to the Holy Spirit: *
  as it was in the beginning, is now, and will be for ever.
      Amen.

The Lessons

One or two Lessons, as appointed, are read, the Reader first saying

A Reading (Lesson) from_____.

A citation giving chapter and verse may be added.

After each Lesson the Reader may say

       The Word of the Lord.
Answer   Thanks be to God.

Or the Reader may say   Here ends the Lesson (Reading).

Silence may be kept after each Reading. One of the following Canticles, or one of those on BCP pages 47-52, or 85-95, is sung or said after each Reading. If three Lessons are used, the Lesson from the Gospel is read after the second Canticle.

le cantamos al Dios Trino:
Padre, Hijo, Espíritu Santo.

¡Digno siempre de alabanza,
Hijo de Dios, luz de vida!
¡Con esta luz vespertina
el universo te canta!

Y a continuación:

Los salmos del día

Al final del salmo (o los salmos) se canta o se dice:

Gloria al Padre, y al Hijo y al Espíritu Santo: *
Como era en el principio, ahora y siempre,
por los siglos de los siglos. Amén.

Las lecturas

Se lee una o dos lecturas, según corresponda; primero, quien lee dice:

Lectura de_____.

Se puede agregar capítulo y versículo.

Después de cada lectura, quien lee puede decir:

Palabra de Dios.
Demos gracias a Dios.

O bien puede decir:

Aquí concluye la lectura.

Se puede guardar silencio después de cada lectura. Entonces, se canta o recita uno de los cánticos que siguen, o uno de los que aparecen en LOC en las páginas 39-49. Si se proclaman tres lecturas, el evangelio se lee después del segundo cántico.

The Song of Mary *Magnificat*

Luke 1:46-55

My soul proclaims the greatness of the Lord,
my spirit rejoices in God my Savior; *
    for he has looked with favor on his lowly servant
From this day all generations will call me blessed: *
    the Almighty has done great things for me,
    and holy is his Name.
He has mercy on those who fear him *
    in every generation.
He has shown the strength of his arm, *
    he has scattered the proud in their conceit.
He has cast down the mighty from their thrones, *
    and has lifted up the lowly.
He has filled the hungry with good things, *
    and the rich he has sent away empty.
He has come to the help of his servant Israel, *
    for he has remembered his promise of mercy,
The promise he made to our fathers, *
    to Abraham and his children for ever.

Glory to the Father, and to the Son, and to the Holy Spirit: *
    as it was in the beginning, is now, and will be
        for ever. Amen.

The Song of Simeon *Nunc dimittis*

Luke 2:29-32

Lord, you now have set your servant free *
    to go in peace as you have promised;
For these eyes of mine have seen the Savior, *
    whom you have prepared for all the world to see:
A Light to enlighten the nations, *
    and the glory of your people Israel.

Glory to the Father, and to the Son, and to the Holy Spirit: *
    as it was in the beginning, is now, and will be for ever.
        Amen.

Cántico de María *Magníficat*

Lucas 1:46-55

Mi alma proclama la grandeza del Señor;
mi espíritu se alegra en Dios mi Salvador *
  que ha notado la humillación de su sierva.
Desde hoy, todas las generaciones me llamarán bendita: *
  Dios Poderoso me ha hecho grandes obras
  y su nombre es santo.
Su misericordia alcanza a sus fieles *
  generación tras generación.
Desplegó la fuerza de su brazo *
  y dispersó a los soberbios de corazón.
Derribó a los poderosos de sus tronos*
  y levantó a la gente humilde.
Colmó de bienes al hambriento *
  y a los ricos despidió sin nada.
Ayudó a su siervo, el pueblo de Israel, *
  porque recuerda la misericordia prometida
a quienes vivieron antes que *nosotros*, *
  a Abrahán y a su descendencia por siempre.

Gloria al Padre, y al Hijo y al Espíritu Santo: *
  Como era en el principio, ahora y siempre por los siglos
  de los siglos. Amén.

Cántico de Simeón *Nunc dimittis*

Lucas 2:29-32

Ahora deja, Señor, que me vaya en paz, *
  conforme a lo que habías prometido;
porque mis ojos han visto al Salvador *
  que has preparado ante los pueblos:
luz que ilumina a las naciones *
  y gloria de Israel, tu pueblo.

Gloria al Padre, y al Hijo y al Espíritu Santo: *
  Como era en el principio, ahora y siempre
    por los siglos de los siglos. Amén.

The Apostles' Creed

Officiant and People together, all standing

I believe in God, the Father almighty,
    creator of heaven and earth.
I believe in Jesus Christ, his only Son, our Lord.
    He was conceived by the power of the Holy Spirit
        and born of the Virgin Mary.
    He suffered under Pontius Pilate,
        was crucified, died, and was buried.
    He descended to the dead.
    On the third day he rose again.
    He ascended into heaven,
        and is seated at the right hand of the Father.
    He will come again to judge the living and the dead.
I believe in the Holy Spirit,
    the holy catholic Church,
    the communion of saints,
    the forgiveness of sins,
    the resurrection of the body,
    and the life everlasting. Amen.

The Prayers

The people stand or kneel

Officiant	The Lord be with you.
People	And also with you.
Officiant	Let us pray.

Officiant and People

Then follows one of these sets of Suffrages

Our Father, who art in heaven,	Our Father in heaven,
hallowed be thy Name,	hallowed be your Name,
thy kingdom come,	your kingdom come,
thy will be done,	your will be done,
on earth as it is in heaven.	on earth as in heaven.

Credo de los apóstoles

Oficiante y pueblo, de pie.

Creo en Dios, Padre todopoderoso,
    creador del cielo y de la tierra.
Creo en Jesucristo, su único Hijo, nuestro Señor,
    que fue concebido por obra y gracia del Espíritu Santo,
        nació de la santa María Virgen,
    padeció bajo el poder de Poncio Pilato,
        fue crucificado, muerto y sepultado,
    descendió a los infiernos,
    al tercer día resucitó de entre los muertos,
    subió a los cielos
        y está sentado a la derecha de Dios, Padre todopoderoso.
    Desde allí ha de venir a juzgar a vivos y muertos.
Creo en el Espíritu Santo,
    la santa iglesia católica,
    la comunión de *los santos,*
    el perdón de los pecados,
    la resurrección de los muertos
    y la vida eterna. Amén.

Oraciones

De pie o de rodillas. Quien oficia dice:

        El Señor esté con ustedes.
Pueblo   **Y también contigo.**
Oficiante   Oremos.

Oficiante y pueblo:

Padre nuestro que estás en el cielo,
    santificado sea tu nombre;
    venga tu reino;
    hágase tu voluntad
        en la tierra como en el cielo.

Give us this day our daily bread. Give us today our daily bread.
And forgive us our trespasses, Forgive us our sins
   as we forgive those   as we forgive those
    who trespass against us.   who sin against us.
And lead us not into temptation, Save us from the time of trial,
   but deliver us from evil.   and deliver us from evil.
For thine is the kingdom, For the kingdom, the power,
   and the power, and the glory,   and the glory are yours,
   for ever and ever. Amen.   now and for ever. Amen.

Then follows one of these sets of Suffrages

A

V.   Show us your mercy, O Lord;
R.   And grant us your salvation.
V.   Clothe your ministers with righteousness;
R.   Let your people sing with joy.
V.   Give peace, O Lord, in all the world;
R.   For only in you can we live in safety.
V.   Lord, keep this nation under your care;
R.   And guide us in the way of justice and truth.
V.   Let your way be known upon earth;
R.   Your saving health among all nations.
V.   Let not the needy, O Lord, be forgotten;
R.   Nor the hope of the poor be taken away.
V.   Create in us clean hearts, O God;
R.   And sustain us with your Holy Spirit.

B

That this evening may be holy, good, and peaceful,
We entreat you, O Lord.

That your holy angels may lead us in paths of peace and
goodwill,
We entreat you, O Lord.

That we may be pardoned and forgiven for our sins and offenses,
We entreat you, O Lord.

Danos hoy nuestro pan de cada día.
Perdona nuestras ofensas,
    como también *nosotros* perdonamos
      a los que nos ofenden.
No nos dejes caer en la tentación
    y líbranos del mal.
Porque tuyo es el reino, el poder y la gloria,
    ahora y por siempre. Amén.

A continuación, se recita una de estas series de sufragios:

A

V.   Muéstranos, Señor, tu gran piedad;
R.   **Y concédenos tu salvación.**
V.   Reviste de justicia a quienes te sirven.
R.   **Que tu pueblo cante jubiloso.**
A.   Danos, Señor, paz en todo el mundo;
R.   **Pues solo en ti vivimos libres de peligro.**
A.   Cuida y protege a esta nación;
R.   **Guíanos por caminos de justicia y de verdad.**
A.   Haz que tus sendas se conozcan en la tierra;
R.   **Tu salud y salvación, en las naciones.**
A.   No dejes que olvidemos a *los necesitados*;
R.   **Ni robemos la esperanza de los pobres.**
A.   Crea en *nosotros* corazones puros;
R.   **Y que tu Espíritu Santo nos sostenga.**

B

Que esta noche sea santa, buena y serena,
Te rogamos, Señor.

Que tus santos ángeles nos guíen en sendas de paz y buena
voluntad,
Te rogamos, Señor.

Que recibamos perdón por nuestras ofensas y pecados,
Te rogamos, Señor.

That there may be peace to your Church and to the whole world,
We entreat you, O Lord.

That we may depart this life in your faith and fear, and not
be condemned before the great judgment seat of Christ,
We entreat you, O Lord.

That we may be bound together by your Holy Spirit in
the communion of [_____and] all your saints,
entrusting one another and all our life to Christ,
We entreat you, O Lord.

The Officiant then says one or more of the following Collects

The Collect of the Day

A Collect for Sundays

Lord God, whose Son our Savior Jesus Christ triumphed over
the powers of death and prepared for us our place in the new
Jerusalem: Grant that we, who have this day given thanks
for his resurrection, may praise you in that City of which he
is the light, and where he lives and reigns for ever and ever.
Amen.

A Collect for Fridays

Lord Jesus Christ, by your death you took away the sting of
death: Grant to us your servants so to follow in faith where
you have led the way, that we may at length fall asleep
peacefully in you and wake up in your likeness; for your
tender mercies' sake. *Amen.*

A Collect for Saturdays

O God, the source of eternal light: Shed forth your unending
day upon us who watch for you, that our lips may praise you,
our lives may bless you, and our worship on the morrow give
you glory; through Jesus Christ our Lord. *Amen.*

Que haya paz en tu iglesia y en el mundo entero,
Te rogamos, Señor.

Que la muerte nos encuentre *anclados* en la fe, y nos
presentemos ante Cristo con la conciencia limpia,
Te rogamos, Señor.

Que tu Santo Espíritu nos una en la comunión de
[_____y] todos tus santos y santas; encomendándonos
mutuamente a Jesucristo y confiándole toda nuestra vida,
Te rogamos, Señor.

Quien oficia dice una o más de las siguientes colectas:

La colecta del día

Colecta para los domingos

Señor Dios, cuyo Hijo Jesucristo nuestro Salvador
venció los poderes de la muerte
preparándonos un lugar en la nueva Jerusalén:
Haz que quienes hoy celebramos su resurrección
podamos alabarte en aquella ciudad
cuya única luz es Jesucristo,
donde vive y reina por siempre jamás. **Amén.**

Colecta para los viernes

Señor Jesucristo:
Con tu muerte has arrancado el aguijón de la muerte;
haz que, siguiendo con fe el camino que trazaste,
al fin podamos dormir en ti
y despertar a tu semejanza,
por tu ternura y misericordia. **Amén.**

Colecta para los sábados

Señor, fuente de luz eterna: derrama en quienes *atentos* te
esperamos el día que no tiene fin para que nuestros labios te
alaben, nuestras vidas te bendigan y en la mañana te adoremos
y rindamos gloria, por Cristo Jesús nuestro Señor. **Amén.**

A Collect for Peace

Most holy God, the source of all good desires, all right judgments, and all just works: Give to us, your servants, that peace which the world cannot give, so that our minds may be fixed on the doing of your will, and that we, being delivered from the fear of all enemies, may live in peace and quietness; through the mercies of Christ Jesus our Savior. *Amen.*

A Collect for Aid against Perils

Be our light in the darkness, O Lord, and in your great mercy defend us from all perils and dangers of this night; for the love of your only Son, our Savior Jesus Christ. *Amen.*

A Collect for Protection

O God, the life of all who live, the light of the faithful, the strength of those who labor, and the repose of the dead: We thank you for the blessings of the day that is past, and humbly ask for your protection through the coming night. Bring us in safety to the morning hours; through him who died and rose again for us, your Son our Savior Jesus Christ. *Amen.*

A Collect for the Presence of Christ

Lord Jesus, stay with us, for evening is at hand and the day is past; be our companion in the way, kindle our hearts, and awaken hope, that we may know you as you are revealed in Scripture and the breaking of bread. Grant this for the sake of your love. *Amen.*

Colecta por la paz

Santísimo Dios, fuente de todo buen deseo,
de todo juicio certero y obra justa:
Otórganos la paz que el mundo no puede conceder
para que tengamos la mente fija solo en hacer tu voluntad
y, así *librados* del temor a todo enemigo,
vivamos en tranquilidad y paz;
por amor de Jesucristo nuestro Salvador. **Amén.**

Colecta por auxilio de todo peligro

Sé nuestra luz en las tinieblas, Señor, y defiéndenos, por tu
piedad, de todos los peligros de esta noche; por amor de tu
Hijo único, Jesucristo nuestro Salvador. **Amén.**

Colecta por la protección divina

Señor, vida de *los* que viven, luz de *los* fieles,
fuerza de trabajadores y reposo de *los* muertos:
Te damos gracias por las bendiciones
recibidas en el día que termina,
y te pedimos humildemente protección
durante la noche que se acerca.
Que tu mano nos proteja hasta el amanecer;
por aquel que murió por *nosotros* y resucitó,
tu Hijo Jesucristo, nuestro Salvador. **Amén.**

Colecta por la presencia de cristo

Quédate con *nosotros*, buen Jesús,
que cae el sol y se acaba el día;
sé nuestro compañero de camino,
aviva nuestros corazones
y despierta en *nosotros* la esperanza,
para reconocerte según te revelas
en las Escrituras y al partir el pan.
En tu amor te lo pedimos. **Amén.**

Then, unless the Eucharist or a form of general intercession is to follow, one of these prayers for mission is added

O God and Father of all, whom the whole heavens adore:
Let the whole earth also worship you, all nations obey you,
all tongues confess and bless you, and men and women
everywhere love you and serve you in peace; through Jesus
Christ our Lord. *Amen.*

or this

Keep watch, dear Lord, with those who work, or watch,
or weep this night, and give your angels charge over
those who sleep. Tend the sick, Lord Christ; give rest to
the weary, bless the dying, soothe the suffering,
pity the afflicted, shield the joyous; and all for your
love's sake. *Amen.*

or the following

O God, you manifest in your servants the signs of your
presence: Send forth upon us the Spirit of love, that in
companionship with one another your abounding grace may
increase among us; through Jesus Christ our Lord. *Amen.*

Here may be sung a hymn or anthem.

Authorized intercessions and thanksgivings may follow.

Before the close of the Office one or both of the following may be used

The General Thanksgiving

Officiant and People

Almighty God, Father of all mercies,
we your unworthy servants give you humble thanks
for all your goodness and loving-kindness
to us and to all whom you have made.

A menos que se continúe con la eucaristía o una intercesión general, se agrega una de las siguientes oraciones por la misión:

Dios y Padre de todo cuanto existe,
a quien el cielo entero adora:
Que toda la tierra también te adore,
todas las naciones te obedezcan,
todas las lenguas te confiesen y bendigan,
y en todas partes mujeres y hombres
te amen y te sirvan en paz;
por Cristo Jesús nuestro Señor. **Amén.**

O esta:

Acompaña, buen Señor, a cada persona
que esta noche trabaja, se desvela o se lamenta,
y haz que tus ángeles cobijen a quienes duermen.
Cuida *al enfermo*, da reposo *al fatigado*,
bendice *al moribundo*, alivia *al* que sufre,
apiádate *del afligido*, y protege *al gozoso*;
por tu amor y tu ternura. **Amén.**

O esta:

Señor, que en tus *siervos* manifiestas
las señales de tu presencia:
Envíanos el Espíritu de amor
para que, en mutua compañía,
tu gracia crezca en abundancia entre *nosotros*,
por Cristo Jesús nuestro Señor. **Amén.**

Aquí puede cantarse un himno o un canto.

Se pueden agregar peticiones y acciones de gracias autorizadas.

Antes de concluir la liturgia, se puede usar una o ambas de las siguientes oraciones:

Acción de gracias de uso general

Oficiante y pueblo:

**Dios de todo poder, Padre de toda piedad,
aunque *servidores indignos*,
con humildad te agradecemos tu bondad y tu ternura
hacia *nosotros* y hacia todo lo que has creado.**

We bless you for our creation, preservation,
and all the blessings of this life;
but above all for your immeasurable love
in the redemption of the world by our Lord Jesus Christ;
for the means of grace, and for the hope of glory.
And, we pray, give us such an awareness of your mercies,
that with truly thankful hearts we may show forth your praise,
not only with our lips, but in our lives,
by giving up our selves to your service,
and by walking before you
in holiness and righteousness all our days;
through Jesus Christ our Lord,
to whom, with you and the Holy Spirit,
be honor and glory throughout all ages. Amen.

A Prayer of St. Chrysostom

Almighty God, you have given us grace at this time with one
accord to make our common supplication to you; and you
have promised through your well-beloved Son that when
two or three are gathered together in his Name you will
be in the midst of them: Fulfill now, O Lord, our desires
and petitions as may be best for us; granting us in this
world knowledge of your truth, and in the age to come life
everlasting. *Amen.*

Then may be said

Let us bless the Lord.
Thanks be to God.

*From Easter Day through the Day of Pentecost "Alleluia, alleluia" may
be added to the preceding versicle and response.*

The Officiant may then conclude with one of the following

The grace of our Lord Jesus Christ, and the love of God, and
the fellowship of the Holy Spirit, be with us all evermore.
Amen. 2 Corinthians 13:14

Te bendecimos por crearnos, preservarnos
y por todas las bendiciones de la vida,
pero sobre todo por tu amor incalculable
al redimir al mundo por nuestro Señor Jesucristo;
por los medios de tu gracia
y la esperanza de vivir en gloria.
Te rogamos que, conscientes de tus favores
y *agradecidos* de todo corazón,
proclamemos tu alabanza no solo con los labios,
sino también con nuestras vidas,
dedicándonos a servirte
y caminando día a día en santidad y rectitud ante ti;
por Jesucristo nuestro Señor.
A él, a ti, y al Espíritu Santo
sean el honor y la gloria por siempre. Amén.

Oración de San Juan Crisóstomo

Dios de todo poder, por tu gracia nos has concedido
que elevemos hoy en armonía una misma súplica;
y nos has prometido por tu Hijo amado que,
cuando dos o tres se reúnan en tu nombre,
allí estarás con *nosotros*.
Cumple ahora, Señor, nuestros deseos y peticiones
como mejor nos convenga,
y danos a conocer tu verdad en este mundo
y en el mundo venidero vida eterna. **Amén.**

Se puede agregar:

Bendigamos al Señor.
Demos gracias a Dios.

*Del Día de Pascua al Día de Pentecostés, al versículo anterior y a la
respuesta se les puede agregar «¡Aleluya, aleluya!».*

Quien oficia puede concluir con una de las siguientes citas bíblicas:

La gracia de nuestro Señor Jesucristo, el amor de Dios y la
comunión del Espíritu Santo nos acompañen siempre.
Amén. *2 Corintios 13:14*

May the God of hope fill us with all joy and peace in believing through the power of the Holy Spirit. *Amen. Romans 15:13*

Glory to God whose power, working in us, can do infinitely more than we can ask or imagine: Glory to him from generation to generation in the Church, and in Christ Jesus for ever and ever. *Amen.   Ephesians 3:20, 21*

El Dios de esperanza nos llene de todo gozo y paz en la fe
por virtud del Espíritu Santo. **Amén.** *Romanos 15:13*

Gloria a Dios cuyo poder, activo en *nosotros*, puede realizar
infinitamente más de lo que podemos pedir o pensar: gloria a
él por siempre en la Iglesia, en Cristo Jesús. **Amén.**
Efesios 3:20, 21

An Order for Compline

The Officiant begins

The Lord Almighty grant us a peaceful night and a perfect end. *Amen.*

Officiant	Our help is in the Name of the Lord;
People	The maker of heaven and earth.

The Officiant may then say

Let us confess our sins to God.

Silence may be kept.

Officiant and People

Almighty God, our heavenly Father:
We have sinned against you,
through our own fault,
in thought, and word, and deed,
and in what we have left undone.
For the sake of your Son our Lord Jesus Christ,
forgive us all our offenses;
and grant that we may serve you in newness of life,
to the glory of your Name. Amen.

Officiant

May the Almighty God grant us forgiveness of all our sins,
and the grace and comfort of the Holy Spirit. *Amen.*

Oración de la Noche

Quien oficia dice:

El Señor nos conceda, en su poder, una noche apacible y un final feliz. **Amén.**

Oficiante Nuestro socorro está en el nombre del Señor;
Pueblo **Que hizo los cielos y la tierra.**

Entonces quien oficia puede decir:

Confesemos a Dios nuestros pecados.

Se puede guardar un período de silencio.

Oficiante y pueblo:

**Dios de poder, nuestro Padre celestial:
Hemos pecado contra ti
por nuestra propia culpa
de pensamiento, palabra y obra
y en lo que hemos dejado sin hacer.
Por amor de tu Hijo Jesucristo,
perdona todas nuestras ofensas;
y haz que te sirvamos con vida renovada
para gloria de tu nombre. Amén.**

Oficiante:

Dios, en su poder, nos perdone de todos nuestros pecados y nos dé la gracia y fortaleza del Espíritu Santo. **Amén.**

The Officiant then says

        O God, make speed to save us.

People   O Lord, make haste to help us.

Officiant and People

Glory to the Father, and to the Son, and to the Holy Spirit: as it was in the beginning, is now, and will be for ever. Amen.

Except in Lent, add   Alleluia.

One or more of the following Psalms are sung or said. Other suitable selections may be substituted.

Psalm 4 *Cum invocarem*

1   Answer me when I call, O God, defender of my cause; *
        you set me free when I am hard-pressed;
        have mercy on me and hear my prayer.

2   "You mortals, how long will you dishonor my glory? *
        how long will you worship dumb idols
        and run after false gods?"

3   Know that the LORD does wonders for the faithful; *
        when I call upon the LORD, he will hear me.

4   Tremble, then, and do not sin; *
        speak to your heart in silence upon your bed.

5   Offer the appointed sacrifices *
        and put your trust in the LORD.

6   Many are saying,
    "Oh, that we might see better times!" *
        Lift up the light of your countenance upon us,
           O LORD.

7   You have put gladness in my heart, *
        more than when grain and wine and oil increase.

Oficiante: Apresúrate, Dios, para salvarnos.
Pueblo: **Date prisa, Señor, en socorrernos.**

Oficiante y pueblo:

Gloria al Padre, y al Hijo y al Espíritu Santo:
Como era en el principio, ahora y para siempre
por los siglos de los siglos. Amén.

Excepto en tiempo de Cuaresma, se agrega:
¡Aleluya!

*Se puede cantar o recitar uno o más de los salmos que siguen, u otras
selecciones que sean apropiadas.*

Salmo 4 *Cum invocarem*

1   Cuando te llame, respóndeme, defensor mío; *
cuando estoy en aprietos, líbrame;
ten compasión y escucha mi plegaria.

2   «¿Hasta cuándo, mortales, ultrajarán mi gloria? *
¿Por qué adoran mentiras, falsedades,
dioses vanos?»

3   Sepan que Dios bendice al fiel; *
el SEÑOR me oirá cuando lo llame.

4   Tiemblen y no pequen; *
mediten en sus lechos en silencio.

5   Ofrezcan sacrificios justos *
y pongan su confianza en Dios.

6   Muchos dicen:
«¡Ojalá vengan épocas mejores!» *
Ilumínanos, Señor, con tu semblante.

7   Has puesto más alegría en mi corazón *
que quienes traen cosechas y vendimias.

8   I lie down in peace; at once I fall asleep; *
        for only you, LORD, make me dwell in safety.

Psalm 31 *In te, Domine, speravi*

1   In you, O LORD, have I taken refuge;
    let me never be put to shame: *
        deliver me in your righteousness.

2   Incline your ear to me; *
        make haste to deliver me.

3   Be my strong rock, a castle to keep me safe,
    for you are my crag and my stronghold; *
        for the sake of your Name, lead me and
            guide me.

4   Take me out of the net that they have secretly set for me, *
        for you are my tower of strength.

5   Into your hands I commend my spirit, *
        for you have redeemed me,
        O LORD, O God of truth.

Psalm 91 *Qui habitat*

1   He who dwells in the shelter of the Most High *
        abides under the shadow of the Almighty.

2   He shall say to the LORD,
    "You are my refuge and my stronghold, *
        my God in whom I put my trust."

3   He shall deliver you from the snare of the hunter *
        and from the deadly pestilence.

4   He shall cover you with his pinions,
    and you shall find refuge under his wings; *
        his faithfulness shall be a shield and buckler.

8   Me acuesto en paz y me duermo enseguida; *
       por ti, SEÑOR, vivo libre de peligros.

Salmo 31 *In te, Domine, speravi*

1   En ti, SEÑOR, espero;
     nunca sea yo avergonzado; *
       en tu justicia líbrame.

2   Inclina tu oído; *
       apresúrate a librarme.

3   Sé mi peñasco, la torre que me salve,
     pues eres mi roca y mi castillo; *
       dirige y guíame, por amor de tu nombre.

4   Sácame de la red que me han tendido, *
       porque tú eres mi torre de defensa.

5   En tus manos encomiendo mi espíritu, *
       porque tú me has redimido,
       SEÑOR, Dios de la verdad.

Salmo 91 *Qui habitat*

1   Quien habita al abrigo del Altísimo *
       vive a la sombra del Todopoderoso.

2   Le dirá al Señor: «Tú eres mi refugio y mi castillo, *
       mi Dios en quien confío».

3   Porque te librará de la trampa del cazador *
       y de la peste destructora.

4   Con sus plumas te cubrirá;
     bajo sus alas te refugiarás; *
       escudo y defensa es su verdad.

5   You shall not be afraid of any terror by night, *
        nor of the arrow that flies by day;

6   Of the plague that stalks in the darkness, *
        nor of the sickness that lays waste at mid-day.

7   A thousand shall fall at your side
    and ten thousand at your right hand, *
        but it shall not come near you.

8   Your eyes have only to behold *
        to see the reward of the wicked.

9   Because you have made the LORD your refuge, *
        and the Most High your habitation,

10 There shall no evil happen to you, *
        neither shall any plague come near your dwelling.

11 For he shall give his angels charge over you, *
        to keep you in all your ways.

12 They shall bear you in their hands, *
        lest you dash your foot against a stone.

13 You shall tread upon the lion and adder; *
        you shall trample the young lion and the serpent
            under your feet.

14 Because he is bound to me in love,
    therefore will I deliver him; *
        I will protect him, because he knows my Name.

15 He shall call upon me, and I will answer him; *
        I am with him in trouble;
        I will rescue him and bring him to honor.

16 With long life will I satisfy him, *
        and show him my salvation.

5   No temerás el terror de la noche *
        ni flecha que vuele de día,

6   ni la pestilencia que acecha en las tinieblas, *
        ni la plaga que azota en pleno día.

7   Mil caerán a tu lado
        y diez mil a tu derecha, *
        pero a ti no te afectará.

8   Con solo abrir los ojos, *
        verás la recompensa del malvado.

9   Porque hiciste del Señor tu refugio *
        y del Altísimo, tu morada.

10 No habrá mal que caiga sobre ti *
        ni calamidad que se acerque a tu morada.

11 Porque ordenará a sus ángeles *
        que te cuiden en todos tus caminos.

12 En sus manos te sostendrán *
        y no habrá piedra que te haga tropezar.

13 Aplastarás al león y a la serpiente; *
        pisarás a la víbora y al tigre.

14 Yo libero a quien me ama; *
        elevo a quien conoce mi nombre.

15 Me llamará y le responderé; *
        en sus angustias, lo acompañaré;
        lo rescataré y lo honraré,

16 lo saciaré con larga vida *
        y le mostraré mi salvación.

Psalm 134 *Ecce nunc*

1   Behold now, bless the LORD, all you servants of the LORD, *
        you that stand by night in the house of the LORD.

2   Lift up your hands in the holy place and bless the LORD; *
        the LORD who made heaven and earth bless
            you out of Zion.

At the end of the Psalms is sung or said

Glory to the Father, and to the Son, and to the Holy Spirit: *
    as it was in the beginning, is now, and will be for ever.
        Amen.

One of the following, or some other suitable passage of Scripture, is read

Lord, you are in the midst of us, and we are called by
your Name: Do not forsake us, O Lord our God.
Jeremiah 14:9, 22

People   Thanks be to God.

or this

Come to me, all who labor and are heavy-laden, and I will
give you rest. Take my yoke upon you, and learn from me;
for I am gentle and lowly in heart, and you will find rest for
your souls. For my yoke is easy, and my burden is light.
Matthew 11:28-30

People   Thanks be to God.

or the following

May the God of peace, who brought again from the dead our
Lord Jesus, the great shepherd of the sheep, by the blood of
the eternal covenant, equip you with everything good that
you may do his will, working in you that which is pleasing
in his sight, through Jesus Christ; to whom be glory for ever
and ever.   *Hebrews 13:20-21*

People   Thanks be to God.

Salmo 134 *Ecce nunc*

1 Bendigan al Señor quienes lo sirven *
    y pasan la noche en la casa de Dios.

2 Alcen las manos hacia el lugar santo; *
    Dios, creador de cielo y tierra, los bendiga
        desde Sion.

Después de los salmos, se canta o se dice:

Gloria al Padre, y al Hijo y al Espíritu Santo: *
Como era en el principio, ahora y para siempre. Amén.

Se lee uno de los siguientes pasajes, u otro que sea apropiado:

Tú, Señor, estás entre *nosotros* y llevamos tu nombre; no
nos abandones, Dios nuestro. *Jeremías 14:9, 22*

Demos gracias a Dios.

O bien:

Vengan a mí, *todos* ustedes que están *cansados* y *cargados*,
y yo *los* haré descansar. Carguen mi yugo y aprendan de
mí, que soy manso y humilde de corazón, y hallarán
descanso. Porque mi yugo es fácil y mi carga, liviana.
Mateo 11:28-30

Demos gracias a Dios.

O bien:

Que el Dios de paz, que resucitó a Jesús nuestro Señor, el
gran pastor de las ovejas, *los* prepare en todo para hacer
su voluntad, por la sangre del pacto eterno, obrando en
ustedes lo que le complace; por Jesucristo, a quien sea la
gloria por los siglos de los siglos. *Hebreos 13:20-21*

Demos gracias a Dios.

or this

Be sober, be watchful. Your adversary the devil prowls around like a roaring lion, seeking someone to devour. Resist him, firm in your faith. *I Peter 5:8-9a*

People   Thanks be to God.

A hymn suitable for the evening may be sung.

Then follows

V.   Into your hands, O Lord, I commend my spirit;
R.   For you have redeemed me, O Lord, O God of truth.
V.   Keep us, O Lord, as the apple of your eye;
R.   Hide us under the shadow of your wings.

Lord, have mercy.
Christ, have mercy.
Lord, have mercy.

Officiant and People

Our Father, who art in heaven,	Our Father in heaven,
hallowed be thy Name,	hallowed be your Name,
thy kingdom come,	your kingdom come,
thy will be done,	your will be done,
on earth as it is in heaven.	on earth as in heaven.
Give us this day our daily bread.	Give us today our daily bread.
And forgive us our trespasses,	Forgive us our sins
as we forgive those	as we forgive those
who trespass against us.	who sin against us.
And lead us not into temptation,	Save us from the time of trial,
but deliver us from evil.	and deliver us from evil.

Officiant   Lord, hear our prayer;
People   And let our cry come to you.
Officiant   Let us pray.

The Officiant then says one of the following Collects

Be our light in the darkness, O Lord, and in your great mercy defend us from all perils and dangers of this night;

O bien:

Sean *sobrios* y estén alertas. El diablo, el adversario,
acecha como un león rugiente, buscando a quien devorar.
Resístanlo, firmes en la fe. *1 Pedro 5:8-9a*
Demos gracias a Dios.

Se puede cantar un himno que sea apropiado para la noche.

Se sigue así:

V. En tus manos, Señor, encomiendo mi espíritu;
R. **Pues tú me has redimido, Dios de la verdad.**
V. Guárdame, Señor, como la niña de tus ojos;
R. **Escóndeme bajo la sombra de tus alas.**

Señor, ten piedad.
Cristo, ten piedad.
Señor, ten piedad.

Padre nuestro que estás en el cielo,
    santificado sea tu nombre;
    venga tu reino;
    hágase tu voluntad
        en la tierra como en el cielo.
Danos hoy nuestro pan de cada día.
Perdona nuestras ofensas,
    como también *nosotros* perdonamos
        a los que nos ofenden.
No nos dejes caer en la tentación
    y líbranos del mal.

Oficiante   Señor, escucha nuestra oración;
Pueblo   **Y atiende nuestra súplica.**
Oficiante   Oremos.

Quien oficia dice una de las siguientes colectas:

Dios de gloria: Sé nuestra luz en las tinieblas y, por tu piedad,
defiéndenos de todos los peligros de esta noche;

for the love of your only Son, our Savior Jesus Christ.
Amen.

Be present, O merciful God, and protect us through
the hours of this night, so that we who are wearied
by the changes and chances of this life may rest in
your eternal changelessness; through Jesus Christ
our Lord. *Amen.*

Look down, O Lord, from your heavenly throne,
and illumine this night with your celestial brightness;
that by night as by day your people
may glorify your holy Name;
through Jesus Christ our Lord. *Amen.*

Visit this place, O Lord,
and drive far from it all snares
of the enemy; let your holy angels dwell
with us to preserve us in peace;
and let your blessing be upon
us always; through Jesus Christ our Lord. *Amen.*

A Collect for Saturdays

We give you thanks, O God,
for revealing your Son Jesus Christ to us
by the light of his resurrection:
Grant that as we sing your glory
at the close of this day, our joy may abound
in the morning as we celebrate the Paschal mystery;
through Jesus Christ our Lord. *Amen.*

One of the following prayers may be added

Keep watch, dear Lord, with those who work, or watch, or
weep this night, and give your angels charge over those who
sleep. Tend the sick, Lord Christ; give rest to the weary, bless
the dying, soothe the suffering, pity the afflicted, shield the
joyous; and all for your love's sake. *Amen.*

por amor de tu único Hijo nuestro Salvador Jesucristo.
Amén.

Dios de piedad:
Acompaña y protégenos a lo largo de esta noche;
que aunque *agobiados* por el cambio e incertidumbre
de esta vida, durmamos en ti que siempre permaneces;
por Cristo Jesús nuestro Señor. **Amén.**

Cuídanos desde tu trono, Dios,
e ilumina esta noche con tu brillo celestial;
para que, tanto de noche como de día,
tu pueblo le rinda gloria a tu santo nombre;
por Cristo Jesús nuestro Señor. **Amén.**

Visita, Señor, este lugar,
y aleja de él las trampas que tiende el enemigo;
que tus ángeles se queden con *nosotros*,
guardándonos en paz;
y que tu bendición siempre esté sobre *nosotros*;
por Jesucristo nuestro Señor. **Amén.**

Colecta para los sábados

Dios de amor:
Te damos gracias porque nos revelaste
a tu Hijo Cristo Jesús por la luz de su resurrección;
concede que *nosotros* que te cantamos alabanzas
al cierre de este día,
celebremos mañana el misterio de su Pascua
con abundante alegría;
por Jesucristo Cristo Jesús nuestro Señor. **Amén.**

Se puede agregar una de las siguientes oraciones:

Acompaña, buen Señor, a cada persona que esta noche
trabaja, se desvela o se lamenta, y haz que tus ángeles cobijen
a quienes duermen. Cuida *al enfermo*, da reposo *al fatigado*,
bendice *al moribundo*, alivia *al que sufre*, apiádate *del
afligido*, y protege *al gozoso*; por tu amor y tu ternura. **Amén.**

or this

O God, your unfailing providence sustains the
world we live in and the life we live: Watch over those,
both night and day, who work while others sleep,
and grant that we may never forget that our common
life depends upon each other's toil;
through Jesus Christ our Lord. *Amen.*

Silence may be kept, and free intercessions and thanksgivings may be offered.

The service concludes with the Song of Simeon with this Antiphon, which is sung or said by all

Guide us waking, O Lord, and guard us sleeping;
that awake we may watch with Christ, and asleep we may
rest in peace.

In Easter Season, add   Alleluia, alleluia, alleluia.

Lord, you now have set your servant free *
    to go in peace as you have promised;

For these eyes of mine have seen the Savior, *
    whom you have prepared for all the world to see:

A Light to enlighten the nations, *
    and the glory of your people Israel.

Glory to the Father, and to the Son, and to the Holy Spirit: *
    as it was in the beginning, is now, and will be for ever.
            Amen.

All repeat the Antiphon

Guide us waking, O Lord, and guard us sleeping; that awake
we may watch with Christ, and asleep we may rest in peace.

O bien:

Dios de amor:
Tu providencia sostiene nuestro mundo y nuestra vida;
protege, tanto de noche como de día,
a quienes trabajan mientras otros duermen,
y no permitas que olvidemos
que nuestra vida depende de labores entrelazadas;
por Cristo Jesús nuestro Señor. **Amén.**

Se pueden agregar peticiones y acciones de gracias espontáneas.

La liturgia concluye con el Cántico de Simeón, precedido por esta antífona que todos cantan o dicen:

Guíanos, Señor, *despiertos,*
y guárdanos *dormidos*;
que, *despiertos*, velemos con Cristo,
y, *dormidos*, descansemos en paz.

Durante el tiempo de Pascua, se agrega:

¡Aleluya, aleluya, aleluya!

Ahora deja, Señor, que me vaya en paz, *
    conforme a lo que habías prometido;

porque mis ojos han visto al Salvador *
    que has preparado ante los pueblos:

luz que ilumina a las naciones *
    y gloria de Israel, tu pueblo.

Gloria al Padre, y al Hijo y al Espíritu Santo: *
    Como era en el principio, ahora y siempre
    por los siglos de los siglos. Amén.

Todos repiten la antífona:

Guíanos, Señor, *despiertos,*
y guárdanos *dormidos*;
que, *despiertos*, velemos con Cristo,
y, *dormidos*, descansemos en paz.

In Easter Season, add   Alleluia, alleluia, alleluia.

Officiant   Let us bless the Lord.
People   Thanks be to God.

The Officiant concludes

The almighty and merciful Lord, Father, Son, and Holy
Spirit, bless us and keep us. *Amen.*

Durante el tiempo de Pascua, se agrega:

¡Aleluya, aleluya, aleluya!

Oficiante: Bendigamos al Señor.
Pueblo: **Demos gracias a Dios.**

Quien oficia concluye así:

Que Dios, poderoso y misericordioso,
Padre, Hijo y Espíritu Santo,
nos bendiga y guarde. **Amén.**

Holy Baptism

A hymn, psalm, or anthem may be sung.

The people standing, the Celebrant says

              Blessed be God: Father, Son, and Holy Spirit.
People   And blessed be his kingdom, now and for ever.
              Amen.

In place of the above, from Easter Day through the Day of Pentecost

Celebrant   Alleluia. Christ is risen.
People   The Lord is risen indeed. Alleluia.

In Lent and on other penitential occasions

Celebrant   Bless the Lord who forgives all our sins;
People   His mercy endures for ever.

The Celebrant then continues

              There is one Body and one Spirit;
People   There is one hope in God's call to us;
Celebrant   One Lord, one Faith, one Baptism;
People   One God and Father of all.

Celebrant   The Lord be with you.
People   And also with you.
Celebrant   Let us pray.

El Santo Bautismo

Se puede cantar un himno, salmo o canto.

El pueblo, de pie; quien preside dice:

Bendito sea Dios: Padre, Hijo y Espíritu Santo.
Y bendito sea su reino ahora y por siempre. Amén.

Del día de Pascua al día de Pentecostés quien preside dice:

¡Aleluya! Cristo ha resucitado.
Es verdad: El Señor ha resucitado. ¡Aleluya!

En Cuaresma y otras ocasiones penitenciales:

Bendito sea el Señor, que perdona todo pecado.
Su misericordia perdura eternamente.

Entonces sigue:

Hay un solo Cuerpo y un solo Espíritu.
Una sola esperanza a la que Dios nos llama.
Un solo Señor, una sola fe, un solo bautismo.
Un solo Dios y Padre de toda la creación.

El Señor esté con ustedes.
Y también contigo.
Oremos.

The Collect of the Day

People   Amen.

At the principal service on a Sunday or other feast, the Collect and Lessons are properly those of the Day. On other occasions they are selected from "At Baptism."

The Lessons

The people sit. One or two Lessons, as appointed, are read, the Reader first saying

A Reading (Lesson) from _____.

A citation giving chapter and verse may be added.

After each Reading, the Reader may say

        The Word of the Lord.
People   Thanks be to God.

or the Reader may say   Here ends the Reading (Epistle).

Silence may follow.

A Psalm, hymn, or anthem may follow each Reading.

Then, all standing, the Deacon or a Priest reads the Gospel, first saying

        The Holy Gospel of our Lord Jesus Christ
        according to _____.
People   Glory to you, Lord Christ.

After the Gospel, the Reader says

        The Gospel of the Lord.
People   Praise to you, Lord Christ.

The Sermon

Or the Sermon may be preached after the Peace.

Colecta del día

Pueblo **Amén.**

Si se estuviera celebrando la liturgia principal del domingo u otra fiesta, se usarán las colectas y las lecturas propias de ese día. En otras ocasiones se elegirán de la sección titulada «En un bautismo».

Las lecturas

El pueblo se sienta. Se lee una o dos lecturas, según corresponda, diciendo primero:

Lectura de_____.

Se puede agregar capítulo y versículo.

Después de cada lectura, el lector *puede decir:*

Palabra de Dios.
Demos gracias a Dios.

O bien puede decir:

Aquí concluye la lectura (la epístola).

Se puede guardar silencio.

Después de cada lectura, se puede seguir con un salmo, un himno u otro canto.

Entonces, con todos *de pie, un diácono (o, en su ausencia, un presbítero) proclama el evangelio, diciendo primero:*

Santo evangelio de nuestro Señor Jesucristo según_____.
¡Gloria a ti, Cristo Señor!

Después del evangelio, quien leyó dice:

El evangelio del Señor.
Te alabamos, Cristo Señor.

Sermón

Se puede dar ahora o después de compartir la paz.

Presentation and Examination of the Candidates

The Celebrant says

The Candidate(s) for Holy Baptism will now be presented.

Adults and Older Children

The candidates who are able to answer for themselves are presented individually by their Sponsors, as follows

Sponsor   I present N. to receive the Sacrament of Baptism.

The Celebrant asks each candidate when presented

         Do you desire to be baptized?
Candidate   I do.

Infants and Younger Children

Then the candidates unable to answer for themselves are presented individually by their Parents and Godparents, as follows

Parents and Godparents

I present N. to receive the Sacrament of Baptism.

When all have been presented the Celebrant asks the parents and godparents

Will you be responsible for seeing that the child you present is brought up in the Christian faith and life?

Parents and Godparents

I will, with God's help.

Celebrant

Will you by your prayers and witness help this child to grow into the full stature of Christ?

Presentación y examen de los candidatos

Presidente:

Que se presenten ahora *los candidatos* para el santo bautismo.

Adultos y *niños* mayores

Los candidatos *que tengan edad suficiente para responder son* presentados *individualmente por sus* padrinos *de la siguiente manera:*

Padrinos **Presento a N. para que reciba el sacramento del bautismo.**

Presidente

(a cada candidato) ¿Deseas bautizarte?
Candidato **Sí.**

Bebés y *niños* de corta edad

Entonces los padres *y* los padrinos *presentan individualmente a* los candidatos *que no puedan responder por sí* mismos *de la siguiente manera:*

Padres y padrinos

Presento a N. para que reciba el sacramento del bautismo.

Una vez que todos *hayan sido* presentados, *quien preside les pregunta a* los padres *y* padrinos:

Presidente ¿Te harás responsable de que esta criatura que presentas se críe en la fe y la vida cristiana?

Padres y padrinos

Lo haré, con la ayuda de Dios.

Presidente ¿Lo ayudarás con tus oraciones y ejemplo a que crezca hasta la estatura de la plenitud de Cristo?

Parents and Godparents

I will, with God's help.

Then the Celebrant asks the following questions of the candidates who can speak for themselves, and of the parents and godparents who speak on behalf of the infants and younger children

Question	Do you renounce Satan and all the spiritual forces of wickedness that rebel against God?
Answer	I renounce them.
Question	Do you renounce the evil powers of this world which corrupt and destroy the creatures of God?
Answer	I renounce them.
Question	Do you renounce all sinful desires that draw you from the love of God?
Answer	I renounce them.
Question	Do you turn to Jesus Christ and accept him as your Savior?
Answer	I do.
Question	Do you put your whole trust in his grace and love?
Answer	I do.
Question	Do you promise to follow and obey him as your Lord?
Answer	I do.

When there are others to be presented, the Bishop says
The other Candidate(s) will now be presented.

Presenters I present *these persons* for Confirmation.

or I present *these persons* to be received into this Communion.

or I present *these persons* who *desire* to reaffirm *their* baptismal vows.

Padres y padrinos
Lo haré, con la ayuda de Dios.

Quien preside les pregunta a los candidatos que pueden responder por sí mismos y a los padres y padrinos que responden a favor de bebés y niños menores:

¿Renuncias a Satanás y a todas las fuerzas malignas que contra Dios se rebelan?
Las renuncio.

¿Renuncias a los poderes malignos de este mundo que corrompen y destruyen a las criaturas de Dios?
Los renuncio.

¿Renuncias todos los deseos pecaminosos que te separan del amor de Dios?
Los renuncio.

¿Te consagras a Jesucristo y lo recibes como tu Salvador?
Me consagro y lo recibo.

¿Pones toda tu confianza en su gracia y amor?
La pongo.

¿Prometes seguir y obedecerlo como tu Señor?
Lo prometo.

Si hubiera más candidatos que presentar, el obispo dice:

Presidente	Ahora se presentarán *otros candidatos.*
Presentadores	Presento a *estas personas* para la confirmación.
O bien:	Presento a *estas personas* para que *sean recibidas* como parte de esta comunión.
O bien:	Presento a *estas personas* que *desean* reafirmar sus votos de bautismo.

The Bishop asks the candidates

Do you reaffirm your renunciation of evil?

Candidate   I do.

Bishop

Do you renew your commitment to Jesus Christ?

Candidate

I do, and with God's grace I will follow him as my Savior and Lord.

After all have been presented, the Celebrant addresses the congregation, saying

Will you who witness these vows do all in your power to support *these persons* in *their* life in Christ?

People   We will.

The Celebrant then says these or similar words

Let us join with *those* who *are* committing *themselves* to Christ and renew our own baptismal covenant.

The Baptismal Covenant

Celebrant	Do you believe in God the Father?
People	I believe in God, the Father almighty, creator of heaven and earth.
Celebrant	Do you believe in Jesus Christ, the Son of God?
People	I believe in Jesus Christ, his only Son, our Lord. He was conceived by the power of the Holy Spirit and born of the Virgin Mary.

Obispo	¿Reafirmas que renuncias al mal?
Candidato	**Lo reafirmo.**
Obispo	¿Renuevas tu entrega a Jesucristo?
Candidato	**La renuevo, y con la gracia de Dios lo seguiré como mi Señor y Salvador.**

Después que todos los candidatos han sido presentados, quien preside dice:

Y ustedes, testigos de estos votos: ¿Harán todo lo que puedan para apoyar a *estas personas* que desde hoy *viven* en Cristo?

Pueblo **¡Lo haremos!**

Quien preside dice lo que sigue, o algo similar:

Unámonos a *quienes* hoy se *consagran* al Señor y renovemos nuestro propio pacto bautismal.

El pacto bautismal

Presidente ¿Crees en Dios el Padre?

Pueblo **Creo en Dios, Padre todopoderoso,
creador del cielo y de la tierra.**

Presidente ¿Crees en Jesucristo, el Hijo de Dios?

Pueblo **Creo en Jesucristo, su único Hijo, nuestro Señor,
que fue concebido por obra y gracia del
Espíritu Santo, nació de la santa María Virgen,**

He suffered under Pontius Pilate,
     was crucified, died, and was buried.
He descended to the dead.
On the third day he rose again.
He ascended into heaven, and is seated
     at the right hand of the Father.
He will come again to judge the living
     and the dead.

Celebrant   Do you believe in God the Holy Spirit?

People   I believe in the Holy Spirit,
     the holy catholic Church,
     the communion of saints,
     the forgiveness of sins,
     the resurrection of the body,
     and the life everlasting.

Celebrant   Will you continue in the apostles' teaching
and fellowship, in the breaking of bread,
and in the prayers?

People   I will, with God's help.

Celebrant   Will you persevere in resisting evil, and,
whenever you fall into sin, repent and return to
the Lord?

People   I will, with God's help.

Celebrant   Will you proclaim by word and example the
Good News of God in Christ?

People   I will, with God's help.

Celebrant   Will you seek and serve Christ in all persons,
loving your neighbor as yourself?

People   I will, with God's help.

Celebrant   Will you strive for justice and peace among all
people, and respect the dignity of every human
being?

People   I will, with God's help.

padeció bajo el poder de Poncio Pilato,
	fue crucificado, muerto y sepultado,
descendió a los infiernos,
al tercer día resucitó de entre los muertos,
subió a los cielos y está sentado a la derecha
	de Dios, Padre todopoderoso.
Desde allí ha de venir a juzgar a vivos y
	muertos.

Presidente ¿Crees en el Espíritu Santo?

Pueblo **Creo en el Espíritu Santo,**
	la santa iglesia católica,
	la comunión de *los santos*,
	el perdón de los pecados,
	la resurrección de los muertos
	y la vida eterna.

Presidente ¿Seguirás fiel a la enseñanza y comunión de *los* apóstoles, en el partir el pan y en las oraciones?

Pueblo **Lo haré, con la ayuda de Dios.**

Presidente ¿Seguirás firme en resistir el mal y, cada vez que caigas en pecado, te arrepentirás y te volverás al Señor?

Pueblo **Lo haré, con la ayuda de Dios.**

Presidente ¿Proclamarás por palabra y ejemplo la buena noticia de Dios en Cristo?

Pueblo **Lo haré, con la ayuda de Dios.**

Presidente ¿Buscarás y servirás a Cristo en toda persona, amando a tu prójimo como a ti mismo?

Pueblo **Lo haré, con la ayuda de Dios.**

Presidente ¿Lucharás por la justicia y la paz en el mundo y respetarás la dignidad de todo ser humano?

Pueblo **Lo haré, con la ayuda de Dios.**

Prayers for the Candidates

The Celebrant then says to the congregation

Let us now pray for *these persons* who *are* to receive the Sacrament of new birth [and for those (this person) who *have* renewed *their* commitment to Christ.]

A Person appointed leads the following petitions

Leader	Deliver *them*, O Lord, from the way of sin and death.
People	Lord, hear our prayer.
Leader	Open *their hearts* to your grace and truth.
People	Lord, hear our prayer.
Leader	Fill *them* with your holy and life-giving Spirit.
People	Lord, hear our prayer.
Leader	Keep *them* in the faith and communion of your holy Church.
People	Lord, hear our prayer.
Leader	Teach *them* to love others in the power of the Spirit.
People	Lord, hear our prayer.
Leader	Send *them* into the world in witness to your love.
People	Lord, hear our prayer.
Leader	Bring *them* to the fullness of your peace and glory.
People	Lord, hear our prayer.

The Celebrant says

Grant, O Lord, that all who are baptized into the death of Jesus Christ your Son may live in the power of his resurrection and look for him to come again in glory; who lives and reigns now and for ever. *Amen.*

Oraciones por *los candidatos*

Presidente   Oremos por *estas personas* que *están* por recibir el sacramento de la nueva vida [y por *estas personas* que *han* renovado su devoción a Cristo].

La persona asignada dirige las siguientes peticiones:

Libera, Señor, a *estas personas* de la senda del pecado y de la muerte.

Señor, escucha nuestra oración.

Ábreles el corazón para que *reciban* tu gracia y tu verdad.

Señor, escucha nuestra oración.

Llénalos del Espíritu que nos aviva y purifica.

Señor, escucha nuestra oración.

Guárdalos en la fe y en comunión con tu santa Iglesia.

Señor, escucha nuestra oración.

Enséñales a amar al prójimo con la fuerza del Espíritu.

Señor, escucha nuestra oración.

Envíalos al mundo para dar testimonio de tu amor.

Señor, escucha nuestra oración.

Tráelos a la plenitud de tu paz y de tu gloria.

Señor, escucha nuestra oración.

Presidente

Concede, Señor, que toda persona bautizada en la muerte de tu Hijo viva en el poder de su resurrección con la esperanza de su regreso en gloria; por Jesucristo, que vive y reina ahora y siempre. **Amén.**

Thanksgiving over the Water

The Celebrant blesses the water, first saying

The Lord be with you.

People And also with you.

Celebrant Let us give thanks to the Lord our God.

People It is right to give him thanks and praise.

Celebrant

We thank you, Almighty God, for the gift of water.
Over it the Holy Spirit moved in the beginning of creation.
Through it you led the children of Israel out of their
bondage in Egypt into the land of promise. In it your Son
Jesus received the baptism of John and was anointed by the
Holy Spirit as the Messiah, the Christ, to lead us, through
his death and resurrection, from the bondage of sin into
everlasting life.

We thank you, Father, for the water of Baptism. In it we
are buried with Christ in his death. By it we share in his
resurrection. Through it we are reborn by the Holy Spirit.
Therefore in joyful obedience to your Son, we bring into his
fellowship those who come to him in faith, baptizing them
in the Name of the Father, and of the Son, and of the Holy
Spirit.

At the following words, the Celebrant touches the water

Now sanctify this water, we pray you, by the power of your
Holy Spirit, that those who here are cleansed from sin and
born again may continue for ever in the risen life of Jesus
Christ our Savior.

To him, to you, and to the Holy Spirit, be all honor and
glory, now and for ever. *Amen.*

Acción de gracias sobre el agua

Quien preside bendice el agua, diciendo primero:

El Señor esté con ustedes.
Y también contigo.

Démosle gracias al Señor nuestro Dios.
Es justo y necesario.

Dios poderoso, te damos gracias por el agua.
Sobre ella se movió tu Espíritu en la aurora de la creación;
por ella guiaste al pueblo de Israel
de la esclavitud de Egipto a la Tierra Prometida;
en ella Jesús fue bautizado por Juan
y ungido por tu Espíritu para ser el Mesías, el Cristo,
y así guiarnos, por su muerte y resurrección, de la esclavitud
del pecado a la vida perdurable.

Te damos gracias Padre, por el agua del bautismo.
En ella nos sepultamos para morir con Cristo;
por ella compartimos su resurrección;
con ella renacemos del Espíritu.
Por eso, con obediencia y alegría,
traemos al rebaño de Cristo
a quienes vienen a Jesús con fe,
bautizándolos en el nombre del Padre,
y del Hijo, y del Espíritu Santo.

Quien preside toca el agua mientras dice:

Ahora santifica esta agua, te pedimos,
mediante el poder de tu Espíritu;
que quienes en ella
sean *lavados* del pecado y nazcan de nuevo,
continúen por siempre en la vida resucitada
de Jesucristo nuestro Salvador.

A él, a ti, y al Espíritu Santo damos todo honor y gloria
ahora y para siempre. **Amén.**

Consecration of the Chrism

The Bishop may then consecrate oil of Chrism, placing a hand on the vessel of oil, and saying

Eternal Father, whose blessed Son was anointed by the Holy Spirit to be the Savior and servant of all, we pray you to consecrate this oil, that those who are sealed with it may share in the royal priesthood of Jesus Christ; who lives and reigns with you and the Holy Spirit, for ever and ever. *Amen.*

The Baptism

Each candidate is presented by name to the Celebrant, or to an assisting priest or deacon, who then immerses, or pours water upon, the candidate, saying

N., I baptize you in the Name of the Father, and of the Son, and of the Holy Spirit. *Amen.*

When this action has been completed for all candidates, the Bishop or Priest, at a place in full sight of the congregation, prays over them, saying

Let us pray.

Heavenly Father, we thank you that by water and the Holy Spirit you have bestowed upon *these* your *servants* the forgiveness of sin, and have raised *them* to the new life of grace. Sustain *them*, O Lord, in your Holy Spirit. Give *them* an inquiring and discerning heart, the courage to will and to persevere, a spirit to know and to love you, and the gift of joy and wonder in all your works. *Amen.*

Consagración del Crisma

Un obispo puede consagrar el crisma poniendo la mano sobre el receptáculo de aceite y diciendo:

Padre Eterno,
cuyo bendito Hijo fue ungido por el Espíritu Santo
para ser Salvador y siervo de la humanidad:
Te rogamos que consagres este crisma
para que toda persona sellada con él
participe del sacerdocio real de Jesucristo;
que vive y reina contigo y el Espíritu Santo ahora y para
siempre. **Amén.**

El bautismo

Se presenta a cada candidato por nombre a quien preside, o a un presbítero o diácono que lo sumerge o le derrama agua diciendo:

N.: Yo te bautizo en el nombre del Padre, y del Hijo, y del
Espíritu Santo. **Amén.**

Cuando estas acciones se completen sobre todos los candidatos, el obispo o presbítero, ora sobre ellos ante todo el pueblo.

Oremos.

Padre celestial: Te damos gracias
porque por agua y el Espíritu Santo
les has concedido a *estos siervos* tuyos
el perdón de los pecados
y *los* has levantado a la vida nueva de gracia.
Sostenlos, Señor, con tu Espíritu Santo.
Dales un corazón inquisitivo y perspicaz,
la valentía de comprometerse y perseverar;
la pasión por conocerte y amarte,
y el don de gozar y maravillarse ante todas tus obras.
Amén.

Then the Bishop or Priest places a hand on the person's head, marking on the forehead the sign of the cross [using Chrism if desired] and saying to each one

N., you are sealed by the Holy Spirit in Baptism and marked as Christ's own for ever. *Amen.*

Or this action may be done immediately after the administration of the water and before the preceding prayer.

When all have been baptized, the Celebrant says

Let us welcome the newly baptized.

Celebrant and People

We receive you into the household of God. Confess the faith of Christ crucified, proclaim his resurrection, and share with us in his eternal priesthood.

If Confirmation, Reception, or the Reaffirmation of Baptismal Vows is not to follow, the Peace is now exchanged

Celebrant   The peace of the Lord be always with you.

People   And also with you.

At Confirmation, Reception, or Reaffirmation

The Bishop says to the congregation

Let us now pray for *these persons* who *have* renewed *their* commitment to Christ.

Silence may be kept.

Then the Bishop says

Almighty God, we thank you that by the death and resurrection of your Son Jesus Christ you have overcome sin and brought us to yourself, and that by the sealing of your Holy Spirit you have bound us to your service.

Un obispo o presbítero impone la mano sobre la cabeza de la persona y la marca en la frente con la señal de la cruz, usando crisma si desea, y le dice:

N., quedas *sellado* por el Espíritu Santo en el bautismo y *marcado* como propiedad de Cristo para siempre.

La marca y declaración puede hacerse inmediatamente después de administrar el agua y antes de decirse la oración post- bautismal.

Cuando se hayan completado todos los bautismos, quien preside dice:

Recibamos a *los* recién *bautizados.*

Pueblo   **Te recibimos en la familia de Dios. Confiesa la fe de Cristo crucificado, proclama su resurrección y participa con *nosotros* de su sacerdocio eterno.**

Si no se continuara con una confirmación, recepción, o reafirmación del pacto bautismal, se da la paz:

Presidente   La paz del Señor esté siempre con ustedes.

Pueblo   **Y también contigo.**

En la confirmación, recepción, o reafirmación del pacto bautismal

El obispo *le dice al pueblo:*

Oremos por *estas personas* que *han* renovado su dedicación a Jesucristo.

Se puede guardar silencio.

El obispo *dice:*

Dios de poder, te damos gracias
porque por la muerte y resurrección de tu Hijo Jesucristo
has triunfado sobre el pecado
y nos has recibido en tu seno;
y porque nos has consagrado
para servirte bajo el sello de tu Espíritu Santo.

Renew in *these* your *servants* the covenant you made with *them* at *their* Baptism. Send *them* forth in the power of that Spirit to perform the service you set before *them*; through Jesus Christ your Son our Lord, who lives and reigns with you and the Holy Spirit, one God, now and for ever. *Amen.*

For Confirmation

The Bishop lays hands upon each one and says

Strengthen, O Lord, your servant N. with your Holy Spirit; empower *him* for your service; and sustain *him* all the days of *his* life. *Amen.*

or this

Defend, O Lord, your servant N. with your heavenly grace, that *he* may continue yours for ever, and daily increase in your Holy Spirit more and more, until *he* comes to your everlasting kingdom. *Amen.*

For Reception

N., we recognize you as a member of the one holy catholic and apostolic Church, and we receive you into the fellowship of this Communion. God, the Father, Son, and Holy Spirit, bless, preserve, and keep you. *Amen.*

For Reaffirmation

N., may the Holy Spirit, who has begun a good work in you, direct and uphold you in the service of Christ and his kingdom. *Amen.*

Then the Bishop says

Almighty and everliving God, let your fatherly hand ever be over *these* your *servants*; let your Holy Spirit ever be with *them*; and so lead *them* in the knowledge and obedience of

Renueva, Señor, en *estos siervos tuyos*
el pacto que hiciste con *ellos* en su bautismo,
y *envíalos* en el poder de tu Espíritu
a llevar a cabo tu misión;
por Jesucristo tu Hijo nuestro Señor,
que vive y reina contigo y el Espíritu Santo:
un solo Dios, ahora y por siempre. **Amén.**

En una confirmación

El obispo *impone las manos sobre cada persona y dice:*

Fortalece, oh Señor, a tu *siervo N.* con tu Espíritu Santo;
empodéralo para servirte; y sostenlo todos los días de su
vida. **Amén.**

O bien:

Defiende, Señor, a tu *siervo N.* con tu gracia celestial,
para que siga siendo *tuyo* para siempre, y acrecienta en *él*
tu Espíritu Santo día tras día hasta que entre en tu reino
sempiterno. **Amén.**

En una recepción

N.: Te reconocemos como miembro de la iglesia, una, santa,
católica y apostólica, y te recibimos como *hermano* en esta
comunión. Que Dios Padre, Hijo y Espíritu Santo te bendiga,
preserve y guarde. **Amén.**

En una reafirmación

N.: Que el Espíritu Santo que en ti empieza a dar buen fruto
te dirija y sostenga para servir a Cristo y su reino. **Amén.**

Entonces el obispo *dice:*

Dios de poder y vida eterna:
Que tu mano tutelar proteja siempre a *estos siervos tuyos*;
y que tu Espíritu Santo *los* acompañe siempre;
Guíalos para que, al conocer y obedecer tu Palabra,

your Word, that *they* may serve you in this life, and dwell with you in the life to come; through Jesus Christ our Lord. *Amen.*

The Peace is then exchanged

Bishop   The peace of the Lord be always with you.
People   And also with you.

At the Eucharist

The service then continues with the Prayers of the People or the Offertory of the Eucharist, at which the Bishop, when present, should be the principal Celebrant.

Except on Principal Feasts, the Proper Preface of Baptism may be used.

Alternative Ending

If there is no celebration of the Eucharist, the service continues with the Lord's Prayer

Our Father, who art in heaven, hallowed be thy Name, thy kingdom come, thy will be done, on earth as it is in heaven. Give us this day our daily bread. And forgive us our trespasses, as we forgive those who trespass against us. And lead us not into temptation, but deliver us from evil. For thine is the kingdom, and the power, and the glory, for ever and ever. Amen.	Our Father in heaven, hallowed be your Name, your kingdom come, your will be done, on earth as in heaven. Give us today our daily bread. Forgive us our sins as we forgive those who sin against us. Save us from the time of trial, and deliver us from evil. For the kingdom, the power, and the glory are yours, now and for ever. Amen.

puedan servirte en esta vida
y morar contigo en la venidera;
por Jesucristo nuestro Señor. **Amén.**

Se puede dar la paz.

Presidente   La paz del Señor esté siempre con ustedes.
Pueblo   **Y también contigo.**

Durante la Santa Comunión

La liturgia continúa con las oraciones del pueblo o el ofertorio de la eucaristía. El obispo, de estar presente, preside.

Excepto en fiestas mayores, se puede usar el prefacio propio del bautismo.

Final alternativo

Si no hay celebración de la Santa Comunión, la liturgia continúa con el Padrenuestro.

Padre nuestro que estás en el cielo,
    santificado sea tu nombre;
    venga tu reino;
    hágase tu voluntad
        en la tierra como en el cielo.
Danos hoy nuestro pan de cada día.
Perdona nuestras ofensas,
    como también nosotros perdonamos
        a los que nos ofenden.
No nos dejes caer en la tentación
    y líbranos del mal.
Porque tuyo es el reino, el poder y la gloria,
    ahora y por siempre. Amén.

All praise and thanks to you, most merciful Father, for adopting us as your own children, for incorporating us into your holy Church, and for making us worthy to share in the inheritance of the saints in light; through Jesus Christ your Son our Lord, who lives and reigns with you and the Holy Spirit, one God, for ever and ever. *Amen.*

Alms may be received and presented, and other prayers may be added, concluding with this prayer

Almighty God, the Father of our Lord Jesus Christ, from whom every family in heaven and earth is named, grant you to be strengthened with might by his Holy Spirit, that, Christ dwelling in your hearts by faith, you may be filled with all the fullness of God. *Amen.*

Presidente

Dios de bondad y clemencia:
Te rendimos gracias y alabanza por adoptarnos
como hijas e hijos tuyos,
hacernos parte del cuerpo de tu santa iglesia
y permitirnos heredar, con los santos y santas,
el reino de la luz;
por tu Hijo Jesucristo nuestro Señor,
que vive y reina contigo y el Espíritu Santo,
un solo Dios por los siglos de los siglos. **Amén.**

*Se pueden presentar ofrendas, y agregar otras oraciones; se concluye
con esta oración:*

Presidente

Dios, Padre poderoso,
fundador de todas las familias del cielo y de la tierra,
los fortalezca con el poder del Espíritu Santo
para que, mediante su fe, Cristo habite en sus corazones
y reciban la plenitud de Dios. **Amén.**

The Holy Eucharist: Rite Two

The Word of God

A hymn, psalm, or anthem may be sung.

The people standing, the Celebrant says

Blessed be God: Father, Son, and Holy Spirit.
People   And blessed be his kingdom, now and for ever. Amen.

In place of the above, from Easter Day through the Day of Pentecost

Celebrant   Alleluia. Christ is risen.
People   The Lord is risen indeed. Alleluia.

In Lent and on other penitential occasions

Celebrant   Bless the Lord who forgives all our sins.
People   His mercy endures for ever.

The Celebrant may say

Almighty God, to you all hearts are open, all desires known, and from you no secrets are hid: Cleanse the thoughts of our hearts by the inspiration of your Holy Spirit, that we may perfectly love you, and worthily magnify your holy Name; through Christ our Lord. *Amen.*

When appointed, the following hymn or some other song of praise is sung or said, all standing

La Santa Eucaristía: Rito II

La palabra de Dios

Se puede cantar un himno, salmo o canto.

El pueblo, de pie; quien preside dice:

Bendito sea Dios: Padre, Hijo y Espíritu Santo.
Y bendito sea su reino ahora y por siempre. Amén.

Del día de Pascua al día de Pentecostés quien preside dice:

¡Aleluya! Cristo ha resucitado.
Es verdad: El Señor ha resucitado. ¡Aleluya!

En Cuaresma y otras ocasiones penitenciales

Bendito sea Dios, que perdona todo pecado.
Su misericordia perdura eternamente.

Quien preside puede decir:

Dios de todo poder: Ante ti, todo corazón queda abierto,
todo deseo revelado, todo secreto expuesto.
Concede que tu Espíritu nos limpie los corazones
y purifique los pensamientos
para que perfectamente te amemos
y dignamente declaremos la grandeza de tu santo nombre.
Por Cristo nuestro Señor. **Amén.**

Cuando se indique, se puede cantar o recitar el himno que sigue, u otro cántico de alabanza. Todos *de pie:*

Glory to God in the highest,
    and peace to his people on earth.

Lord God, heavenly King,
almighty God and Father,
    we worship you, we give you thanks,
    we praise you for your glory.

Lord Jesus Christ, only Son of the Father,
Lord God, Lamb of God,
you take away the sin of the world:
    have mercy on us;
you are seated at the right hand of the Father:
    receive our prayer.

For you alone are the Holy One,
you alone are the Lord,
you alone are the Most High,
    Jesus Christ,
    with the Holy Spirit,
    in the glory of God the Father. Amen.

On other occasions the following is used

Lord, have mercy.		Kyrie eleison.
Christ, have mercy.	*or*	*Christe eleison.*
Lord, have mercy.		Kyrie eleison.

or this

Holy God,
Holy and Mighty,
Holy Immortal One,
Have mercy upon us.

Gloria a Dios en las alturas,
y en la tierra paz y buena voluntad a quienes Dios ama.

Por tu inmensa gloria te alabamos, te bendecimos,
te adoramos, te glorificamos, te damos gracias
Señor Dios, Rey celestial,
Dios Padre todopoderoso.

Señor Jesucristo, Hijo único del Padre,
Señor Dios, Cordero de Dios:
Tú que quitas el pecado del mundo;
recibe nuestra súplica.
Tú que estás sentado a la diestra del Padre;
ten piedad de *nosotros*;

porque solo tú eres Santo,
solo tú Señor,
solo tú Altísimo,
Jesucristo,
con el Espíritu Santo,
en la gloria de Dios Padre. Amén.

En otras ocasiones puede cantarse o recitarse

Señor, ten piedad.		Kyrie, eleison.
Cristo, ten piedad.	*O bien:*	**Christe, eleison.**
Señor, ten piedad.		Kyrie, eleison

O lo siguiente:

Santo Dios,
Santo poderoso,
Santo inmortal,
Ten piedad de *nosotros*.

The Collect of the Day

The Celebrant says to the people

	The Lord be with you.
People	And also with you.
Celebrant	Let us pray.

The Celebrant says the Collect.

People	Amen.

The Lessons

The people sit. One or two Lessons, as appointed, are read, the Reader first saying

A Reading (Lesson) from _____.

A citation giving chapter and verse may be added.

After each Reading, the Reader may say

	The Word of the Lord.
People	Thanks be to God.

or the Reader may say   Here ends the Reading (Epistle).

Silence may follow.

A Psalm, hymn, or anthem may follow each Reading.

Then, all standing, the Deacon or a Priest reads the Gospel, first saying

The Holy Gospel of our Lord Jesus Christ according to _____.
People Glory to you, Lord Christ.

After the Gospel, the Reader says

	The Gospel of the Lord.
People	Praise to you, Lord Christ.

La colecta del día

Quien preside dice:

El Señor esté con ustedes.
Y también contigo.
Oremos.

Quien preside dice la colecta.

Amén.

Las lecturas

El pueblo se sienta. Se leen una o dos lecturas, según se indique; quien lee dice:

Lectura de_____.

Se puede agregar capítulo y versículo.

Después de cada lectura, quien lee puede decir:

Palabra de Dios.
Demos gracias a Dios.

O bien:

Aquí concluye la lectura.

Se puede guardar silencio.

Después de cada lectura, se puede cantar o leer un salmo, un himno o un canto.

Todos *de pie;* un diácono, *o en su ausencia* un presbítero, *lee el evangelio, diciendo primero:*

Santo evangelio de nuestro Señor Jesucristo según_____.
Gloria a ti, Cristo Señor.

Después del evangelio, quien lee dice:

El evangelio del Señor.
Te alabamos, Cristo Señor.

The Sermon

On Sundays and other Major Feasts there follows, all standing

The Nicene Creed

We believe in one God,
>   the Father, the Almighty,
>   maker of heaven and earth,
>   of all that is, seen and unseen.

We believe in one Lord, Jesus Christ,
>   the only Son of God,
>   eternally begotten of the Father,
>   God from God, Light from Light,
>   true God from true God,
>   begotten, not made,
>   of one Being with the Father.
>   Through him all things were made.
>   For us and for our salvation
>   he came down from heaven:
>   by the power of the Holy Spirit
>   he became incarnate from the Virgin Mary,
>   and was made man.
>   For our sake he was crucified under Pontius Pilate;
>   he suffered death and was buried.
>   On the third day he rose again
>   in accordance with the Scriptures;
>   he ascended into heaven
>   and is seated at the right hand of the Father.
>   He will come again in glory to judge the living
>   and the dead, and his kingdom will have no end.

We believe in the Holy Spirit, the Lord, the giver of life,
>   who proceeds from the Father and the Son.
>   With the Father and the Son he is worshiped and glorified.
>   He has spoken through the Prophets.
>   We believe in one holy catholic and apostolic Church.
>   We acknowledge one baptism for the forgiveness of sins.
>   We look for the resurrection of the dead,
>   and the life of the world to come. Amen.

El sermón

Los domingos y en otras fiestas mayores, todos *se ponen de pie y dicen:*

El Credo Niceno

Creemos en un solo Dios,
    Padre todopoderoso,
    Creador del cielo y de la tierra,
    de todo lo visible e invisible.

Creemos en un solo Señor, Jesucristo,
    Hijo único de Dios,
    nacido del Padre antes de todos los siglos:
    Dios de Dios, Luz de Luz,
    Dios verdadero de Dios verdadero,
    engendrado, no creado,
    de la misma naturaleza que el Padre,
    por quien todo fue hecho;
    que por *nosotros,* y por nuestra salvación bajó del cielo,
    y por obra del Espíritu Santo
        se encarnó de María, la Virgen,
        y se hizo humano.
    Por nuestra causa fue crucificado
        en tiempos de Poncio Pilato;
    padeció y fue sepultado,
    resucitó al tercer día, según las escrituras,
    subió al cielo,
        y está sentado a la derecha del Padre;
    de nuevo vendrá con gloria para juzgar
        a vivos y muertos,
    y su reino no tendrá fin.

Creemos en el Espíritu Santo, Señor y dador de vida,
    que procede del Padre y del Hijo,
    que con el Padre y el Hijo recibe
    una misma adoración y gloria,
    y que habló por los profetas.
    Creemos en la iglesia,
    que es una, santa, católica y apostólica.
    Reconocemos un solo bautismo
    para el perdón de los pecados.
    Esperamos la resurrección de los muertos
        y la vida del mundo futuro. Amén.

The Prayers of the People

Prayer is offered with intercession for

The Universal Church, its members, and its mission
The Nation and all in authority
The welfare of the world
The concerns of the local community
Those who suffer and those in any trouble
The departed (with commemoration of a saint when appropriate)

Any of the forms which follow may be used.

Adaptations or insertions suitable to the occasion may be made.

Any of the forms may be conformed to the language of the Rite being used.

A bar in the margin indicates petitions which may be omitted.

The Celebrant may introduce the Prayers with a sentence of invitation related to the occasion, or the season, or the Proper of the Day.

Form I

Deacon or other leader

With all our heart and with all our mind, let us pray to the Lord, saying, "Lord, have mercy."

For the peace from above, for the loving-kindness of God, and for the salvation of our souls, let us pray to the Lord.
Lord, have mercy.

For the peace of the world, for the welfare of the holy Church of God, and for the unity of all peoples, let us pray to the Lord.
Lord, have mercy.

For our Bishop, and for all the clergy and people, let us pray to the Lord.
Lord, have mercy.

Las oraciones del pueblo

El pueblo ofrece oraciones por:

La iglesia universal, sus miembros y su misión
La nación y todas las autoridades
El bienestar del mundo
Las necesidades de la comunidad local
Las personas que sufren o pasan dificultades
Quienes han fallecido (con la conmemoración de un santo o
santa cuando sea apropiado)

Se puede usar cualquiera de las fórmulas que se enumeran más abajo.

Se pueden hacer adaptaciones o interpolaciones según la ocasión.

*La barra vertical que aparece al margen indica peticiones que pueden
omitirse.*

*Quien preside puede comenzar la oración con una invitación de
acuerdo a la ocasión, el tiempo litúrgico, o el propio del día.*

Fórmula I

Un diácono u otro líder dice:

Con toda la mente y de todo corazón, oremos al Señor
diciendo: «Señor, ten piedad».

Por la paz del cielo, por la bondad de Dios y por la
salvación de nuestras almas, oremos al Señor.
Señor, ten piedad.

Por la paz del mundo, por el bienestar de la santa Iglesia
de Dios y por la unidad de todas las naciones, oremos al
Señor.
Señor, ten piedad.

Por *nuestros obispos*, y por todo el clero y el pueblo de la
iglesia, oremos al Señor.
Señor, ten piedad.

For our President, for the leaders of the nations, and for all in authority, let us pray to the Lord.
Lord, have mercy.

For this city (town, village, _____), for every city and community, and for those who live in them, let us pray to the Lord.
Lord, have mercy.

For seasonable weather, and for an abundance of the fruits of the earth, let us pray to the Lord.
Lord, have mercy.

For the good earth which God has given us, and for the wisdom and will to conserve it, let us pray to the Lord.
Lord, have mercy.

For those who travel on land, on water, or in the air [or through outer space], let us pray to the Lord.
Lord, have mercy.

For the aged and infirm, for the widowed and orphans, and for the sick and the suffering, let us pray to the Lord.
Lord, have mercy.

For _____, let us pray to the Lord.
Lord, have mercy.

For the poor and the oppressed, for the unemployed and the destitute, for prisoners and captives, and for all who remember and care for them, let us pray to the Lord.
Lord, have mercy.

For all who have died in the hope of the resurrection, and for all the departed, let us pray to the Lord.
Lord, have mercy.

For deliverance from all danger, violence, oppression, and degradation, let us pray to the Lord.
Lord, have mercy.

Por presidentes y dirigentes de las naciones y por toda autoridad, oremos al Señor.
Señor, ten piedad.

Por esta ciudad (este pueblo, esta aldea, este____), por toda ciudad y comunidad, y por sus habitantes, oremos al Señor.
Señor, ten piedad.

Por buen clima y por cosechas abundantes, oremos al Señor.
Señor, ten piedad.

Por la madre tierra que Dios nos ha brindado, y por la sabiduría y voluntad de preservarla, oremos al Señor.
Señor, ten piedad.

Por quienes viajan por tierra, mar y aire [y en el espacio], oremos al Señor.
Señor, ten piedad.

Por toda persona anciana, enferma o sufriente, por *viudos* y por *huérfanos*, oremos al Señor.
Señor, ten piedad.

Por_____, oremos al Señor.
Señor, ten piedad.

Por las personas pobres y oprimidas, desempleadas e indigentes, encarceladas y cautivas, y por *todos los* que las recuerdan y las cuidan, oremos al Señor.
Señor, ten piedad.

Por toda persona que ha muerto en la esperanza de la resurrección y por toda persona fallecida, oremos al Señor.
Señor, ten piedad.

Por la salvación de todo peligro, violencia, opresión y degradación, oremos al Señor.
Señor, ten piedad.

For the absolution and remission of our sins and offenses, let us pray to the Lord.
Lord, have mercy.

That we may end our lives in faith and hope, without suffering and without reproach, let us pray to the Lord.
Lord, have mercy.

Defend us, deliver us, and in thy compassion protect us, O Lord, by thy grace.
Lord, have mercy.

In the communion of [_____and of all the] saints, let us commend ourselves, and one another, and all our life, to Christ our God.
To thee, O Lord our God.

Silence

The Celebrant adds a concluding Collect.

Form II

In the course of the silence after each bidding, the People offer their own prayers, either silently or aloud.

I ask your prayers for God's people throughout the world; for our Bishop(s) _____; for this gathering; and for all ministers and people.
Pray for the Church.

Silence

I ask your prayers for peace; for goodwill among nations; and for the well-being of all people.
Pray for justice and peace.

Silence

I ask your prayers for the poor, the sick, the hungry, the oppressed, and those in prison.
Pray for those in any need or trouble.

Por el perdón de nuestros pecados y ofensas, oremos al Señor.
Señor, ten piedad.

Que a la hora de nuestra muerte tengamos fe y esperanza,
sin sufrimientos ni reproches, oremos al Señor.
Señor, ten piedad.

Defiéndenos, libéranos y en tu compasión protégenos,
Señor, por tu gracia.
Señor, ten piedad.

En comunión con [_____y todos los]
santos y santas, encomendémonos, y toda nuestra vida a
Cristo nuestro Dios.
A ti, Señor Dios nuestro.

Se guarda silencio.

Quien preside agrega una colecta de cierre.

Fórmula II

Durante el silencio que sigue a cada invitación, el pueblo ofrece sus propias oraciones, en voz alta o en silencio.

Pido sus oraciones por el pueblo de Dios en todo el
mundo; por *nuestro obispo,*_____; por esta congregación;
por *todos los* que ministran, y por toda persona.
Oren por la iglesia.

El pueblo ora.

Pido sus oraciones por la paz, por la buena voluntad entre
las naciones, y por el bienestar de todo el mundo.
Oren por la justicia y la paz.

El pueblo ora.

Pido sus oraciones por toda persona pobre, enferma,
hambrienta, oprimida o encarcelada.
Oren por toda persona en necesidad o dificultad.

Silence

I ask your prayers for all who seek God, or a deeper knowledge of him.
Pray that they may find and be found by him.

Silence

I ask your prayers for the departed [especially _____].
Pray for those who have died.

Silence

Members of the congregation may ask the prayers or the thanksgivings of those present

I ask your prayers for _____.

I ask your thanksgiving for _____.

Silence

Praise God for those in every generation in whom Christ has been honored [especially _____ whom we remember today].
Pray that we may have grace to glorify Christ in our own day.

Silence

The Celebrant adds a concluding Collect.

Form III

The Leader and People pray responsively

Father, we pray for your holy Catholic Church;
That we all may be one.

Grant that every member of the Church may truly and humbly serve you;
That your Name may be glorified by all people.

We pray for all bishops, priests, and deacons;
That they may be faithful ministers of your Word and Sacraments.

El pueblo ora.

Pido sus oraciones por toda persona que busca o quiere tener un mejor conocimiento de Dios.
Oren por que encuentren y sean *encontrados* por Dios.

El pueblo ora.

Pido sus oraciones por toda persona fallecida, [especialmente_____].
Oren por *todos los* que han muerto.

El pueblo ora.

Pido sus oraciones por_____.

El pueblo ora.

Pido acciones de gracias por_____.

El pueblo ora.

Alaben a Dios por quienes, a lo largo de la historia, han vivido en lealtad a Jesucristo [especialmente por_____, a quien hoy recordamos]. Oren por que sepamos vivir hoy como vivieron *ellos* en su día.

El pueblo ora.

Quien preside agrega una colecta de cierre.

Fórmula III

Quien dirige y el pueblo oran en forma responsorial.

Padre, oramos por tu santa iglesia católica.
Que seamos una.

Concede que cada miembro de la iglesia te sirva leal y humildemente.
Que el mundo glorifique tu nombre.

Rogamos por todo el clero al servicio de la Iglesia.
Que ministren fielmente tu palabra y sacramentos.

We pray for all who govern and hold authority in the nations of the world;
That there may be justice and peace on the earth.

Give us grace to do your will in all that we undertake;
That our works may find favor in your sight.

Have compassion on those who suffer from any grief or trouble;
That they may be delivered from their distress.

Give to the departed eternal rest;
Let light perpetual shine upon them.

We praise you for your saints who have entered into joy;
May we also come to share in your heavenly kingdom.

Let us pray for our own needs and those of others.

Silence

The People may add their own petitions.

The Celebrant adds a concluding Collect.

Form IV

Deacon or other leader

Let us pray for the Church and for the world.

Grant, Almighty God, that all who confess your Name may be united in your truth, live together in your love, and reveal your glory in the world.

Silence

Lord, in your mercy
Hear our prayer.

Guide the people of this land, and of all the nations, in the ways of justice and peace; that we may honor one another and serve the common good.

Silence

Rogamos por toda persona que gobierna y ejerce
autoridad en las naciones del mundo.
Que florezca la justicia y la paz en la tierra.

Llénanos de gracia para cumplir tu voluntad en lo que hagamos.
Que nuestras obras sean agradables ante tu vista.

Ten compasión de quienes sufren cualquier dificultad o angustia.
Que sean *librados* de sus aflicciones.

Otorga paz eterna a quienes han fallecido.
Que les brille tu luz perpetua.

Te alabamos por los santos y santas que han entrado en tu gozo.
Que también *nosotros* seamos parte de tu reino eterno.

Oremos por nuestras necesidades y las de nuestro prójimo.

El pueblo ora.

El pueblo puede agregar sus propias peticiones.

Quien preside agrega una colecta de cierre.

Fórmula IV

Un diácono u otro líder dice:

Oremos por la Iglesia y por el mundo.
Dios de todo poder: Concede que quienes confiesan tu
nombre se unan en tu verdad, convivan en tu amor y
manifiesten tu gloria en el mundo.

El pueblo ora.

Señor, en tu piedad,
Escucha nuestra oración.

Guía al pueblo de este lugar, y a todas las naciones en los
caminos de justicia y paz para que nos respetemos
mutuamente y sirvamos el bien común.

El pueblo ora.

Lord, in your mercy
Hear our prayer.

Give us all a reverence for the earth as your own creation,
that we may use its resources rightly in the service of others
and to your honor and glory.

Silence

Lord, in your mercy
Hear our prayer.

Bless all whose lives are closely linked with ours, and grant
that we may serve Christ in them, and love one another as he
loves us.

Silence

Lord, in your mercy
Hear our prayer.

Comfort and heal all those who suffer in body, mind, or
spirit; give them courage and hope in their troubles, and
bring them the joy of your salvation.

Silence

Lord, in your mercy
Hear our prayer.

We commend to your mercy all who have died, that your will
for them may be fulfilled; and we pray that we may share
with all your saints in your eternal kingdom.

Silence

Lord, in your mercy
Hear our prayer.

The Celebrant adds a concluding Collect.

Señor, en tu piedad,
Escucha nuestra oración.

Otórganos reverencia por la tierra, obra de tus manos,
para que usemos sus recursos sabiamente para tu gloria y
el servicio a los demás.

El pueblo ora.

Señor, en tu piedad,
Escucha nuestra oración.

Bendice todas las vidas entretejidas con las nuestras; y
concede que sirvamos a Cristo en ellas, amándonos como
él nos ama.

El pueblo ora.

Señor, en tu piedad,
Escucha nuestra oración.

Consuela y sana a quienes sufren en cuerpo, mente o
espíritu; en sus tribulaciones otórgales valentía y
esperanza, y muéstrales el gozo de tu salvación.

El pueblo ora.

Señor, en tu piedad,
Escucha nuestra oración.

A tu gracia encomendamos toda persona fallecida, para
que se les cumpla lo que has dispuesto; y *juntos*
participemos en tu reino eterno.

El pueblo ora.

Señor, en tu piedad,
Escucha nuestra oración.

Quien preside agrega una colecta de cierre.

Form V

Deacon or other leader

In peace, let us pray to the Lord, saying, "Lord, have mercy" (*or* "Kyrie eleison").

For the holy Church of God, that it may be filled with truth and love, and be found without fault at the day of your coming, we pray to you, O Lord.

Here and after every petition the People respond

Kyrie eleison.   or   *Lord, have mercy.*

For N. our Presiding Bishop, for N. (N.) our own Bishop(s), for all bishops and other ministers, and for all the holy people of God, we pray to you, O Lord.

For all who fear God and believe in you, Lord Christ, that our divisions may cease, and that all may be one as you and the Father are one, we pray to you, O Lord.

For the mission of the Church, that in faithful witness it may preach the Gospel to the ends of the earth, we pray to you, O Lord.

For those who do not yet believe, and for those who have lost their faith, that they may receive the light of the Gospel, we pray to you, O Lord.

For the peace of the world, that a spirit of respect and forbearance may grow among nations and peoples, we pray to you, O Lord.

For those in positions of public trust [especially _____], that they may serve justice, and promote the dignity and freedom of every person, we pray to you, O Lord.

For all who live and work in this community [especially _____], we pray to you, O Lord.

Fórmula V

Un diácono u otro líder dice:

En paz oremos al Señor diciendo «Señor, ten piedad» (o «Kyrie, eleison»).

Por la santa iglesia de Dios, que rebose de verdad y amor, y la halles sin falta el día de tu venida, te rogamos, Señor.

Después de esta y cada petición, el pueblo responde:

Señor, ten piedad.   *O bien:*   **Kyrie, eleison.**

Por N., *nuestro obispo* presidente, por N. *nuestro obispo,* por *todo obispo y ministro,* y por todo el pueblo santo de Dios, te rogamos, Señor.

Por quienes respetan a Dios y creen en ti, Señor Jesucristo, para que acaben nuestras divisiones y seamos uno como tú y el Padre son uno, te rogamos, Señor.

Por la misión de la Iglesia, para que en fiel testimonio proclame la buena noticia hasta los confines de la tierra, te rogamos, Señor.

Por quienes todavía no creen, y por quienes han perdido su fe, para que reciban la luz del evangelio, te rogamos, Señor.

Por la paz del mundo, para que florezca entre los pueblos un espíritu de respeto y tolerancia, te rogamos, Señor.

Por quienes ocupan cargos públicos [especialmente _____], para que hagan justicia y promuevan la dignidad y libertad de toda persona, te rogamos, Señor.

Por toda persona que vive y trabaja en esta comunidad, [especialmente_____], te rogamos, Señor.

For a blessing upon all human labor, and for the right use of the riches of creation, that the world may be freed from poverty, famine, and disaster, we pray to you, O Lord.

For the poor, the persecuted, the sick, and all who suffer; for refugees, prisoners, and all who are in danger; that they may be relieved and protected, we pray to you, O Lord.

For this *congregation* [for those who are present, and for those who are absent], that we may be delivered from hardness of heart, and show forth your glory in all that we do, we pray to you, O Lord.

For our enemies and those who wish us harm; and for all whom we have injured or offended, we pray to you, O Lord.

For ourselves; for the forgiveness of our sins, and for the grace of the Holy Spirit to amend our lives, we pray to you, O Lord.

For all who have commended themselves to our prayers; for our families, friends, and neighbors; that being freed from anxiety, they may live in joy, peace, and health, we pray to you, O Lord.

For _____, we pray to you, O Lord.

For all who have died in the communion of your Church, and those whose faith is known to you alone, that, with all the saints, they may have rest in that place where there is no pain or grief, but life eternal, we pray to you, O Lord.

Rejoicing in the fellowship of [the ever-blessed Virgin Mary, (*blessed N.*) and] all the saints, let us commend ourselves, and one another, and all our life to Christ our God.
To you, O Lord our God.

Silence

The Celebrant adds a concluding Collect, or the following Doxology

Por tu bendición sobre toda labor humana y por el uso debido de la abundancia de la creación; para liberar el mundo de la pobreza, el hambre y las calamidades, te rogamos, Señor.

Por toda persona pobre, perseguida, enferma y sufriente; por *refugiados, prisioneros,* y toda persona en peligro; que hallen alivio y protección, te rogamos, Señor.
Por esta *congregación* [presentes y ausentes,] que se nos ablande el corazón y manifestemos tu gloria en todo lo que hacemos, te rogamos, Señor.

Por *nuestros enemigos* y *los* que quieren hacernos daño; y por toda persona que hayamos ofendido o herido, te rogamos, Señor.

Por *nosotros mismos*; por que perdones nuestros pecados y la gracia de tu Espíritu transforme nuestras vidas.

Por toda persona que ha pedido nuestras oraciones; por nuestras familias, amistades y *vecinos*; que se libren de toda ansiedad y vivan con alegría, paz y salud, te rogamos, Señor.

Por_____, te rogamos, Señor.

Por quienes han muerto en la comunión de tu iglesia, y por las personas cuya fe solo tú conoces, para que, con todos los santos y santas, puedan descansar en vida eterna libradas de penas y aflicciones, te rogamos, Señor.

En jubilosa comunión con [la bienaventurada Virgen María, *(bendito N.)* y] todos tus santos y santas, encomendémonos *unos a otros,* y toda nuestra vida a Cristo nuestro Dios.
A ti, Señor Dios.

Se guarda silencio.

Quien preside agrega una colecta de cierre (ver páginas 168-173) o esta doxología:

For yours is the majesty, O Father, Son, and Holy Spirit;
yours is the kingdom and the power and the glory, now and
for ever. *Amen.*

Form VI

The Leader and People pray responsively

In peace, we pray to you, Lord God.

Silence

For all people in their daily life and work;
*For our families, friends, and neighbors, and for those who
are alone.*

For this community, the nation, and the world;
For all who work for justice, freedom, and peace.

For the just and proper use of your creation;
For the victims of hunger, fear, injustice, and oppression.

For all who are in danger, sorrow, or any kind of trouble;
*For those who minister to the sick, the friendless, and the
needy.*

For the peace and unity of the Church of God;
*For all who proclaim the Gospel, and all who seek
the Truth.*

For [N. our Presiding Bishop, and N. (N.) our Bishop(s); and
for] all bishops and other ministers;
For all who serve God in his Church.

For the special needs and concerns of this congregation.

Silence

The People may add their own petitions

Hear us, Lord;
For your mercy is great.

Porque tuya es la majestad, Padre, Hijo y Espíritu Santo; tuyo es el reino, el poder y la gloria, ahora y por siempre. **Amén.**

Fórmula VI

Un diácono u otro líder y el pueblo oran en forma responsorial.

En paz oramos a ti, Señor Dios.

Se guarda silencio.

Por toda la gente en su trabajo y vida cotidiana.
Por nuestras familias, amistades y *vecinos,* y por quienes están *solos.*

Por esta comunidad, esta nación y el mundo;
Por toda persona que trabaja por la justicia, la libertad y la paz.

Por el uso responsable de tu creación;
Por las víctimas de hambre, temor, injusticia y opresión.

Por quienes enfrentan peligro, pesar o cualquier dificultad.
Por quienes ministran *al* que le falta salud, *amigos* o recursos.

Por la paz y unidad de la iglesia de Dios;
Por quienes proclaman el evangelio y quienes buscan la verdad.

Por [*N. nuestro obispo* presidente, y *N.* (y *N.) nuestro(s) obispo(s)*; y por] *todos los obispos* y *ministros;*
Por toda persona que sirve a Dios en su iglesia.

Por las necesidades de esta congregación.

Se guarda silencio.

El pueblo puede añadir sus propias peticiones.

Escúchanos, Señor;
Porque grande es tu misericordia.

We thank you, Lord, for all the blessings of this life.

Silence

The People may add their own thanksgivings

We will exalt you, O God our King;
And praise your Name for ever and ever.

We pray for all who have died, that they may have a place in
your eternal kingdom.

Silence

The People may add their own petitions

Lord, let your loving-kindness be upon them;
Who put their trust in you.

We pray to you also for the forgiveness of our sins.

Silence may be kept.

Leader and People

Have mercy upon us, most merciful Father;
in your compassion forgive us our sins,
known and unknown,
things done and left undone;
and so uphold us by your Spirit
that we may live and serve you in newness of life,
to the honor and glory of your Name;
through Jesus Christ our Lord. Amen.

The Celebrant concludes with an absolution or a suitable Collect.

The Collect at the Prayers

For the concluding Collect, the Celebrant selects

(a)   a Collect appropriate to the Season or occasion being
      celebrated;

Te damos gracias, Señor, por todas las bendiciones de esta vida.

El pueblo ora y puede añadir expresiones de gratitud.

Te alabamos, Dios nuestro Rey.
Y celebramos tu nombre eternamente.

Oramos por quienes han fallecido, que tengan un lugar en tu reino eterno.

El pueblo ora y puede añadir sus propias peticiones.

Señor, *cúbrelos* con tu bondad.
A quienes ponen su confianza en ti.

Oramos también por el perdón de nuestros pecados.

Se guarda silencio.

El líder y el pueblo dicen:

**Padre de misericordia: Apiádate de *nosotros*;
en tu compasión perdona nuestros pecados
conocidos e ignorados
lo que hicimos y lo que dejamos sin hacer;
y sostennos por tu Espíritu
para vivir y servirte con vidas renovadas,
para honor y gloria de tu nombre;
por Jesucristo nuestro Señor. Amén.**

Quien preside concluye con una absolución o una colecta adecuada.

Colectas de cierre a las oraciones del pueblo

Para concluir las oraciones del pueblo, quien preside elige una de las siguientes:

(a) Una colecta que sea apropiada para el tiempo litúrgico o la ocasión que se celebre;

(b) a Collect expressive of some special need in the life of the local congregation;

(c) a Collect for the mission of the Church;

(d) a general Collect such as the following:

1

Lord, hear the prayers of *thy* people; and what we have asked faithfully, grant that we may obtain effectually, to the glory of *thy* Name; through Jesus Christ our Lord. *Amen.*

2

Heavenly Father, you have promised to hear what we ask in the Name of your Son: Accept and fulfill our petitions, we pray, not as we ask in our ignorance, nor as we deserve in our sinfulness, but as you know and love us in your Son Jesus Christ our Lord. *Amen.*

3

Almighty and eternal God, ruler of all things in heaven and earth: Mercifully accept the prayers of your people, and strengthen us to do your will; through Jesus Christ our Lord. *Amen.*

4

Almighty God, to whom our needs are known before we ask, help us to ask only what accords with your will; and those good things which we dare not, or in our blindness cannot ask, grant us for the sake of your Son Jesus Christ our Lord. *Amen.*

(b)   Una colecta que exprese alguna necesidad especial de la congregación local;

(c)   Una colecta por la misión de la iglesia;

(d)   Una colecta general, tal como las que siguen:

1

Escucha, Señor, las oraciones de tu pueblo;
y, lo que con fe te hemos pedido,
concede que lo recibamos
para gloria de tu santo nombre;
por Jesucristo nuestro Señor. **Amén.**

2

Padre celestial: Nos has prometido
oír lo que pidamos en nombre de tu Hijo.
Te rogamos que aceptes y cumplas nuestras peticiones,
no en la ignorancia en que las hacemos
ni como merecemos en nuestra culpa,
sino según nos conoces y nos amas
mediante tu Hijo Jesucristo. **Amén.**

3

Dios eterno y poderoso,
gobernante de todas las cosas en el cielo y en la tierra:
Acepta en tu piedad las oraciones de tu pueblo
y danos fuerza para hacer tu voluntad;
por Jesucristo nuestro Señor. **Amén.**

4

Dios de todo poder,
que sabes de antemano lo que necesitamos:
Ayúdanos a pedir solo de acuerdo a tu voluntad;
y concédenos todo lo bueno
que por temor o ignorancia no pedimos;
por amor de tu Hijo Jesucristo. **Amén.**

5

O Lord our God, accept the fervent prayers of your people; in the multitude of your mercies, look with compassion upon us and all who turn to you for help; for you are gracious, O lover of souls, and to you we give glory, Father, Son, and Holy Spirit, now and for ever. *Amen.*

6

Lord Jesus Christ, you said to your apostles, "Peace I give to you; my own peace I leave with you:" Regard not our sins, but the faith of your Church, and give to us the peace and unity of that heavenly City, where with the Father and the Holy Spirit, you live and reign, now and for ever. *Amen.*

7

Hasten, O Father, the coming of *thy* kingdom; and grant that we *thy* servants, who now live by faith, may with joy behold *thy* Son at his coming in glorious majesty; even Jesus Christ, our only Mediator and Advocate. *Amen.*

8

Almighty God, by your Holy Spirit you have made us one with your saints in heaven and on earth: Grant that in our earthly pilgrimage we may always be supported by this fellowship of love and prayer, and know ourselves to be surrounded by their witness to your power and mercy. We ask this for the sake of Jesus Christ, in whom all our intercessions are acceptable through the Spirit, and who lives and reigns for ever and ever. *Amen.*

5

Recibe, Dios, nuestras fervientes oraciones
y en tu gran misericordia
apiádate de quienes te piden auxilio;
pues estás lleno de gracia y de amor entrañable,
y a ti rendimos gloria, Santísima Trinidad,
ahora y por siempre. **Amén**

6

Señor Jesucristo, que dijiste a tus apóstoles,
«La paz les dejo, mi paz les doy»:
No te fijes en nuestros pecados,
sino en la fe de tu iglesia,
y danos la paz y la unidad de esa ciudad celestial
donde, con el Padre y el Espíritu Santo,
vives y reinas ahora y por siempre. **Amén.**

7

Apresura, Padre, la llegada de tu reino;
y concede que quienes por fe te servimos y vivimos,
contemplemos a tu Hijo con alegría
cuando vuelva en gloriosa majestad;
por Jesucristo, nuestro abogado y mediador. **Amén.**

8

Dios de poder: Por tu Espíritu Santo
nos has hecho uno con todos tus santos y santas;
concédenos que, al caminar por este mundo,
siempre tengamos su amor, sus plegarias,
y el testimonio que dan de tu poder y tu piedad.
Te lo pedimos por amor de Jesucristo,
en quien toda petición es aceptable. **Amén.**

Confession of Sin

A Confession of Sin is said here if it has not been said earlier. On occasion, the Confession may be omitted.

One of the sentences from the Penitential Order on BCP page 351 may be said.

The Deacon or Celebrant says

Let us confess our sins against God and our neighbor.

Silence may be kept.

Minister and People

Most merciful God,
we confess that we have sinned against you
in thought, word, and deed,
by what we have done,
and by what we have left undone.
We have not loved you with our whole heart;
we have not loved our neighbors as ourselves.
We are truly sorry and we humbly repent.
For the sake of your Son Jesus Christ,
have mercy on us and forgive us;
that we may delight in your will,
and walk in your ways,
to the glory of your Name. Amen.

The Bishop when present, or the Priest, stands and says

Almighty God have mercy on you, forgive you all your
sins through our Lord Jesus Christ, strengthen you in all
goodness, and by the power of the Holy Spirit keep you in
eternal life. *Amen.*

The Peace

All stand. The Celebrant says to the people

> The peace of the Lord be always with you.
People   And also with you.

Then the Ministers and People may greet one another in the name of the Lord.

La confesión de pecado

De no haberse hecho antes, ahora se hace la confesión de pecado. En ciertas ocasiones, se puede omitir.

Se puede decir una de las frases del Orden Penitencial en LOC en la página 237.

El diácono, o quien preside, dice:

Confesemos nuestros pecados contra Dios y nuestroprójimo.

Se puede guardar un período de silencio.

**Dios de misericordia,
confesamos que hemos pecado contra ti
de pensamiento, palabra y obra,
por lo que hemos hecho
y por lo que hemos dejado sin hacer.
No te hemos amado de todo corazón;
no hemos amado al prójimo como a *nosotros mismos*.
Sincera y humildemente nos arrepentimos.
Por tu Hijo Jesucristo,
ten piedad de *nosotros* y perdónanos;
así tu voluntad será nuestra alegría
y caminaremos en tus sendas
para gloria de tu nombre. Amén.**

Quien preside declara:

Dios Todopoderoso tenga misericordia de ustedes,
perdone todos sus pecados por Jesucristo nuestro Señor,
los fortalezca en toda bondad
y por el poder del Espíritu Santo
los guarde en la vida eterna. **Amén.**

La paz

De pie. Quien preside dice:

La paz del Señor sea siempre con ustedes.
Y también contigo.

El pueblo puede saludarse en nombre del Señor.

The Holy Communion

Offertory Sentences

One of the following, or some other appropriate sentence of Scripture, may be used

Offer to God a sacrifice of thanksgiving, and make good your vows to the Most High.   *Psalm 50:14*

Ascribe to the Lord the honor due his Name; bring offerings and come into his courts.   *Psalm 96:8*

Walk in love, as Christ loved us and gave himself for us, an offering and sacrifice to God.   *Ephesians 5:2*

I appeal to you, brethren, by the mercies of God, to present yourselves as a living sacrifice, holy and acceptable to God, which is your spiritual worship.   *Romans 12:1*

If you are offering your gift at the altar, and there remember that your brother has something against you, leave your gift there before the altar and go; first be reconciled to your brother, and then come and offer your gift.   *Matthew 5:23, 24*

Through Christ let us continually offer to God the sacrifice of praise, that is, the fruit of lips that acknowledge his Name. But do not neglect to do good and to share what you have, for such sacrifices are pleasing to God.   *Hebrews 13:15, 16*

O Lord our God, you are worthy to receive glory and honor and power; because you have created all things, and by your will they were created and have their being.
Revelation 4:11

Yours, O Lord, is the greatness, the power, the glory, the victory, and the majesty. For everything in heaven and on earth is yours. Yours, O Lord, is the kingdom, and you are exalted as head over all.   *1 Chronicles 29:11*

La Santa Comunión

Versículos para la presentación de ofrendas

Se puede usar uno de los siguientes, u otro versículo de la Biblia que sea apropiado:

Ofrézcanle a Dios su agradecimiento y cumplan sus votos con el Altísimo. *Salmo 50:14*

Rindan al Señor la gloria de su nombre; traigan ofrendas y vengan a su templo. *Salmo 96:8*

Anden en amor, como Cristo nos amó y se entregó por *nosotros* como ofrenda y sacrificio a Dios. *Efesios 5:2*

Les ruego, hermanos y hermanas, por la misericordia de Dios, que se ofrezcan como una ofrenda viva, santa, y agradable a Dios, pues eso es su adoración espiritual. *Romanos 12:1*

Si al llevar tu ofrenda al altar te acuerdas de algo que tu *hermano* tiene contra ti, deja la ofrenda delante del altar, y ve primero a reconciliarte; y entonces vuelve y presenta tu ofrenda. *Mateo 5:23,24*

Por medio de Cristo, ofrezcamos siempre a Dios un sacrificio de alabanza; es decir: el fruto de labios que confiesan su nombre. Y no se olviden de hacer el bien y de compartir lo que tienen, porque esas son las ofrendas sagradas que le agradan a Dios. *Hebreos 13:15,16*

Digno eres tú, Señor y Dios nuestro, de recibir la gloria, la honra y el poder; porque tú has creado todas las cosas, y por tu voluntad surgieron y tienen su existencia. *Apocalipsis 4:11*

Tuyos son, Señor, la grandeza, el poder, la gloria, la victoria y la majestad; porque tuyo es cuanto hay en cielo y tierra. Tuyo es el reino, Señor, y tú te enalteces y encabezas todas las cosas. *1 Crónicas 29:11*

Let us with gladness present the offerings and oblations of our life and labor to the Lord.

During the Offertory, a hymn, psalm, or anthem may be sung.

Representatives of the congregation bring the people's offerings of bread and wine, and money or other gifts, to the deacon or celebrant. The people stand while the offerings are presented and placed on the Altar.

The Great Thanksgiving

Eucharistic Prayer A

The people remain standing. The Celebrant, whether bishop or priest, faces them and sings or says

	The Lord be with you.
People	And also with you.
Celebrant	Lift up your hearts.
People	We lift them to the Lord.
Celebrant	Let us give thanks to the Lord our God.
People	It is right to give him thanks and praise.

Then, facing the Holy Table, the Celebrant proceeds

It is right, and a good and joyful thing, always and everywhere to give thanks to you, Father Almighty, Creator of heaven and earth.

Here a Proper Preface is sung or said on all Sundays, and on other occasions as appointed.

Therefore we praise you, joining our voices with Angels and Archangels and with all the company of heaven, who for ever sing this hymn to proclaim the glory of your Name:

O esta invitación:

Presentemos al Señor con alegría las ofrendas de nuestra vida y nuestro trabajo.

Durante la presentación de ofrendas se puede cantar un himno, salmo o canto.

Las ofrendas del pueblo (pan y vino, y dinero u otras ofrendas) se traen directamente al diácono, o en su ausencia, a quien preside. El pueblo permanece de pie mientras se presentan las ofrendas y se colocan sobre la santa mesa.

La Gran Plegaria Eucarística

Plegaria Eucarística A

El pueblo sigue de pie. Quien preside, de cara al pueblo, canta o dice:

El Señor esté con ustedes.
Y también contigo.
Elevemos los corazones.
Los elevamos al Señor.
Demos gracias al Señor, nuestro Dios.
Es justo y necesario.

Frente a la santa mesa, quien preside continúa con estas palabras:

Es en verdad justo y necesario
en todo tiempo y lugar darte gracias,
Padre de todo poder, creador de cielo y tierra.

Aquí se canta o se dice un prefacio propio, en los domingos y en otras ocasiones en que se indique.

Por tanto te alabamos uniendo nuestras voces
con ángeles, arcángeles y todos los coros celestiales
que por siempre cantan este himno
para proclamar la gloria de tu nombre:

Holy, holy, holy Lord, God of power and might,
heaven and earth are full of your glory.
Hosanna in the highest.
Blessed is he who comes in the name of the Lord.
Hosanna in the highest.

The people stand or kneel.

Then the Celebrant continues

Holy and gracious Father: In your infinite love you made us
for yourself; and, when we had fallen into sin and become
subject to evil and death, you, in your mercy, sent Jesus
Christ, your only and eternal Son, to share our human
nature, to live and die as one of us, to reconcile us to you, the
God and Father of all.

He stretched out his arms upon the cross, and offered himself
in obedience to your will, a perfect sacrifice for the whole
world.

*At the following words concerning the bread, the Celebrant is to hold it
or lay a hand upon it; and at the words concerning the cup, to hold or
place a hand upon the cup and any other vessel containing wine to be
consecrated.*

On the night he was handed over to suffering and death, our
Lord Jesus Christ took bread; and when he had given thanks
to you, he broke it, and gave it to his disciples, and said,
"Take, eat: This is my Body, which is given for you. Do this
for the remembrance of me."

After supper he took the cup of wine; and when he had given
thanks, he gave it to them, and said, "Drink this, all of you:
This is my Blood of the new Covenant, which is shed for you
and for many for the forgiveness of sins. Whenever you drink
it, do this for the remembrance of me."

Santo, santo, santo es el Señor, Dios del universo.
Llenos están el cielo y la tierra de tu gloria.
Hosanna en el cielo.
Bendito quien viene en nombre del Señor.
Hosanna en el cielo.

El pueblo, de pie o de rodillas.

Quien preside continúa:

Padre santo y bondadoso:
Con amor infinito nos creaste para ti;
y cuando caímos en el pecado
y quedamos bajo el poder del mal y de la muerte,
tú nos tuviste misericordia:
Enviaste a Jesucristo, tu Hijo único y eterno,
a compartir la naturaleza humana,
a vivir y morir como *nosotros*
y a reconciliarnos contigo, Dios y Padre de *todos*.

Sobre la cruz Jesús extendió sus brazos
y, obedeciendo tu voluntad,
se ofreció como sacrificio perfecto para el mundo entero.

Cuando quien preside se refiere al pan, lo alza o le impone una mano;
cuando se refiere al vino lo alza o le impone una mano.

La noche en que lo entregaron
al sufrimiento y a la muerte,
nuestro Señor Jesucristo tomó pan;
y después de darte gracias, lo partió
y se lo dio a sus discípulos, y dijo:
«Tomen y coman:
Esto es mi cuerpo, que se entrega por ustedes.
Hagan esto en memoria mía».

Después de cenar tomó el vino;
y después de darte gracias, se lo dio y dijo:
«Beban *todos*: Esto es mi sangre de la nueva alianza,
que por ustedes y por *todos*
se derrama para el perdón de los pecados.
Cada vez que lo beban, hagan esto en memoria mía».

Therefore we proclaim the mystery of faith:

Celebrant and People

Christ has died.
Christ is risen.
Christ will come again.

The Celebrant continues

We celebrate the memorial of our redemption, O Father, in this sacrifice of praise and thanksgiving. Recalling his death, resurrection, and ascension, we offer you these gifts.

Sanctify them by your Holy Spirit to be for your people the Body and Blood of your Son, the holy food and drink of new and unending life in him. Sanctify us also that we may faithfully receive this holy Sacrament, and serve you in unity, constancy, and peace; and at the last day bring us with all your saints into the joy of your eternal kingdom.

All this we ask through your Son Jesus Christ. By him, and with him, and in him, in the unity of the Holy Spirit all honor and glory is yours, Almighty Father, now and for ever. *AMEN.*

Continue with the Lord's Prayer on page 200.

Eucharistic Prayer B

The people remain standing. The Celebrant, whether bishop or priest, faces them and sings or says

	The Lord be with you.
People	And also with you.
Celebrant	Lift up your hearts.
People	We lift them to the Lord.
Celebrant	Let us give thanks to the Lord our God.
People	It is right to give him thanks and praise.

Por tanto, proclamamos el misterio de la fe:

Cristo ha muerto.
Cristo ha resucitado.
Cristo volverá.

Quien preside continúa:

Mediante este sacrificio y acción de gracias, Padre nuestro,
celebramos nuestra liberación.
Y recordando que Cristo murió, resucitó y subió al cielo,
te ofrecemos estas ofrendas.

Santifícalas por tu Espíritu;
que sean para tu pueblo el cuerpo y la sangre de tu Hijo,
la santa comida y bebida de la vida nueva y sin fin
que tenemos en él.
Santifícanos también a *nosotros*
para que fielmente recibamos este santo sacramento,
y te sirvamos firmes, *unidos,* y en paz;
y en el día final llévanos con todo tu pueblo santo
al gozo de tu reino eterno.

Todo esto te lo pedimos por tu Hijo Jesucristo.
Por él, con él y en él, en la unidad del Espíritu Santo,
tuyos son todo el honor y la gloria,
Padre todopoderoso, ahora y siempre. **AMÉN.**

Se continúa con el Padrenuestro en la página 201.

Plegaria eucarística B

El pueblo sigue de pie. Quien preside, de cara al pueblo, canta o dice:

El Señor esté con ustedes.
Y también contigo.
Elevemos los corazones.
Los elevamos al Señor.
Demos gracias al Señor, nuestro Dios.
Es justo y necesario.

Then, facing the Holy Table, the Celebrant proceeds

It is right, and a good and joyful thing, always and everywhere to give thanks to you, Father Almighty, Creator of heaven and earth.

Here a Proper Preface is sung or said on all Sundays, and on other occasions as appointed.

Therefore we praise you, joining our voices with Angels and Archangels and with all the company of heaven, who for ever sing this hymn to proclaim the glory of your Name:

Celebrant and People

Holy, holy, holy Lord, God of power and might,
heaven and earth are full of your glory.
Hosanna in the highest.
Blessed is he who comes in the name of the Lord.
Hosanna in the highest.

The people stand or kneel.

Then the Celebrant continues

We give thanks to you, O God, for the goodness and love which you have made known to us in creation; in the calling of Israel to be your people; in your Word spoken through the prophets; and above all in the Word made flesh, Jesus, your Son. For in these last days you sent him to be incarnate from the Virgin Mary, to be the Savior and Redeemer of the world. In him, you have delivered us from evil, and made us worthy to stand before you. In him, you have brought us out of error into truth, out of sin into righteousness, out of death into life.

At the following words concerning the bread, the Celebrant is to hold it or lay a hand upon it; and at the words concerning the cup, to hold or place a hand upon the cup and any other vessel containing wine to be consecrated.

On the night before he died for us, our Lord Jesus Christ took bread; and when he had given thanks to you, he broke it, and gave it to his disciples, and said, "Take, eat:

Quien preside continúa:

Es en verdad justo y necesario
en todo tiempo y lugar darte gracias,
Padre de todo poder, creador de cielo y tierra.

Aquí se canta o se dice un prefacio propio, en los domingos y en otras ocasiones en que se indique.

Por tanto te alabamos uniendo nuestras voces
con ángeles, arcángeles y todos los coros celestiales
que por siempre cantan este himno
para proclamar la gloria de tu nombre:

Santo, santo, santo es el Señor, Dios del universo.
Llenos están el cielo y la tierra de tu gloria.
Hosanna en el cielo.
Bendito quien viene en nombre del Señor.
Hosanna en el cielo.

El pueblo, de pie o de rodillas. Quien preside continúa:

Te damos gracias, Señor, por la bondad y el amor
que nos mostraste al crear el universo;
al llamar a Israel a ser tu pueblo;
al revelar tu Palabra a través de profetas;
y sobre todo al encarnar tu Palabra en Jesús tu Hijo.
Porque en estos días finales lo enviaste
para encarnarse de la Virgen María
y ser el Salvador y Redentor del mundo.
En él nos libraste del mal
y nos hiciste *dignos* de estar de pie en tu presencia.
En él nos llevaste del error a la verdad,
del pecado a la rectitud, de la muerte a la vida.

Cuando quien preside se refiere al pan, lo alza o le impone una mano; cuando se refiere al vino lo alza o le impone una mano.

En la noche en que lo entregaron
al sufrimiento y a la muerte,
nuestro Señor Jesucristo tomó pan;
y después de darte gracias, lo partió
y se lo dio a sus discípulos, y dijo:
«Tomen y coman:

This is my Body, which is given for you. Do this for the remembrance of me."

After supper he took the cup of wine; and when he had given thanks, he gave it to them, and said, "Drink this, all of you: This is my Blood of the new Covenant, which is shed for you and for many for the forgiveness of sins. Whenever you drink it, do this for the remembrance of me."

Therefore, according to his command, O Father,

Celebrant and People

We remember his death,
We proclaim his resurrection,
We await his coming in glory;

The Celebrant continues

And we offer our sacrifice of praise and thanksgiving to you, O Lord of all; presenting to you, from your creation, this bread and this wine.

We pray you, gracious God, to send your Holy Spirit upon these gifts that they may be the Sacrament of the Body of Christ and his Blood of the new Covenant. Unite us to your Son in his sacrifice, that we may be acceptable through him, being sanctified by the Holy Spirit. In the fullness of time, put all things in subjection under your Christ, and bring us to that heavenly country where, with [_____ and] all your saints, we may enter the everlasting heritage of your sons and daughters; through Jesus Christ our Lord, the firstborn of all creation, the head of the Church, and the author of our salvation.

By him, and with him, and in him, in the unity of the Holy Spirit all honor and glory is yours, Almighty Father, now and for ever. *AMEN.*

Esto es mi cuerpo, que se entrega por ustedes.
Hagan esto en memoria mía».

Al final de la cena tomó el vino,
y dándote gracias se lo dio y dijo:
«Beban *todos*: Esto es mi sangre de la nueva alianza,
que por ustedes y por *todos* se derrama
para el perdón de los pecados.
Cada vez que lo beban, hagan esto en memoria mía».

Por tanto, Padre, según su mandato,

**Recordamos su muerte,
proclamamos su resurrección
y esperamos su venida en gloria.**

Te ofrecemos nuestro sacrificio
de alabanza y agradecimiento
a ti, Señor de todo lo creado;
y te ofrecemos de tu creación, este pan y este vino.

Te rogamos, Dios de toda bondad,
que envíes tu Espíritu Santo sobre estas ofrendas
para que sean el sacramento del cuerpo de Cristo
y su sangre de la nueva alianza.
Únenos a tu Hijo en su sacrificio,
para que seamos aceptables por medio de él,
santificados por el Espíritu Santo.

En la plenitud del tiempo,
pon todo bajo el mando de tu Ungido,
y llévanos a aquella patria celestial
en la que con [_____y] tus santos y santas
recibamos la herencia eterna de tu pueblo;
por Jesucristo nuestro Señor,
primogénito de toda la creación,
cabeza de la Iglesia y autor de nuestra salvación.

Por él, con él y en él, en la unidad del Espíritu Santo,
tuyos son todo el honor y la gloria,
Padre todopoderoso, ahora y siempre. **AMÉN.**

Continue with the Lord's Prayer on page 200.

Eucharistic Prayer C

In this prayer, the lines in italics are spoken by the People.

The Celebrant, whether bishop or priest, faces them and sings or says

The Lord be with you.
And also with you.

Lift up your hearts.
We lift them to the Lord.

Let us give thanks to the Lord our God.
It is right to give him thanks and praise.

Then, facing the Holy Table, the Celebrant proceeds

God of all power, Ruler of the Universe, you are worthy of glory and praise.
Glory to you for ever and ever.

At your command all things came to be: the vast expanse of interstellar space, galaxies, suns, the planets in their courses, and this fragile earth, our island home.
By your will they were created and have their being.

From the primal elements you brought forth the human race, and blessed us with memory, reason, and skill. You made us the rulers of creation. But we turned against you, and betrayed your trust; and we turned against one another.
Have mercy, Lord, for we are sinners in your sight.

Again and again, you called us to return. Through prophets and sages you revealed your righteous Law. And in the fullness of time you sent your only Son, born of a woman, to fulfill your Law, to open for us the way of freedom and peace.
By his blood, he reconciled us.
By his wounds, we are healed.

Se continúa con el Padrenuestro en la página 201.

Plegaria eucarística C

Quien preside, de cara al pueblo, canta o dice:

El Señor esté con ustedes.
Y también contigo.
Elevemos los corazones.
Los elevamos al Señor.
Demos gracias al Señor, nuestro Dios.
Es justo y necesario.

Quien preside continúa:

Dios de todo poder, Rey del universo:
Tú eres digno de gloria y alabanza.
Te alabamos ahora y siempre.

A tu mandato nació todo el universo:
La inmensidad del espacio, galaxias, soles,
los planetas en sus órbitas
y esta tierra frágil, nuestro hogar insular.
Por tu voluntad nacieron y tienen su existencia.

De la materia primordial generaste la raza humana
y le otorgaste memoria, razón y destreza.
Nos encomendaste la creación.
Pero nos rebelamos, traicionamos tu confianza
y nos hicimos *enemigos unos* de *otros*.
Ten piedad, Señor, que somos pecadores ante ti.

Persistente, muchas veces nos llamaste a regresar.
Mediante profetas y personas sabias
nos revelaste tu justa ley.
Y en la plenitud del tiempo enviaste a tu único Hijo,
nacido de una mujer, para cumplir tu ley
y abrirnos la senda de la libertad y la paz.
Su sangre nos reconcilia. Sus heridas nos sanan.

And therefore we praise you, joining with the heavenly chorus, with prophets, apostles, and martyrs, and with all those in every generation who have looked to you in hope, to proclaim with them your glory, in their unending hymn:

Celebrant and People

Holy, holy, holy Lord, God of power and might,
heaven and earth are full of your glory.
Hosanna in the highest.
Blessed is he who comes in the name of the Lord.
Hosanna in the highest.

The Celebrant continues

And so, Father, we who have been redeemed by him, and made a new people by water and the Spirit, now bring before you these gifts. Sanctify them by your Holy Spirit to be the Body and Blood of Jesus Christ our Lord.

At the following words concerning the bread, the Celebrant is to hold it, or lay a hand upon it; and at the words concerning the cup, to hold or place a hand upon the cup and any other vessel containing wine to be consecrated.

On the night he was betrayed he took bread, said the blessing, broke the bread, and gave it to his friends, and said, "Take, eat: This is my Body, which is given for you. Do this for the remembrance of me."

After supper, he took the cup of wine, gave thanks, and said, "Drink this, all of you: This is my Blood of the new Covenant, which is shed for you and for many for the forgiveness of sins. Whenever you drink it, do this for the remembrance of me."

Remembering now his work of redemption, and offering to you this sacrifice of thanksgiving,
We celebrate his death and resurrection,
as we await the day of his coming.

Por todo eso te alabamos, uniéndonos al coro de los cielos,
a profetas, apóstoles y mártires, y a toda persona que,
a lo largo de la historia, ha vislumbrado en ti su esperanza;
junto a *ellos* te glorificamos con su himno sin fin:

Santo, santo, santo es el Señor, Dios del universo.
Llenos están el cielo y la tierra de tu gloria.
Hosanna en el cielo.
Bendito quien viene en nombre del Señor.
Hosanna en el cielo.

El pueblo, de pie o de rodillas.

Quien preside continúa:

Y así, Padre, *redimidos* por él
y *hechos* un pueblo nuevo por el agua y el Espíritu,
te ofrecemos estas ofrendas.
Santifícalas con tu Espíritu Santo
para que sean el cuerpo y la sangre
de Jesucristo nuestro Señor.

Cuando quien preside se refiere al pan, lo alza o le impone una mano;
cuando se refiere al vino lo alza o le impone una mano.

En la noche que lo traicionaron, Jesús tomó pan,
lo bendijo, lo partió y se lo dio a sus *amigos* diciendo:
«Tomen y coman: Esto es mi cuerpo,
que se entrega por ustedes. Hagan esto en memoria mía.»

Después de cenar tomó el vino, dio gracias, y dijo:
«Beban *todos*: Esto es mi sangre de la nueva alianza,
que por ustedes y por *todos* se derrama
para el perdón de los pecados.
Cada vez que lo beban, háganlo en memoria mía.»

Recordando su obra redentora
con este sacrificio de alabanza,
Recordamos su muerte y resurrección
y esperamos el día de su regreso.

Lord God of our Fathers; God of Abraham, Isaac, and
Jacob; God and Father of our Lord Jesus Christ: Open our
eyes to see your hand at work in the world about us. Deliver
us from the presumption of coming to this Table for solace
only, and not for strength; for pardon only, and not for
renewal. Let the grace of this Holy Communion make us one
body, one spirit in Christ, that we may worthily serve the
world in his name.
Risen Lord, be known to us in the breaking of the Bread.

Accept these prayers and praises, Father, through Jesus
Christ our great High Priest, to whom, with you and the
Holy Spirit, your Church gives honor, glory, and worship,
from generation to generation. *AMEN.*

Continue with the Lord's Prayer on page 200.

Eucharistic Prayer D

*The people remain standing. The Celebrant, whether bishop or priest,
faces them and sings or says*

	The Lord be with you.
People	And also with you.
Celebrant	Lift up your hearts.
People	We lift them to the Lord.
Celebrant	Let us give thanks to the Lord our God.
People	It is right to give him thanks and praise.

Then, facing the Holy Table, the Celebrant proceeds

It is truly right to glorify you, Father, and to give you thanks;
for you alone are God, living and true, dwelling in light
inaccessible from before time and for ever.

Señor Dios de nuestros padres y madres,
Dios de Abraham, Isaac, y Jacob,
Dios de Sara, Rebeca, Raquel y Lea,
Dios del pueblo de Israel,
Dios y Padre de Jesucristo nuestro Señor:
Ábrenos los ojos para reconocer tu mano en el mundo.
No permitas que vengamos a esta mesa
buscando solo consuelo sin fortaleza,
o perdón sin renovación de vida.
Que esta Santa Comunión nos haga un cuerpo
y un espíritu en Cristo,
para que fielmente sirvamos al mundo en su nombre.
Señor resucitado, revélate al partir el pan.

Padre: Recibe estas plegarias y alabanzas
por Jesucristo, nuestro Sumo Sacerdote;
a ti, a él y al Espíritu Santo,
tu Iglesia rinde gloria, honor y adoración
por los siglos de los siglos. **AMÉN.**

Se continúa con el Padrenuestro en la página 201.

Plegaria eucarística D

Quien preside, de cara al pueblo, canta o dice:

El Señor esté con ustedes.
Y también contigo.
Elevemos los corazones.
Los elevamos al Señor.
Demos gracias al Señor, nuestro Dios.
Es justo y necesario.

Quien preside continúa:

¡Justo es glorificarte y darte gracias!
Porque tú, Padre, eres el único Dios vivo y verdadero,
en tu morada de luz inaccesible,
desde antes del principio y para siempre.

Fountain of life and source of all goodness, you made all things and fill them with your blessing; you created them to rejoice in the splendor of your radiance.

Countless throngs of angels stand before you to serve you night and day; and, beholding the glory of your presence, they offer you unceasing praise. Joining with them, and giving voice to every creature under heaven, we acclaim you, and glorify your Name, as we sing (say),

Celebrant and People

Holy, holy, holy Lord, God of power and might,
heaven and earth are full of your glory.
Hosanna in the highest.
Blessed is he who comes in the name of the Lord.
Hosanna in the highest.

The people stand or kneel.

Then the Celebrant continues

We acclaim you, holy Lord, glorious in power. Your mighty works reveal your wisdom and love. You formed us in your own image, giving the whole world into our care, so that, in obedience to you, our Creator, we might rule and serve all your creatures. When our disobedience took us far from you, you did not abandon us to the power of death. In your mercy you came to our help, so that in seeking you we might find you. Again and again you called us into covenant with you, and through the prophets you taught us to hope for salvation.

Father, you loved the world so much that in the fullness of time you sent your only Son to be our Savior. Incarnate by the Holy Spirit, born of the Virgin Mary, he lived as one of us, yet without sin. To the poor he proclaimed the good news of salvation; to prisoners, freedom; to the sorrowful, joy. To fulfill your purpose he gave himself up to death; and, rising from the grave, destroyed death, and made the whole creation new.

Eres fuente de vida y todo bien;
creaste todas las cosas y las colmaste de tu bendición
para que se gocen en el esplendor de tu presencia.

Un sinnúmero de ángeles te rodea para servirte día y noche
y, admirando tu gloria, te alaban sin cesar.
Junto con ellos, y dándole voz a toda tu creación,
te aclamamos y glorificamos cantando (diciendo):

Santo, santo, santo es el Señor, Dios del universo.
Llenos están el cielo y la tierra de tu gloria.
Hosanna en el cielo.
Bendito quien viene en nombre del Señor.
Hosanna en el cielo.

El pueblo, de pie o de rodillas.

Quien preside continúa:

Te aclamamos, Dios de santidad, poder y gloria.
Tus proezas revelan tu sabiduría y amor.
Nos formaste a tu imagen
y nos pusiste a cargo de este mundo
para que, en fiel mayordomía,
gobernemos y sirvamos a toda tu creación.
Cuando, desobedientes, nos alejamos de ti,
no nos abandonaste al poder de la muerte,
sino que en tu misericordia nos tendiste la mano
para que, al buscarte, te encontremos.
Con insistencia nos llamaste a una alianza
y por voz de tus profetas nos enseñaste
a esperar con fe nuestra liberación.

Dios de ternura, tanto amaste al mundo,
que en la plenitud de los tiempos
nos enviaste a tu Hijo único para redimirnos.
Se encarnó por el Espíritu Santo, nació de la Virgen María
y vivió como uno de *nosotros*, pero sin pecado.
A la gente pobre le anunció la salvación;
a la gente en prisión, la libertad;
a la gente afligida, la alegría.
Para cumplir tus designios se entregó a la muerte
y, levantándose del sepulcro,
destruyó la muerte y renovó toda la creación.

And, that we might live no longer for ourselves, but for him who died and rose for us, he sent the Holy Spirit, his own first gift for those who believe, to complete his work in the world, and to bring to fulfillment the sanctification of all.

At the following words concerning the bread, the Celebrant is to hold it or lay a hand upon it; and at the words concerning the cup, to hold or place a hand upon the cup and any other vessel containing wine to be consecrated.

When the hour had come for him to be glorified by you, his heavenly Father, having loved his own who were in the world, he loved them to the end; at supper with them he took bread, and when he had given thanks to you, he broke it, and gave it to his disciples, and said, "Take, eat: This is my Body, which is given for you. Do this for the remembrance of me."

After supper he took the cup of wine; and when he had given thanks, he gave it to them, and said, "Drink this, all of you. This is my Blood of the new Covenant, which is shed for you and for many for the forgiveness of sins. Whenever you drink it, do this for the remembrance of me."

Father, we now celebrate this memorial of our redemption. Recalling Christ's death and his descent among the dead, proclaiming his resurrection and ascension to your right hand, awaiting his coming in glory; and offering to you, from the gifts you have given us, this bread and this cup, we praise you and we bless you.

Celebrant and People

We praise you, we bless you,
we give thanks to you,
and we pray to you, Lord our God.

Y para que no vivamos ya para *nosotros mismos*
sino para aquel que nos salvó,
nos envió el Espíritu Santo, su primer fruto a los creyentes,
para completar su misión en este mundo
y hacernos, a *todos*, un pueblo santo.

Cuando quien preside se refiere al pan, lo alza o le impone una mano;
cuando se refiere al vino, lo alza o le impone una mano.

Padre celestial, cuando llegó la hora de recibir tu gloria,
tu Hijo no abandonó a sus *amigos*,
sino que *los* amó hasta el fin.
Cuando estaban cenando tomó pan, te dio gracias,
lo partió y se lo dio a sus *discípulos* diciendo:
«Tomen y coman:
Esto es mi cuerpo, que se entrega por ustedes.
Hagan esto en memoria mía».

Después de cenar tomó el cáliz de vino, te dio gracias,
y se la dio a sus *discípulos* diciendo:
«Beban *todos*: Esto es mi sangre de la nueva alianza,
que por ustedes y por *todos* se derrama
para el perdón de los pecados.
Cada vez que lo beban, hagan esto en memoria mía».

Por tanto, Padre, celebramos y recordamos nuestra
liberación; recordamos que Cristo murió y descendió
entre los muertos; proclamamos que resucitó y subió
a tu lado y esperamos su triunfal regreso; y de lo mucho
que nos has dado, te ofrecemos este pan y este cáliz,
te alabamos y te bendecimos.

Te alabamos, te bendecimos,
te damos gracias
y oramos a ti, Señor Dios nuestro.

The Celebrant continues

Lord, we pray that in your goodness and mercy your Holy
Spirit may descend upon us, and upon these gifts, sanctifying
them and showing them to be holy gifts for your holy people,
the bread of life and the cup of salvation, the Body and Blood
of your Son Jesus Christ.

Grant that all who share this bread and cup may become one
body and one spirit, a living sacrifice in Christ, to the praise
of your Name.

Remember, Lord, your one holy catholic and apostolic
Church, redeemed by the blood of your Christ. Reveal its
unity, guard its faith, and preserve it in peace.

[Remember (*NN.* and) all who minister in your Church.]
[Remember all your people, and those who seek your truth.]
[Remember _____.]
[Remember all who have died in the peace of Christ, and
those whose faith is known to you alone; bring them into the
place of eternal joy and light.]

And grant that we may find our inheritance with [the Blessed
Virgin Mary, with patriarchs, prophets, apostles, and martyrs,
(with _____) and] all the saints who have found favor with
you in ages past. We praise you in union with them and give
you glory through your Son Jesus Christ our Lord.

Through Christ, and with Christ, and in Christ, all honor
and glory are yours, Almighty God and Father, in the unity
of the Holy Spirit, for ever and ever. *AMEN.*

Quien preside continúa:

Y te pedimos por tu gracia y bondad
que tu Santo Espíritu
descienda sobre *nosotros* y sobre estas ofrendas,
las santifique, y nos muestre
que son santas ofrendas para tu pueblo santo,
el pan de vida y el cáliz de la salvación,
el cuerpo y sangre de tu Hijo Jesucristo.

Haz que, al compartir este pan y este cáliz,
seamos uno en cuerpo y en espíritu,
una ofrenda viva en Cristo para alabanza de tu nombre.

No te olvides, Señor,
de tu santa iglesia católica y apostólica,
redimida por la sangre de tu Ungido.
Haz visible su unidad, constante su fe
y permanente su paz.

[Recuerda (a *NN.* y) a quienes ministran en tu iglesia.]
[Recuerda a todo tu pueblo y a *cuantos* buscan tu verdad.]
[Recuerda a_____.]
[Recuerda a quienes han muerto en la paz de Cristo
y a toda persona cuya fe solo tú conoces;
condúcenos a aquel lugar
donde el gozo y la luz nunca se acaban.]

Y otórganos llegar a nuestra herencia [con la bienaventurada
Virgen María, matriarcas y patriarcas, profetas, profetisas,
apóstoles y mártires, (con_____) y] con todas las santas
y santos que en antaño te complacieron, con quienes te
alabamos y glorificamos, por tu Hijo Jesucristo, nuestro
Señor. Por Cristo, con Cristo y en Cristo, tuyos son todo el
honor y toda la gloria, Dios Padre de poder supremo, en la
unidad del Espíritu Santo, por siempre jamás. **AMÉN**

The Lord's Prayer

And now, as our Savior
Christ has taught us,
we are bold to say,

As our Savior Christ
has taught us,
we now pray,

People and Celebrant

Our Father, who art in heaven,
    hallowed be thy Name,
    thy kingdom come,
    thy will be done,
       on earth as it is in heaven.
Give us this day our daily bread.
And forgive us our trespasses,
    as we forgive those
    who trespass against us.
And lead us not into temptation,
    but deliver us from evil.
For thine is the kingdom,
    and the power, and the glory,
    for ever and ever. Amen.

Our Father in heaven,
    hallowed be your Name,
    your kingdom come,
    your will be done,
       on earth as in heaven.
Give us today our daily bread.
Forgive us our sins
    as we forgive those
    who sin against us.
Save us from the time of trial,
    and deliver us from evil.
For the kingdom, the power,
    and the glory are yours,
    now and for ever. Amen.

The Breaking of the Bread

The Celebrant breaks the consecrated Bread.

A period of silence is kept.

Then may be sung or said

[Alleluia.] Christ our Passover is sacrificed for us;
Therefore let us keep the feast. [Alleluia.]

*In Lent, Alleluia is omitted, and may be omitted at other times except
during Easter Season.*

*In place of, or in addition to, the preceding, some other suitable
anthem may be used.*

Facing the people, the Celebrant says the following Invitation

El Padrenuestro

Presidente

Siguiendo la enseñanza de nuestro Salvador, oremos diciendo:

Presidente y Pueblo

Padre nuestro que estás en el cielo,
santificado sea tu nombre;
venga tu reino;
hágase tu voluntad
en la tierra como en el cielo.
Danos hoy nuestro pan de cada día.
Perdona nuestras ofensas,
como también *nosotros* perdonamos
a los que nos ofenden.
No nos dejes caer en la tentación
y líbranos del mal.
Porque tuyo es el reino, el poder y la gloria,
ahora y por siempre. Amén.

La fracción del pan

Quien preside parte el pan consagrado.

Se guarda silencio.

Después se puede cantar o decir:

[¡Aleluya!] Cristo, nuestra Pascua, se sacrificó por *nosotros*;
Celebremos la fiesta. [¡Aleluya!]

En Cuaresma se omite el aleluya; también puede omitirse en otros tiempos litúrgicos, excepto el de Pascua.

Puede usarse cualquier otro canto apropiado, ya sea para reemplazar o complementar el Aleluya.

De cara al pueblo, quien preside invita:

The Gifts of God for the People of God.

and may add   Take them in remembrance that Christ died
for you, and feed on him in your hearts by
faith, with thanksgiving.

*The ministers receive the Sacrament in both kinds, and then
immediately deliver it to the people.*

*The Bread and the Cup are given to the communicants with these
words*

The Body (Blood) of our Lord Jesus Christ keep you in
everlasting life. [*Amen.*]

or with these words

The Body of Christ, the bread of heaven. [*Amen.*]
The Blood of Christ, the cup of salvation. [*Amen.*]

*During the ministration of Communion, hymns, psalms, or anthems
may be sung.*

*When necessary, the Celebrant consecrates additional bread and wine,
using the form on BCP page 408.*

After Communion, the Celebrant says

Let us pray.

Celebrant and People

Eternal God, heavenly Father,
you have graciously accepted us as living members
of your Son our Savior Jesus Christ,
and you have fed us with spiritual food
in the Sacrament of his Body and Blood.
Send us now into the world in peace,
and grant us strength and courage
to love and serve you
with gladness and singleness of heart;
through Christ our Lord. Amen.

Las ofrendas de Dios para el pueblo de Dios.

Y puede agregar:

Tómenlas en memoria de que Cristo murió por ustedes y aliméntense de él en sus corazones, con fe y agradecimiento.

Los ministros reciben el pan y vino e inmediatamente lo comparten con el pueblo.

El pan y el cáliz se comparten con quienes van a comulgar, con estas palabras:

El cuerpo (La sangre) de nuestro Señor Jesucristo te guarde en la vida eterna. [**Amén.**]

O con estas palabras:

El cuerpo de Cristo, pan del cielo. [**Amén.**]
La sangre de Cristo, cáliz de salvación. [**Amén**]

Mientras se comparte la Comunión, se pueden cantar himnos, salmos o cantos.

Si fuera necesario, quien preside consagra más pan y vino utilizando la fórmula en LOC en la página 273.

Después de la Comunión, quien preside dice:

Oremos.

Presidente y pueblo:

**Dios eterno, Padre celestial:
En tu gracia nos has aceptado como miembros *vivos*
de tu Hijo nuestro Salvador Jesucristo,
y nos has alimentado con comida espiritual
en el sacramento de su cuerpo y de su sangre.
Envíanos ahora en paz al mundo
y danos fortaleza y valentía
para amarte y servirte con alegría y de todo corazón;
por Cristo nuestro Señor. Amén.**

or the following

Almighty and everliving God,
we thank you for feeding us with the spiritual food
of the most precious Body and Blood
of your Son our Savior Jesus Christ;
and for assuring us in these holy mysteries
that we are living members of the Body of your Son,
and heirs of your eternal kingdom.
And now, Father, send us out
to do the work you have given us to do,
to love and serve you
as faithful witnesses of Christ our Lord.
To him, to you, and to the Holy Spirit,
be honor and glory, now and for ever. Amen.

The Bishop when present, or the Priest, may bless the people.

The Deacon, or the Celebrant, dismisses them with these words

	Let us go forth in the name of Christ.
People	Thanks be to God.

or this

Deacon	Go in peace to love and serve the Lord.
People	Thanks be to God.

or this

Deacon	Let us go forth into the world, rejoicing in the power of the Spirit.
People	Thanks be to God.

or this

Deacon	Let us bless the Lord.
People	Thanks be to God.

From the Easter Vigil through the Day of Pentecost "Alleluia, alleluia" may be added to any of the dismissals.

The People respond   Thanks be to God. Alleluia, alleluia.

O bien:

Dios poderoso y eterno:
Te damos gracias por habernos alimentado
con la cena espiritual del inestimable cuerpo y sangre
de tu Hijo nuestro Salvador Jesucristo;
y por asegurarnos, en estos santos misterios,
que somos miembros *vivos* del cuerpo de tu Hijo
y *herederos* de tu reino eterno.
Y ahora, Padre, envíanos al mundo
a cumplir la misión que nos has encomendado
para amar y servirte
en fiel testimonio de Cristo nuestro Señor.
A él, a ti, y al Espíritu Santo
sean honor y gloria, ahora y siempre. Amén.

Quien preside puede bendecir al pueblo.

*El diácono, o en su ausencia, quien preside, puede despedir al pueblo
con estas palabras:*

Salgamos en el nombre de Cristo.
Demos gracias a Dios.

O bien:

Vayamos en paz para amar y servir al Señor.
Demos gracias a Dios.

O bien:

Salgamos con gozo al mundo
en el poder del Espíritu.
Demos gracias a Dios.

O bien:

Bendigamos al Señor.
Demos gracias a Dios.

*Desde la vigilia pascual hasta el Día de Pentecostés se puede agregar
«¡Aleluya, aleluya!» a cualquiera de las despedidas:*

Demos gracias a Dios. ¡Aleluya, aleluya!

Proper Prefaces

Preface of the Lord's Day

To be used on Sundays as appointed, but not on the succeeding weekdays

1. Of God the Father

For you are the source of light and life; you made us in your image, and called us to new life in Jesus Christ our Lord.

or this

2. Of God the Son

Through Jesus Christ our Lord; who on the first day of the week overcame death and the grave, and by his glorious resurrection opened to us the way of everlasting life.

or the following

3. Of God the Holy Spirit

For by water and the Holy Spirit you have made us a new people in Jesus Christ our Lord, to show forth your glory in all the world.

Prefaces for Seasons

To be used on Sundays and weekdays alike, except as otherwise appointed for Holy Days and Various Occasions

Advent

Because you sent your beloved Son to redeem us from sin and death, and to make us heirs in him of everlasting life; that when he shall come again in power and great triumph to judge the world, we may without shame or fear rejoice to behold his appearing.

Prefacios propios

Prefacios del día del señor

Para ser usado los domingos que se indique, pero no en los días de semana subsiguientes.

1. De Dios Padre

Porque tú eres la fuente de luz y vida;
nos hiciste a tu imagen
y nos llamaste a nueva vida en Jesucristo nuestro Señor.

O bien:

2. De Dios Hijo

Por Jesucristo nuestro Señor;
quien el primer día de la semana
venció a la muerte y a la tumba,
y por su gloriosa resurrección,
nos abrió el camino de la vida eterna.

O bien:

3. De Dios Espíritu Santo

Porque, por agua y el Espíritu Santo,
nos has hecho un pueblo nuevo
en Jesucristo nuestro Señor
para manifestar tu gloria en todo el mundo.

Prefacios para los varios tiempos litúrgicos

Para tanto los domingos como los días de semana, excepto que se indique lo contrario para días santos y ocasiones varias.

Adviento

Porque enviaste a tu Hijo amado a redimirnos de la muerte y el pecado y hacernos herederos de la vida eterna; y así, cuando él regrese con poder triunfante a juzgar al mundo, podamos, sin temor ni vergüenza, contemplar con gozo su venida.

Incarnation

Because you gave Jesus Christ, your only Son, to be born for us; who, by the mighty power of the Holy Spirit, was made perfect Man of the flesh of the Virgin Mary his mother; so that we might be delivered from the bondage of sin, and receive power to become your children.

Epiphany

Because in the mystery of the Word made flesh, you have caused a new light to shine in our hearts, to give the knowledge of your glory in the face of your Son Jesus Christ our Lord.

Lent

Through Jesus Christ our Lord, who was tempted in every way as we are, yet did not sin. By his grace we are able to triumph over every evil, and to live no longer for ourselves alone, but for him who died for us and rose again.

or this

You bid your faithful people cleanse their hearts, and prepare with joy for the Paschal feast; that, fervent in prayer and in works of mercy, and renewed by your Word and Sacraments, they may come to the fullness of grace which you have prepared for those who love you.

Holy Week

Through Jesus Christ our Lord. For our sins he was lifted high upon the cross, that he might draw the whole world to himself; and, by his suffering and death, he became the source of eternal salvation for all who put their trust in him.

Encarnación

Porque nos diste a Jesucristo, tu Hijo único,
que por el poder del Espíritu Santo
se hizo perfectamente humano
de la misma carne que la Virgen María, su madre;
para liberarnos de la esclavitud del pecado,
y recibir el poder de ser tu familia.

Epifanía

Porque, en el misterio de la Palabra encarnada,
has encendido una nueva luz en nuestros corazones
para dar a conocer tu gloria
en el rostro de tu Hijo Jesucristo.

Cuaresma

Por Jesucristo nuestro Señor que,
aunque como *nosotros* fue tentado en todo, en nada pecó.
Por su gracia podemos derrotar el mal
y, dejando nuestra vida de egoísmo,
vivir por él, que por *nosotros* murió y resucitó.

O bien:

Tú le pides a tu pueblo fiel que purifique el corazón
y se prepare con gozo para la fiesta de Pascua.
Para que así, en oración fervorosa y obras de misericordia,
y *renovados* por tu palabra y sacramentos,
conozcamos la plenitud de gracia
que tú has dispuesto para quienes te aman.

Semana Santa

Por Jesucristo nuestro Señor.
Por nuestros pecados fue crucificado
para atraer a sí mismo a todo el mundo;
y, por su agonía y muerte,
se convirtió en manantial de salvación eterna
para quienes en él confían.

Easter

But chiefly are we bound to praise you for the glorious resurrection of your Son Jesus Christ our Lord; for he is the true Paschal Lamb, who was sacrificed for us, and has taken away the sin of the world. By his death he has destroyed death, and by his rising to life again he has won for us everlasting life.

Ascension

Through your dearly beloved Son Jesus Christ our Lord. After his glorious resurrection he openly appeared to his disciples, and in their sight ascended into heaven, to prepare a place for us; that where he is, there we might also be, and reign with him in glory.

Pentecost

Through Jesus Christ our Lord. In fulfillment of his true promise, the Holy Spirit came down [on this day] from heaven, lighting upon the disciples, to teach them and to lead them into all truth; uniting peoples of many tongues in the confession of one faith, and giving to your Church the power to serve you as a royal priesthood, and to preach the Gospel to all nations.

Prefaces for Other Occasions

Trinity Sunday

For with your co-eternal Son and Holy Spirit, you are one God, one Lord, in Trinity of Persons and in Unity of Being; and we celebrate the one and equal glory of you, O Father, and of the Son, and of the Holy Spirit.

Pascua

Pero sobre todo debemos alabarte
por la gloriosa resurrección
de tu Hijo Jesucristo, nuestro Señor.
Él es el verdadero cordero pascual,
que por *nosotros* fue sacrificado,
para librar del pecado al mundo entero.
Por su muerte, la muerte aniquiló
y, al resucitar a nueva vida, nos ganó la vida eterna.

Ascensión

Por Jesucristo nuestro Señor.
Después de su resurrección gloriosa,
apareció claramente a sus *discípulos*
y antes sus ojos ascendió a los cielos
para prepararnos un lugar;
para que donde él está, también *nosotros* estemos
y reinemos con él en gloria.

Pentecostés

Por Jesucristo nuestro Señor. Para cumplir la promesa de
tu Hijo, el Espíritu Santo descendió [este día] sobre sus
discípulos para enseñarles y *guiarlos* a toda verdad, uniendo
así pueblos de diversas lenguas en afirmar la misma fe, y
empoderando a tu pueblo para servirte como un sacerdocio
ungido y predicar el evangelio a todas las naciones.

Prefacios para otras ocasiones

Domingo de la Santísima Trinidad

Porque con el Hijo y el Espíritu Santo
eres Dios y Señor, trino y uno:
Tres personas coeternas en una sustancia;
y celebramos la gloria que tú, el Hijo, y el Espíritu Santo
comparten como iguales.

All Saints

For in the multitude of your saints, you have surrounded us with a great cloud of witnesses, that we might rejoice in their fellowship, and run with endurance the race that is set before us; and, together with them, receive the crown of glory that never fades away.

A Saint

For the wonderful grace and virtue declared in all your saints, who have been the chosen vessels of your grace, and the lights of the world in their generations.

or this

Because in the obedience of your saints you have given us an example of righteousness, and in their eternal joy a glorious pledge of the hope of our calling.

or this

Because you are greatly glorified in the assembly of your saints. All your creatures praise you, and your faithful servants bless you, confessing before the rulers of this world the great Name of your only Son.

Apostles and Ordinations

Through the great shepherd of your flock, Jesus Christ our Lord; who after his resurrection sent forth his apostles to preach the Gospel and to teach all nations; and promised to be with them always, even to the end of the ages.

Dedication of a Church

Through Jesus Christ our great High Priest, in whom we are built up as living stones of a holy temple, that we might offer before you a sacrifice of praise and prayer which is holy and pleasing in your sight.

Todos los Santos y Santas

Porque en la multitud de tus santos y santas
nos has rodeado de una gran nube de testigos,
para que en su comunión tengamos gozo y, perseverantes,
corramos la carrera que tenemos por delante
y recibamos una corona de gloria que nunca se marchita.

Un santo o santa

Por la gracia y virtud maravillosas
declaradas en tus santos y santas,
que designaste instrumentos de tu gracia
y luces del mundo a sus *contemporáneos*.

O bien:

Porque en la obediencia de tus santos y santas
nos das ejemplos de gran rectitud y, en su gozo eterno,
la promesa gloriosa que nuestra vocación anhela.

O bien:

Porque tus santos y santas te alaban y te glorifican.
Todas tus criaturas te celebran y tus fieles te bendicen,
declarando el nombre de tu Hijo ante todos los poderes de
este mundo.

Apóstoles y ordenaciones

Por el pastor perfecto del rebaño, Jesucristo nuestro Señor;
quien después de resucitar,
envió a sus apóstoles a predicar el evangelio
y a enseñar a todas las naciones;
y prometió que siempre *los* acompañaría,
hasta el fin del mundo.

Dedicación de una iglesia

Por Jesucristo, nuestro gran Sumo Sacerdote,
en quien, como piedras vivas, somos *edificados*
formando un santo templo,
para ofrecer nuestra alabanza y oración,
una ofrenda agradable ante tu vista.

Baptism

Because in Jesus Christ our Lord you have received us as
your sons and daughters, made us citizens of your kingdom,
and given us the Holy Spirit to guide us into all truth.

Marriage

Because in the love of wife and husband, you have given us
an image of the heavenly Jerusalem, adorned as a bride for
her bridegroom, your Son Jesus Christ our Lord; who loves
her and gave himself for her, that he might make the whole
creation new.

Commemoration of the Dead

Through Jesus Christ our Lord; who rose victorious
from the dead, and comforts us with the blessed hope of
everlasting life. For to your faithful people, O Lord, life
is changed, not ended; and when our mortal body lies in
death, there is prepared for us a dwelling place eternal in the
heavens.

Bautismo

Porque en Jesucristo nuestro Señor
nos has recibido como hijas e hijos tuyos,
nos has hecho *conciudadanos* de tu reino
y nos has dado el Espíritu Santo
para que nos guíe a toda verdad.

Matrimonio

Porque en el amor de una pareja
nos has dado una imagen de la Jerusalén celestial,
adornada como una novia para su novio,
tu Hijo Jesucristo nuestro Señor,
quien ama a la Iglesia y por ella se entregó,
para así renovar toda la creación.

Conmemoración de difuntos y difuntas

Por Jesucristo nuestro Señor;
quien se levantó victorioso de entre los muertos,
y nos consuela con la esperanza de la vida eterna.
Porque para tus fieles, Señor, la vida no termina,
sino que cambia;
y cuando nuestro cuerpo mortal duerma en su tumba,
habrá preparada para *nosotros*
una morada celestial y eterna.

The Celebration and Blessing of a Marriage

At the time appointed, the persons to be married, with their witnesses, assemble in the church or some other appropriate place.

During their entrance, a hymn, psalm, or anthem may be sung, or instrumental music may be played.

Then the Celebrant, facing the people and the persons to be married, with the woman to the right and the man to the left, addresses the congregation and says

Dearly beloved: We have come together in the presence of God to witness and bless the joining together of this man and this woman in Holy Matrimony. The bond and covenant of marriage was established by God in creation, and our Lord Jesus Christ adorned this manner of life by his presence and first miracle at a wedding in Cana of Galilee. It signifies to us the mystery of the union between Christ and his Church, and Holy Scripture commends it to be honored among all people.

The union of husband and wife in heart, body, and mind is intended by God for their mutual joy; for the help and comfort given one another in prosperity and adversity; and, when it is God's will, for the procreation of children and their nurture in the knowledge and love of the Lord. Therefore marriage is not to be entered into unadvisedly or lightly, but reverently, deliberately, and in accordance with the purposes for which it was instituted by God.

Celebración y bendición de un matrimonio

A la hora designada, la pareja y los testigos se reúnen en la iglesia o en otro lugar apropiado.

Mientras entran, se puede cantar un himno, salmo o canto, o se puede tocar música instrumental.

Quien preside de cara al pueblo y a los novios, con la mujer a su derecha y el hombre a su izquierda, se dirige a la congregación con estas palabras:

Queridos hermanos y hermanas: Nos hemos reunido en presencia de Dios para ser testigos y bendecir la unión de esta mujer y este hombre en santo matrimonio. El vínculo y convenio del matrimonio fue establecido por Dios en la creación, y nuestro Señor Jesucristo honró esta forma de vida con su presencia y primer milagro en una boda en Caná de Galilea. El matrimonio representa el misterio de la unión entre Cristo y su iglesia, y la sagrada escritura encomienda a que sea respetado por todo el mundo.

Es la intención de Dios que la unión del esposo y la esposa en corazón, cuerpo y mente sea para gozo mutuo; para la ayuda y consuelo entre ambos, tanto en la adversidad como en la prosperidad; y, cuando sea la voluntad de Dios, para la procreación de hijas e hijos y su crianza en el conocimiento y el amor del Señor. Por lo tanto no debe contraerse el matrimonio sin consciencia o ligeramente, sino de forma reverente y deliberada, conforme a los propósitos por los que Dios lo estableció.

Into this holy union N.N. and N.N. now come to be joined. If any of you can show just cause why they may not lawfully be married, speak now; or else for ever hold your peace.

Then the Celebrant says to the persons to be married

I require and charge you both, here in the presence of God, that if either of you know any reason why you may not be united in marriage lawfully, and in accordance with God's Word, you do now confess it.

The Declaration of Consent

The Celebrant says to the woman

N., will you have this man to be your husband; to live together in the covenant of marriage? Will you love him, comfort him, honor and keep him, in sickness and in health; and, forsaking all others, be faithful to him as long as you both shall live?

The Woman answers

I will.

The Celebrant says to the man

N., will you have this woman to be your wife; to live together in the covenant of marriage? Will you love her, comfort her, honor and keep her, in sickness and in health; and, forsaking all others, be faithful to her as long as you both shall live?

The Man answers

I will.

The Celebrant then addresses the congregation, saying

Will all of you witnessing these promises do all in your power to uphold these two persons in their marriage?

People We will.

Tal es la santa unión en la que *N.N.* y *N.N.* hoy vienen para ser unidos. Si alguien de entre ustedes pudiera demostrar causa justa que les impida casarse según la ley, que hable ahora, o que guarde silencio para siempre.

Entonces quien preside les dice a los novios:

Les exijo y ordeno a ustedes dos, en la presencia de Dios: Si uno de ustedes conoce cualquier motivo por el que no pueden unirse en matrimonio según la ley y de acuerdo con la palabra de Dios, que ahora lo declare.

La declaración de consentimiento

Quien preside le dice a la mujer:

N., ¿tomas a este hombre como esposo para vivir juntos en el convenio del matrimonio? ¿Lo amarás, consolarás, honrarás y cuidarás en salud o enfermedad y, excluyendo a toda otra persona, le serás fiel mientras los dos vivan?

La mujer responde:

Sí, así lo haré.

Quien preside le dice al hombre:

N., ¿tomas a esta mujer como tu esposa para vivir juntos en el convenio del matrimonio? ¿La amarás, consolarás, honrarás y cuidarás en salud o enfermedad y, excluyendo a toda otra persona, le serás fiel mientras los dos vivan?

El hombre responde:

Sí, así lo haré.

Quien preside se dirige a la congregación:

Ustedes *todos*, testigos de estas promesas, ¿harán todo lo posible por apoyar a estas dos personas en su matrimonio?

Pueblo **Sí, así lo haremos.**

If there is to be a presentation or a giving in marriage, it takes place at this time. See BCP page 437.

A hymn, psalm, or anthem may follow.

The Ministry of the Word

The Celebrant then says to the people

The Lord be with you.
People   And also with you.

Let us pray.

O gracious and everliving God, you have created us male and female in your image: Look mercifully upon this man and this woman who come to you seeking your blessing, and assist them with your grace, that with true fidelity and steadfast love they may honor and keep the promises and vows they make; through Jesus Christ our Savior, who lives and reigns with you in the unity of the Holy Spirit, one God, for ever and ever. *Amen.*

Then one or more of the following passages from Holy Scripture is read. If there is to be a Communion, a passage from the Gospel always concludes the Readings.

Genesis 1:26-28 (Male and female he created them)
Genesis 2:4-9, 15-24 (A man cleaves to his wife and they become one flesh)
Song of Solomon 2:10-13; 8:6-7 (Many waters cannot quench love)
Tobit 8:5b-8 (*New English Bible*) (That she and I may grow old together)

1 Corinthians 13:1-13 (Love is patient and kind)
Ephesians 3:14-19 (The Father from whom every family is named)
Ephesians 5:1-2, 21-33 (Walk in love, as Christ loved us)

Si se presentara a los novios o se entregara a la novia, se lo hace ahora. Consule LOC en la página 299.

Puede cantarse un himno, salmo o canto.

Ministerio de la palabra

Entonces quien preside le dice al pueblo:

El Señor esté con ustedes.
Y también contigo.

Oremos.

Dios bondadoso y eterno:
Nos creaste, hombre y mujer, a tu imagen;
mira con compasión a esta mujer y a este hombre
que vienen buscando tu bendición.
Ayúdalos con tu gracia para que honren y cumplan
los votos y promesas que hacen hoy
con lealtad verdadera y amor firme;
por Jesucristo nuestro Salvador,
que vive y reina contigo
en la unidad del Espíritu Santo,
un solo Dios, ahora y por siempre. **Amén.**

Se lee uno o más de los siguientes pasajes de las Sagradas Escrituras. Si habrá comunión, siempre se concluye con un pasaje del evangelio.

Génesis 1:26-28 (Hombre y mujer los creó)
Génesis 2:4-9, 15-24 (Por tanto, el hombre se unirá a su mujer y serán una sola carne)
Cantares 2:10-13; 8:6-7 (Las poderosas aguas no pueden apagar el amor)
Tobías 8:5b-8 (Haznos llegar juntos a la vejez)

1 Corintios 13:1-13 (El amor es paciente y bondadoso)
Efesios 3:14-19 (El Padre de quien toma nombre toda familia)
Efesios 5:1-2, 21-33 (Anden en amor, como Cristo también nos amó)

Colossians 3:12-17 (Love which binds everything together in harmony)
1 John 4:7-16 (Let us love one another for love is of God)

Between the Readings, a Psalm, hymn, or anthem may be sung or said. Appropriate Psalms are 67, 127, and 128.

When a passage from the Gospel is to be read, all stand, and the Deacon or Minister appointed says

> The Holy Gospel of our Lord Jesus Christ according to_____.

People   Glory to you, Lord Christ.

Matthew 5:1-10 (The Beatitudes)
Matthew 5:13-16 (You are the light... Let your light so shine)
Matthew 7:21, 24-29 (Like a wise man who built his house upon the rock)
Mark 10:6-9, 13-16 (They are no longer two but one)
John 15:9-12 (Love one another as I have loved you)

After the Gospel, the Reader says

> The Gospel of the Lord.

People   Praise to you, Lord Christ.

A homily or other response to the Readings may follow.

The Marriage

The Man, facing the woman and taking her right hand in his, says

In the Name of God, I, N., take you, N., to be my wife, to have and to hold from this day forward, for better for worse, for richer for poorer, in sickness and in health, to love and to cherish, until we are parted by death. This is my solemn vow.

Colosenses 3:12-17 (El amor es el vínculo perfecto)
1 Juan 4:7-16 (Amémonos *unos a otros* porque el amor es de Dios)

Entre las lecturas se puede leer o cantar un salmo, himno o canto. Los salmos apropiados son el 67, 127 y 128. Si se lee el evangelio, todos de pie. La persona del clero designada dice:

Santo evangelio de Nuestro Señor Jesucristo según _____.
Gloria a ti, Cristo Señor.

Mateo 5:1-10 (Las bienaventuranzas)
Mateo 5:13-16 (Ustedes son la luz… Así alumbre su luz)
Mateo 7:21, 24-29 (Como una persona prudente que edificó su casa sobre la peña)
Marcos 10:6-9, 13-16 (Ya no son más dos, sino uno)
Juan 15:9-12 (Ámense los unos a los otros como yo los he amado)

Después del evangelio, quien leyó dice:

El evangelio del Señor.
Te alabamos, Cristo Señor.

Puede predicarse un sermón breve o incluirse alguna otra forma de reflexión sobre las lecturas.

El matrimonio

El hombre, de cara a la mujer, toma su mano derecha y dice:

En el nombre de Dios, yo, N.,
te tomo a ti, N., como mi esposa,
para vivir y contar contigo
de hoy en adelante
en las buenas y en las malas,
en riqueza y en pobreza,
en salud y en enfermedad,
para amar y quererte
hasta que la muerte nos separe.
Este es mi voto solemne.

Then they loose their hands, and the Woman, still facing the man, takes his right hand in hers, and says

In the Name of God, I, *N.*,
take you, *N.*, to be my husband,
to have and to hold
from this day forward,
for better for worse, for richer for poorer,
in sickness and in health,
to love and to cherish,
until we are parted by death.
This is my solemn vow.

They loose their hands.

The Priest may ask God's blessing on a ring or rings as follows

Bless, O Lord, *this ring* to be a *sign*
of the vows by which this man
and this woman have bound
themselves to each other;
through Jesus Christ our Lord. *Amen.*

The giver places the ring on the ring-finger of the other's hand and says

N., I give you this ring as a symbol of my vow,
and with all that I am, and all that I have,
I honor you, in the Name of the Father,
and of the Son, and of the Holy Spirit
(*or* in the Name of God).

Then the Celebrant joins the right hands of husband and wife and says

Now that *N.* and *N.* have given themselves
to each other by solemn vows,
with the joining of hands and the giving and
 receiving of *a ring*, I pronounce that they are
husband and wife, in the Name of the Father,
and of the Son, and of the Holy Spirit.

Those whom God has joined together let no one put asunder.

People   Amen.

Se sueltan las manos; la mujer, aun de cara al hombre, toma su mano derecha y dice:

En el nombre de Dios, yo, N.,
te tomo a ti, N., como mi esposo,
para vivir y contar contigo
de hoy en adelante
en las buenas y en las malas,
en riqueza y en pobreza,
en salud y en enfermedad,
para amar y quererte
hasta que la muerte nos separe.
Este es mi voto solemne.

Se sueltan las manos.

Quien preside puede pedir la bendición de Dios sobre el anillo usando estas palabras:

Bendice, Señor, *este anillo*
como *signo* de los votos
por los que este hombre y esta mujer
se han unido en un vínculo de amor;
por Cristo Jesús nuestro Señor. **Amén.**

La persona que da el anillo lo coloca en el dedo anular de la otra y dice:

Te doy este anillo como símbolo de mi voto,
y con todo lo que soy y con todo lo que tengo,
te honro en el nombre del Padre y del Hijo
y del Espíritu Santo (*o en el nombre de Dios*).

Quien preside une las manos derechas del hombre y la mujer y dice:

Ya que N. y N. se han entregado mutuamente con votos solemnes, tomados de la mano, dando y recibiendo *un anillo*, los declaro esposa y esposo, en el nombre del Padre y del Hijo y del Espíritu Santo.

Los que Dios ha unido, nadie los separe.

Amén.

The Prayers

All standing, the Celebrant says

Let us pray together in the words our Savior taught us.

People and Celebrant

Our Father, who art in heaven,	Our Father in heaven,
hallowed be thy Name,	hallowed be your Name,
thy kingdom come,	your kingdom come,
thy will be done,	your will be done,
on earth as it is in heaven.	on earth as in heaven.
Give us this day our daily bread.	Give us today our daily bread.
And forgive us our trespasses,	Forgive us our sins
as we forgive those	as we forgive those
who trespass against us.	who sin against us.
And lead us not into temptation,	Save us from the time of trial,
but deliver us from evil.	and deliver us from evil.
For thine is the kingdom,	For the kingdom, the power,
and the power, and the glory,	and the glory are yours,
for ever and ever. Amen.	now and for ever. Amen.

If Communion is to follow, the Lord's Prayer may be omitted here.

The Deacon or other person appointed reads the following prayers, to which the People respond, saying, Amen.

If there is not to be a Communion, one or more of the prayers may be omitted.

Let us pray.

Eternal God, creator and preserver of all life, author of salvation, and giver of all grace: Look with favor upon the world you have made, and for which your Son gave his life, and especially upon this man and this woman whom you make one flesh in Holy Matrimony. *Amen.*

Give them wisdom and devotion in the ordering of their common life, that each may be to the other a strength in need, a counselor in perplexity, a comfort in sorrow, and a companion in joy. *Amen.*

Las oraciones

Todos de pie. Quien preside dice:

Oremos como nuestro Salvador nos enseñó:

Padre nuestro que estás en el cielo,
santificado sea tu nombre;
venga tu reino;
hágase tu voluntad
en la tierra como en el cielo.
Danos hoy nuestro pan de cada día.
Perdona nuestras ofensas,
como también *nosotros* perdonamos
a los que nos ofenden.
No nos dejes caer en la tentación
y líbranos del mal.
Porque tuyo es el reino, el poder y la gloria,
ahora y por siempre. Amén.

Si sigue la Santa Comunión, el Padrenuestro se puede omitir.

Una persona designada lee las siguientes oraciones; el pueblo responde a cada oración diciendo «Amén».

Si no hay comunión, se puede omitir una o más de las oraciones.

Oremos.

Dios eterno, creador y protector de toda vida,
autor de la salvación y dador de toda gracia:
Mira bondadosamente a tu creación
por la cual tu Hijo dio su vida,
y en especial a esta mujer y a este hombre
a quienes unes hoy en santo matrimonio. **Amén.**

Dales sabiduría y devoción al ordenar su vida en común,
para que se fortalezcan mutuamente, se aconsejen en sus
desafíos, se consuelen en sus pesares, y se acompañen en sus
alegrías. **Amén.**

Grant that their wills may be so
knit together in your will, and their spirits
in your Spirit, that they may grow
in love and peace with you and one another all the days
of their life. *Amen.*

Give them grace, when they hurt each other,
to recognize and acknowledge their fault,
and to seek each other's
forgiveness and yours. *Amen.*

Make their life together
a sign of Christ's love to
this sinful and broken world,
that unity may overcome estrangement,
forgiveness heal guilt, and joy conquer despair. *Amen.*

Bestow on them, if it is your will, the gift and heritage of
children, and the grace to bring them up to know you, to
love you, and to serve you. *Amen.*

Give them such fulfillment of their mutual affection that they
may reach out in love and concern for others. *Amen.*

Grant that all married persons who have witnessed these
vows may find their lives strengthened and their loyalties
confirmed. *Amen.*

Grant that the bonds of our common humanity,
by which all your children are united one to another,
and the living to the dead, may be so transformed
by your grace, that your will may be done on earth as
it is in heaven; where, O Father, with your Son
and the Holy Spirit, you live and reign in perfect unity,
now and for ever. *Amen.*

Concede que entretejan sus voluntades con la tuya,
y sus almas con tu Espíritu,
para que crezcan juntos y contigo
en amor y paz todos los días de su vida;
por Cristo Jesucristo nuestro Señor. **Amén.**

Dales gracia, cuando se lastimen,
para reconocer y admitir su error,
pedirse perdón y buscar el tuyo. **Amén.**

Haz que su vida en común
sea un signo del amor de Cristo
hacia este mundo pecador y quebrantado
y que así la unidad venza la división,
el perdón sane la culpa
y la alegría conquiste la desesperanza. **Amén.**

Concédeles, si es tu voluntad, la bendición de hijas e hijos; y
dales la gracia de *criarlos* para conocerte, amarte y servirte.
Amén.

Haz que sientan tanto gozo por su afecto mutuo que se
entreguen a amar y servir a los demás. **Amén.**

Concede que toda persona casada
que ha presenciado estos votos
encuentre su vida fortalecida y sus votos confirmados. **Amén.**

Transforma, con tu gracia,
nuestros vínculos de hermandad
y los lazos entre *vivos* y *difuntos*
para que así tu voluntad
se cumpla en la tierra y en el cielo;
donde tú, Padre, vives y reinas en perfecta unidad
con tu Hijo y con el Espíritu Santo, ahora y por siempre. **Amén.**

The Blessing of the Marriage

The people remain standing. The husband and wife kneel, and the Priest says one of the following prayers

Most gracious God, we give you thanks for your tender love in sending Jesus Christ to come among us, to be born of a human mother, and to make the way of the cross to be the way of life. We thank you, also, for consecrating the union of man and woman in his Name. By the power of your Holy Spirit, pour out the abundance of your blessing upon this man and this woman. Defend them from every enemy. Lead them into all peace. Let their love for each other be a seal upon their hearts, a mantle about their shoulders, and a crown upon their foreheads. Bless them in their work and in their companionship; in their sleeping and in their waking; in their joys and in their sorrows; in their life and in their death. Finally, in your mercy, bring them to that table where your saints feast for ever in your heavenly home; through Jesus Christ our Lord, who with you and the Holy Spirit lives and reigns, one God, for ever and ever. *Amen.*

or this

O God, you have so consecrated the covenant of marriage that in it is represented the spiritual unity between Christ and his Church: Send therefore your blessing upon these your servants, that they may so love, honor, and cherish each other in faithfulness and patience, in wisdom and true godliness, that their home may be a haven of blessing and peace; through Jesus Christ our Lord,

La Bendición del matrimonio

El pueblo sigue de pie. La pareja se arrodilla y quien preside dice una de las siguientes oraciones:

Dios de infinita bondad:
Te damos gracias por el tierno amor que mostraste
al enviar a Jesucristo entre *nosotros*
para nacer de una madre humana
y hacer, del camino de la cruz, el camino de la vida.

Te damos gracias también por consagrar,
en su nombre, la unión de hombre y mujer.
Por el poder de tu Espíritu Santo
derrama abundantes bendiciones sobre esta pareja.
Defiéndelos de todo enemigo.
Condúcelos siempre por sendas de paz.
Que el amor que se tienen
sea un sello sobre sus corazones,
un manto sobre sus hombros
y una corona sobre su cabezas.
Bendícelos en su trabajo y en su hogar;
al dormir y al despertar;
en sus alegrías y en sus tristezas;
en la vida y en la muerte.
Y al final, en tu misericordia,
tráelos al banquete eterno de tu hogar celestial
donde festejan tus santos y santas;
por Jesucristo nuestro Señor, que vive y reina contigo
y con el Espíritu Santo un solo Dios, ahora y por siempre. **Amén.**

O bien:

Dios, que has consagrado el convenio del matrimonio
para representar la unión espiritual
entre Cristo y su Iglesia:
Bendice a estos tus servidores
para que se amen, quieran y honren
con tal fidelidad y paciencia, tal sabiduría y reverencia,
que su hogar sea un refugio de bendición y de paz;
por Jesucristo nuestro Señor,

who lives and reigns with you and the Holy Spirit, one God, now and for ever. *Amen.*

The husband and wife still kneeling, the Priest adds this blessing

God the Father, God the Son, God the Holy Spirit, bless, preserve, and keep you; the Lord mercifully with his favor look upon you, and fill you with all spiritual benediction and grace; that you may faithfully live together in this life, and in the age to come have life everlasting. *Amen.*

The Peace

The Celebrant may say to the people

The peace of the Lord be always with you.
People   And also with you.

The newly married couple then greet each other, after which greetings may be exchanged throughout the congregation.

When Communion is not to follow, the wedding party leaves the church. A hymn, psalm, or anthem may be sung, or instrumental music may be played.

At the Eucharist

The liturgy continues with the Offertory, at which the newly married couple may present the offerings of bread and wine.

Preface of Marriage

At the Communion, it is appropriate that the newly married couple receive Communion first, after the ministers.

In place of the usual postcommunion prayer, the following is said

O God, the giver of all that is true and lovely and gracious: We give you thanks for binding us together in these holy mysteries of the Body and Blood of your Son Jesus Christ. Grant that by your Holy Spirit, N. and N., now joined in Holy Matrimony, may become one in heart and soul,

que contigo y el Espíritu Santo vive y reina,
un solo Dios, ahora y por siempre. **Amén.**

Quien preside añade esta bendición:

Dios Padre, Dios Hijo y Dios Espíritu Santo
los bendiga, guarde y preserve;
que el Señor, compasivo y generoso,
los tenga presentes
y les colme de toda bendición y gracia espiritual
para que convivan fielmente en esta vida
y vivan por siempre en el mundo venidero. **Amén.**

La paz

Quien preside puede decir al pueblo:

La paz del Señor esté siempre con ustedes.
Y también contigo.

La pareja se saluda y la congregación puede saludarse mutuamente.

Si no sigue la comunión, el cortejo nupcial se retira de la iglesia.
Se puede cantar un himno, salmo o canto, o se puede tocar música
instrumental.

Durante la eucaristía

El rito continúa con la presentación de ofrendas. La pareja puede
presentar las ofrendas.

Se usa el prefacio de matrimonio.

Durante la comunión, es apropiado que la pareja reciba la comunión
primero, después de los ministros.

En vez de la oración de poscomunión usual, se dice lo siguiente:

Dios creador, fuente de toda verdad, belleza y bondad:
Te damos gracias por unirnos en estos santos misterios
del cuerpo y sangre de tu Hijo Jesucristo.
Concede por tu Santo Espíritu, que *N.* y *N.*,
unidos en santo matrimonio,

live in fidelity and peace, and obtain those eternal joys
prepared for all who love you; for the sake of Jesus Christ our
Lord. *Amen.*

*As the wedding party leaves the church, a hymn, psalm, or anthem may
be sung; or instrumental music may be played.*

lleguen a ser uno de alma y corazón,
vivan en fidelidad y paz,
y obtengan los gozos eternos
preparados para quienes te aman;
por amor de Cristo Jesús nuestro Señor. **Amén.**

The Blessing of a Civil Marriage

The Rite begins as prescribed for celebrations of the Holy Eucharist, using the Collect and Lessons appointed in the Marriage service.

After the Gospel (and homily), the husband and wife stand before the Celebrant, who addresses them in these or similar words

N. and N., you have come here today to seek the blessing of God and of his Church upon your marriage. I require, therefore, that you promise, with the help of God, to fulfill the obligations which Christian Marriage demands.

The Celebrant then addresses the husband, saying

N., you have taken N. to be your wife. Do you promise to love her, comfort her, honor and keep her, in sickness and in health; and, forsaking all others, to be faithful to her as long as you both shall live?

The Husband answers I do.

The Celebrant then addresses the wife, saying

N., you have taken N. to be your husband. Do you promise to love him, comfort him, honor and keep him, in sickness and in health; and, forsaking all others, to be faithful to him as long as you both shall live?

La Bendición de un matrimonio civil

El rito comienza de la manera indicada para la celebración de la santa eucaristía, usando la colecta y las lecturas designadas en el rito de matrimonio. Si se ha de incluir la Santa Comunión, se proclama el evangelio seguido por una homilía.

El esposo y la esposa se ponen de pie frente a quien preside, que se dirige a ellos con estas estas u otras palabras similares:

N. y N., ustedes han venido hoy pidiendo la bendición de Dios y la Iglesia sobre su matrimonio. Les pido, por lo tanto, que prometan cumplir, con la ayuda de Dios, las obligaciones que el matrimonio cristiano exige.

Quien preside le dice al hombre:

N., que has tomado a N. por esposa: ¿La amarás, consolarás, honrarás y cuidarás en salud o enfermedad y, excluyendo a toda otra persona, le serás fiel mientras los dos vivan?

El hombre responde:

Sí, así lo haré.

Quien preside le dice a la mujer:

N., que has tomado a N. por esposo: ¿Lo amarás, consolarás, honrarás y cuidarás en salud o enfermedad y, excluyendo a toda otra persona, le serás fiel mientras los dos vivan?

The Wife answers   I do.

The Celebrant then addresses the congregation, saying

Will you who have witnessed these promises do all in your power to uphold these two persons in their marriage?

People   We will.

If a ring or rings are to be blessed, the wife extends her hand (and the husband extends his hand) toward the Priest, who says

Bless, O Lord, *this ring* to be *a sign* of the vows by which this man and this woman have bound themselves to each other; through Jesus Christ our Lord. *Amen.*

The Celebrant joins the right hands of the husband and wife and says

Those whom God has joined together let no one put asunder.

The Congregation responds   Amen.

The service continues with The Prayers on page 226.

La mujer responde:

Sí, así lo haré.

Quien preside se dirige a la congregación con estas palabras:

Ustedes, que presencian estas promesas, ¿harán todo lo posible por apoyar a estas dos personas en su matrimonio?

Sí, lo haremos.

Si hay anillo que bendecir, la mujer extiende su mano (y el hombre la suya) hacia quien preside, que dice:

Bendice, Señor, *este anillo*
como *signo* de los votos
por los que este hombre y esta mujer
se han unido en un vínculo de amor;
por Cristo Jesús nuestro Señor. **Amén.**

Quien preside une las manos derechas del hombre y la mujer y dice:

Los que Dios ha unido, nadie los separe.
Amén.

La liturgia continúa con Las Oraciones en la página 227.

The Reconciliation of a Penitent

Form One

The Penitent begins

Bless me, for I have sinned.

The Priest says

The Lord be in your heart and upon your lips that you may truly and humbly confess your sins: In the Name of the Father, and of the Son, and of the Holy Spirit. *Amen.*

Penitent

I confess to Almighty God, to his Church, and to you, that I have sinned by my own fault in thought, word, and deed, in things done and left undone; especially_____. For these and all other sins which I cannot now remember, I am truly sorry. I pray God to have mercy on me. I firmly intend amendment of life, and I humbly beg forgiveness of God and his Church, and ask you for counsel, direction, and absolution.

La Reconciliación
de penitentes

Fórmula I

Penitente

Bendíceme, porque he pecado.

Presbítero

El Señor esté en tu corazón y en tus labios para que confieses
verdadera y humildemente tus pecados: En el nombre del
Padre, y del Hijo, y del Espíritu Santo. **Amén.**

Penitente

Confieso a Dios Todopoderoso, a su Iglesia y a ti,
que he pecado por mi propia culpa,
de pensamiento, palabra y obra,
por lo que he hecho y he dejado sin hacer;
especialmente_____.
De estos y cualquier otro pecado
que ahora no puedo recordar,
me arrepiento sinceramente.
Pido a Dios que tenga misericordia de mí.
Me propongo firmemente a corregir mi vida,
y humildemente le pido perdón a Dios y su Iglesia;
y a ti te pido consejo, dirección y absolución.

Here the Priest may offer counsel, direction, and comfort.
The Priest then pronounces this absolution

Our Lord Jesus Christ, who has left power to his Church to absolve all sinners who truly repent and believe in him, of his great mercy forgive you all your offenses; and by his authority committed to me, I absolve you from all your sins: In the Name of the Father, and of the Son, and of the Holy Spirit. *Amen.*

or this

Our Lord Jesus Christ, who offered himself to be sacrificed for us to the Father, and who conferred power on his Church to forgive sins, absolve you through my ministry by the grace of the Holy Spirit, and restore you in the perfect peace of the Church. *Amen.*

The Priest adds

The Lord has put away all your sins.

Penitent Thanks be to God.

The Priest concludes

Go (*or* abide) in peace, and pray for me, a sinner.

Declaration of Forgiveness
to be used by a Deacon or Lay Person

Our Lord Jesus Christ, who offered himself to be sacrificed for us to the Father, forgives your sins by the grace of the Holy Spirit. *Amen.*

Form Two

The Priest and Penitent begin as follows

Have mercy on me, O God, according to your loving-
    kindness; in your great compassion blot out my offenses.
Wash me through and through from my wickedness, and
    cleanse me from my sin.

El presbítero puede ofrecer consejo, dirección y consuelo y declara esta absolución:

Nuestro Señor Jesucristo, le ha dado poder a su Iglesia para absolver a *pecadores* que verdaderamente se arrepienten y creen en él. En su gran misericordia te perdone todas tus ofensas; y por la autoridad a mí conferida, yo te absuelvo de todos tus pecados en el nombre del Padre, y del Hijo, y del Espíritu Santo, **Amén.**

O bien:

Nuestro Señor Jesucristo, que se ofreció al Padre en sacrificio por *nosotros* y confirió a su Iglesia el poder de perdonar pecados, por la gracia del Espíritu Santo te absuelva mediante mi ministerio, y te restaure a la paz perfecta de la iglesia. **Amén.**

Presbítero El Señor ha quitado todos tus pecados.
Penitente Demos gracias a Dios.
Presbítero Ve (o vive) en paz y reza por mí, *un pecador.*

Declaración de perdón
para ser utilizada por un diácono o *persona laica:*

Nuestro Señor Jesucristo, que se ofreció a sí mismo al Padre en sacrificio por *nosotros*, perdona tus pecados por la gracia del Espíritu Santo. **Amén.**

Fórmula II

Presbítero y penitente juntos

Ten misericordia de mí, Dios, según tu gran amor;
     en tu inmensa bondad borra todas mis ofensas.
De mi maldad lávame enteramente,
     y límpiame de mi pecado.

For I know my transgressions only too well, and my sin is
ever before me.

Holy God, Holy and Mighty, Holy Immortal One, have
mercy upon us.

Penitent　　　　　*Pray for me, a sinner.*

Priest

May God in his love enlighten your heart, that you may
remember in truth all your sins and his unfailing mercy. *Amen.*

*The Priest may then say one or more of these or other appropriate
verses of Scripture, first saying*

Hear the Word of God to all who truly turn to him.

Come unto me, all ye that travail and are heavy laden, and I
will refresh you.　　*Matthew 11:28*

God so loved the world, that he gave his only-begotten Son,
to the end that all that believe in him should not perish, but
have everlasting life.　　*John 3:16*

This is a true saying, and worthy of all men to be received,
that Christ Jesus came into the world to save sinners.
1 Timothy 1:15

If any man sin, we have an Advocate with the Father, Jesus
Christ the righteous; and he is the perfect offering for our
sins, and not for ours only, but for the sins of the whole
world.　　*I John 2:1-2*

The Priest then continues

Now, in the presence of Christ, and of me, his minister,
confess your sins with a humble and obedient heart to
Almighty God, our Creator and our Redeemer.

Porque bien conozco mis transgresiones,
y mi pecado está siempre delante de mí.

Santo Dios, Santo y Poderoso, Santo Inmortal,
ten piedad de *nosotros.*

Penitente   Reza por mí, *un pecador.*

Presbítero   Dios en su amor ilumine tu corazón, para que de
veras recuerdes todos tus pecados y su inagotable
misericordia. **Amén.**

*Quien oye la confesión puede decir uno o más de estos u otros
versículos apropiados de la Escritura, primero diciendo:*

Escucha la Palabra de Dios a *todos* quienes
verdaderamente se vuelven a él.

Vengan a mí *todos los* que están *cargados* y *agobiados* y yo
les daré descanso.   *Mateo 11:28*

Tanto amó Dios al mundo, que dio a su Hijo unigénito,
para que quienes creen en él no perezcan sino que tengan
vida eterna.   *Juan 3:16*

Palabra verdadera y digna de ser aceptada por *todos*: que
Cristo Jesús vino al mundo para salvar a *pecadores.*
1 Timoteo 1:15

Si alguien ha pecado, tenemos un abogado ante el Padre,
Jesucristo el justo; quien es la ofrenda perfecta por nuestro
pecados, y no solo por los nuestros, sino también por los
del mundo entero.   *1 Juan 2: 1-2*

Presbítero

Ahora, en presencia de Cristo y delante de mí, su *ministro*,
con corazón humilde y obediente confiesa tus pecados a
Dios Todopoderoso, nuestro Creador y nuestro Redentor.

Holy God, heavenly Father, you formed me from the dust in your image and likeness, and redeemed me from sin and death by the cross of your Son Jesus Christ. Through the water of baptism you clothed me with the shining garment of his righteousness, and established me among your children in your kingdom. But I have squandered the inheritance of your saints, and have wandered far in a land that is waste.

Especially, I confess to you and to the Church...

Here the penitent confesses particular sins.

Therefore, O Lord, from these and all other sins I cannot now remember, I turn to you in sorrow and repentance. Receive me again into the arms of your mercy, and restore me to the blessed company of your faithful people; through him in whom you have redeemed the world, your Son our Savior Jesus Christ. Amen.

The Priest may then offer words of comfort and counsel.

Priest

Will you turn again to Christ as your Lord?

Penitent   *I will.*

Priest

Do you, then, forgive those who have sinned against you?

Penitent   *I forgive them.*

Priest

May Almighty God in mercy receive your confession of sorrow and of faith, strengthen you in all goodness, and by the power of the Holy Spirit keep you in eternal life. *Amen.*

Santo Dios, Padre celestial,
me formaste del polvo a tu imagen y semejanza,
y por la cruz de tu Hijo Jesucristo
me redimiste del pecado y de la muerte.
Por el agua del bautismo me revestiste
con el manto resplandeciente de su justicia
y me incluiste entre tus hijos e hijas en tu reino.
Pero yo he malgastado la herencia de tus *santos*,
y me he extraviado en una tierra estéril.

En particular, confieso a ti y a la iglesia…

Aquí el *penitente confiesa pecados particulares.*

Por tanto, Señor,
vuelvo a ti con arrepentimiento y tristeza,
dejando atrás estos y otros pecados
que no puedo ahora recordar.
Recíbeme de nuevo en los brazos de tu misericordia
y restáurame a la bendita comunidad de tu pueblo fiel;
por Aquel por quien has redimido al mundo,
tu Hijo nuestro Salvador Jesucristo. Amén.

Se pueden ofrecer palabras de consuelo y consejo.

Presbítero   ¿Quieres volver a Cristo como tu Señor?

Penitente   Sí, quiero.

Presbítero   ¿Perdonas entonces a quienes han pecado contra ti?

Penitente   Sí, *los* perdono.

Presbítero

Dios Todopoderoso en misericordia acepte tu confesión de dolor y de fe, te fortalezca en toda bondad, y por el poder del Espíritu Santo te guarde en la vida eterna. **Amén.**

The Priest then lays a hand upon the penitent's head (or extends a hand over the penitent), saying one of the following

Our Lord Jesus Christ, who offered himself to be sacrificed for us to the Father, and who conferred power on his Church to forgive sins, absolve you through my ministry by the grace of the Holy Spirit, and restore you in the perfect peace of the Church. *Amen.*

or this

Our Lord Jesus Christ, who has left power to his Church to absolve all sinners who truly repent and believe in him, of his great mercy forgive you all your offenses; and by his authority committed to me, I absolve you from all your sins: In the Name of the Father, and of the Son, and of the Holy Spirit. *Amen.*

The Priest concludes

Now there is rejoicing in heaven; for you were lost, and are found; you were dead, and are now alive in Christ Jesus our Lord. Go (or abide) in peace. The Lord has put away all your sins.

Penitent   *Thanks be to God.*

Declaration of Forgiveness
to be used by a Deacon or Lay Person

Our Lord Jesus Christ, who offered himself to be sacrificed for us to the Father, forgives your sins by the grace of the Holy Spirit. *Amen.*

El presbítero *impone o extiende una mano sobre la cabeza* del penitente *diciendo una de las siguientes fórmulas:*

Nuestro Señor Jesucristo, que se ofreció al Padre en sacrificio por *nosotros* y confirió a su Iglesia el poder de perdonar pecados, por la gracia del Espíritu Santo te absuelva mediante mi ministerio, y te restaure a la paz perfecta de la iglesia. **Amén.**

O bien:

Nuestro Señor Jesucristo ha dado poder a su iglesia para absolver a pecadores que verdaderamente se arrepienten y creen en él. En su gran misericordia te perdone todas tus ofensas; y por la autoridad a mí conferida, yo te absuelvo de todos tus pecados en el nombre del Padre, y del Hijo y del Espíritu Santo. **Amén.**

El presbítero concluye con estas palabras:

Ahora se alegra el cielo; porque te habías perdido y ahora has sido *hallado*; estabas *muerto* y ahora vives en Cristo Jesús nuestro Señor. Ve (*o vive*) en paz. El Señor ha quitado todos tus pecados.

Penitente Demos gracias a Dios.

Declaración de perdón para ser utilizada por un diácono o *persona laica:*

Nuestro Señor Jesucristo, que se ofreció a sí mismo al Padre en sacrificio por *nosotros*, perdona tus pecados por la gracia del Espíritu Santo. **Amén.**

Ministration to the Sick

In case of illness, the Minister of the Congregation is to be notified.

At the Ministration, one or more parts of the following service are used, as appropriate; but when two or more are used together, they are used in the order indicated. The Lord's Prayer is always included.

Part One of this service may always be led by a deacon or lay person.

When the Laying on of Hands or Anointing takes place at a public celebration of the Eucharist, it is desirable that it precede the distribution of Holy Communion, and it is recommended that it take place immediately before the exchange of the Peace.

The Celebrant begins the service with the following or some other greeting

Peace be to this house (place), and to all who dwell in it.

Part I. Ministry of the Word

One or more of the following or other passages of Scripture are read

General

2 Corinthians 1:3-5 (God comforts us in affliction)
Psalm 91 (He will give his angels charge over you)
Luke 17:11-19 (Your faith has made you well)

Ministerio a los enfermos

En caso de enfermedad, se debe notificar al ministro de la congregación.

En el ministerio se utilizan una o más partes del siguiente rito, según corresponda; pero cuando se usan dos o más juntas, se usan en el orden indicado. Siempre se incluye el Padrenuestro.

La primera parte de este rito siempre la puede dirigir un diácono o una persona laica.

Cuando se realiza la imposición de manos o la unción en una celebración pública de la Eucaristía, es preferible que preceda a la distribución de la Sagrada Comunión, y se recomienda que se haga inmediatamente antes de darse la paz.

Quien oficia comienza el rito con el siguiente o algún otro saludo:

Paz a esta casa (lugar) y a *todos* los que *la* habitan.

Parte I. Ministerio de la Palabra

Se leen uno o más de los siguientes u otros pasajes de las Escrituras.

General

2 Corintios 1: 3-5 (Dios nos consuela en la aflicción)
Salmo 91 (Él dará a sus ángeles cargo sobre ti)
Lucas 17: 11-19 (Tu fe te ha sanado)

Penitence

Hebrews 12:1-2	(Looking to Jesus, the perfecter of our faith)
Psalm 103	(He forgives all your sins)
Matthew 9:2-8	(Your sins are forgiven)

When Anointing is to follow

James 5:14-16	(Is any among you sick?)
Psalm 23	(You have anointed my head with oil)
Mark 6:7, 12-13	(They anointed with oil many that were sick)

When Communion is to follow

1 John 5:13-15	(That you may know that you have eternal life)
Psalm 145:14-22	(The eyes of all wait upon you, O Lord)
John 6:47-51	(I am the bread of life)

After any Reading, the Celebrant may comment on it briefly.

Prayers may be offered according to the occasion.

The Priest may suggest the making of a special confession, if the sick person's conscience is troubled, and use the form for the Reconciliation of a Penitent.

Or else the following general confession may be said

Most merciful God,
we confess that we have sinned against you
in thought, word, and deed,
by what we have done,
and by what we have left undone.
We have not loved you with our whole heart;
we have not loved our neighbors as ourselves.
We are truly sorry and we humbly repent.
For the sake of your Son Jesus Christ,
have mercy on us and forgive us;
that we may delight in your will,
and walk in your ways,
to the glory of your Name. Amen.

Penitencia

Hebreos 12: 1-2 (Mirando a Jesús, el consumador de nuestra fe)
Salmo 103 (Él perdona todos tus pecados)
Mateo 9: 2-8 (Tus pecados son perdonados)

Cuando ha de seguir la unción

Santiago 5: 14-16 (¿Está alguno enfermo entre vosotros?)
Salmo 23 (Unges mi cabeza…)
Marcos 6: 7,12-13(Ungieron con aceite a muchos enfermos)

Cuando ha de seguir la comunión

1 Juan 5: 13-15 (Para que sepas que tienes vida eterna)
Salmo 145: 14-22 (Los ojos de *todos* esperan en ti, oh Señor)
Juan 6: 47-51 (Yo soy el pan de vida)

Después de cualquier lectura, quien oficia la puede explicar brevemente.

Se pueden ofrecer oraciones según la ocasión.

Un presbítero *puede sugerir la realización de una confesión especial, si la conciencia de la persona está afligida, y utilizar una de las fórmulas para la reconciliación de penitentes.*

O de lo contrario se puede decir la siguiente confesión general:

Dios de misericordia,
confesamos que hemos pecado contra ti
de pensamiento, palabra y obra,
por lo que hemos hecho
y por lo que hemos dejado sin hacer.
No te hemos amado de todo corazón;
no hemos amado al prójimo como a *nosotros mismos*.
Sincera y humildemente nos arrepentimos.
Por tu Hijo Jesucristo,
ten piedad de *nosotros* y perdónanos;
así tu voluntad será nuestra alegría
y caminaremos en tus sendas
para gloria de tu nombre. Amén.

The Priest alone says

Almighty God have mercy on you, forgive you all your sins through our Lord Jesus Christ, strengthen you in all goodness, and by the power of the Holy Spirit keep you in eternal life. *Amen.*

A deacon or lay person using the preceding form substitutes "us" for "you" and "our" for "your."

Part II. Laying on of Hands and Anointing

If oil for the Anointing of the Sick is to be blessed, the Priest says

O Lord, holy Father, giver of health and salvation: Send your Holy Spirit to sanctify this oil; that, as your holy apostles anointed many that were sick and healed them, so may those who in faith and repentance receive this holy unction be made whole; through Jesus Christ our Lord, who lives and reigns with you and the Holy Spirit, one God, for ever and ever. *Amen.*

The following anthem is said

Savior of the world, by your cross and precious blood you have redeemed us;
Save us, and help us, we humbly beseech you, O Lord.

The Priest then lays hands upon the sick person, and says one of the following

N., I lay my hands upon you in the Name of the Father, and of the Son, and of the Holy Spirit, beseeching our Lord Jesus Christ to sustain you with his presence, to drive away all sickness of body and spirit, and to give you that victory of life and peace which will enable you to serve him both now and evermore. *Amen.*

Dios Todopoderoso tenga misericordia de *ti*, perdone todos *tus* pecados por nuestro Señor Jesucristo, *te* fortalezca en toda bondad y por el poder del Espíritu Santo *te* guarde en la vida eterna. **Amén.**

Un diácono o persona laica que usa la fórmula anterior sustituye «ti» con «nosotros», «tus» con «nuestros» y «te» con «nos».

Parte II. Imposición de manos y unción

Si el presbítero va a bendecir el óleo para la unción, dice:

Oh Señor, Padre santo, dador de salud y salvación:
Envía tu Espíritu Santo para santificar este aceite;
para que, así como tus santos apóstoles
ungieron a *muchos enfermos* y *los* sanaban,
también sean *sanados los* que en fe y arrepentimiento
reciben esta santa unción;
por Jesucristo nuestro Señor,
que vive y reina contigo y el Espíritu Santo,
un solo Dios, por los siglos de los siglos. **Amén.**

Se dice la siguiente antífona:

Salvador del mundo,
por tu cruz y sangre preciosa nos has redimido;
Sálvanos y ayúdanos, te suplicamos humildemente, Señor.

El presbítero luego impone las manos sobre la persona enferma y dice una de las siguientes frases:

N., te impongo las manos
en el nombre del Padre, y del Hijo, y del Espíritu Santo,
suplicando a nuestro Señor Jesucristo
que te sostenga con su presencia,
que aleje toda enfermedad de cuerpo y de espíritu,
y te conceda la victoria de vida y paz
que te permitirá servirlo ahora y siempre. **Amén.**

or this

N., I lay my hands upon you in the Name of our Lord and Savior Jesus Christ, beseeching him to uphold you and fill you with his grace, that you may know the healing power of his love. *Amen.*

If the person is to be anointed, the Priest dips a thumb in the holy oil, and makes the sign of the cross on the sick person's forehead, saying

N., I anoint you with oil in the Name of the Father, and of the Son, and of the Holy Spirit. *Amen.*

The Priest may add

As you are outwardly anointed with this holy oil, so may our heavenly Father grant you the inward anointing of the Holy Spirit. Of his great mercy, may he forgive you your sins, release you from suffering, and restore you to wholeness and strength. May he deliver you from all evil, preserve you in all goodness, and bring you to everlasting life; through Jesus Christ our Lord. *Amen.*

In cases of necessity, a deacon or lay person may perform the anointing, using oil blessed by a bishop or priest.

If Communion is not to follow, the Lord's Prayer is now said.

The Priest concludes

The Almighty Lord, who is a strong tower to all who put their trust in him, to whom all things in heaven, on earth, and under the earth bow and obey: Be now and evermore your defense, and make you know and feel that the only Name under heaven given for health and salvation is the Name of our Lord Jesus Christ. *Amen.*

Part III. Holy Communion

If the Eucharist is to be celebrated, the Priest begins with the [Peace and] Offertory.

O bien:

N., te impongo las manos
en el nombre de nuestro Señor y Salvador Jesucristo,
suplicándole que te sostenga y te llene de su gracia,
para que conozcas el poder sanador de su amor. **Amén.**

*Si la persona va a ser ungida, el presbítero moja el pulgar en el óleo
de los enfermos y hace la señal de la cruz en la frente de la persona
enferma, diciendo:*

N., te unjo con aceite en el nombre del Padre y del Hijo y del
Espíritu Santo. **Amén.**

Y puede agregar:

Así como estás *ungido* exteriormente con este aceite santo,
así nuestro Padre celestial te conceda
la unción interior del Espíritu Santo.
Que en su gran misericordia te perdone tus pecados,
te libre del sufrimiento
y te devuelva la integridad y la fuerza.
Que te libre de todo mal, te guarde en toda bondad
y te traiga la vida eterna;
por Jesucristo nuestro Señor. **Amén.**

*De ser necesario, un diácono o una persona laica puede realizar la
unción, usando aceite bendecido por un obispo o presbítero.*

Si no ha de seguir la comunión, se dice ahora el Padrenuestro.

Quien oficia concluye:

Que Dios Todopoderoso,
torre fuerte de quien en él confía,
el Señor a quien obedece toda la creación,
sea hoy y siempre tu defensa
y te haga saber y sentir
que no hay otro nombre bajo el cielo
para la salud y salvación, sino el de Jesucristo. **Amén.**

Parte III. Santa comunión

*Si se va a celebrar la Eucaristía, el presbítero comienza con [la Paz y]
la presentación de ofrendas. Si en la Comunión se va a administrar*

If Communion is to be administered from the reserved Sacrament, the form for Communion under Special Circumstances is used, beginning with the [Peace and] Lord's Prayer on BCP page 398.

If the sick person cannot receive either the consecrated Bread or the Wine, it is suitable to administer the Sacrament in one kind only.

One of the usual postcommunion prayers is said, or the following

Gracious Father, we give you praise and thanks for this Holy Communion of the Body and Blood of your beloved Son Jesus Christ, the pledge of our redemption; and we pray that it may bring us forgiveness of our sins, strength in our weakness, and everlasting salvation; through Jesus Christ our Lord. *Amen.*

The service concludes with a blessing or with a dismissal

Let us bless the Lord.
Thanks be to God.

If a person desires to receive the Sacrament, but, by reason of extreme sickness or physical disability, is unable to eat and drink the Bread and Wine, the Celebrant is to assure that person that all the benefits of Communion are received, even though the Sacrament is not received with the mouth.

Prayers for the Sick

For a Sick Person

O Father of mercies and God of all comfort, our only help in time of need: We humbly beseech thee to behold, visit, and relieve thy sick servant N. for whom our prayers are desired. Look upon *him* with the eyes of thy mercy; comfort *him* with a sense of thy goodness; preserve *him* from the temptations of the enemy; and give *him* patience under *his* affliction. In thy good time, restore *him* to health, and enable *him* to lead the residue of *his* life in thy fear, and to thy glory; and grant that finally *he* may dwell with thee in life everlasting; through Jesus Christ our Lord. *Amen.*

*el Sacramento reservado, se usa la fórmula para Comunión en
Circunstancias Especiales, comenzando con [la Paz y] el Padrenuestro en
LOC en la página 266.*

*Si la persona enferma no puede recibir el pan consagrado o el vino,
conviene administrar el sacramento solo en una especie.*

Se dice una de las oraciones de poscomunión o la siguiente plegaria:

Padre de bondad y amor:
Te alabamos y te damos gracias por esta santa comunión
del cuerpo y sangre de tu Hijo amado Jesucristo,
garantía de nuestra redención;
te pedimos que este sacramento
nos traiga el perdón de los pecados,
fortaleza en las debilidades y salvación eterna;
por Jesucristo nuestro Señor. **Amén.**

El servicio concluye con una bendición o con una despedida.

Bendigamos al Señor.
Demos gracias a Dios.

*Si una persona desea recibir el sacramento, pero, debido a extrema
enfermedad o discapacidad física no pudiera comer ni beber el pan y el
vino, quien preside debe asegurarle que recibe todos los beneficios de la
comunión aunque no reciba el sacramento por la boca.*

Oraciones por *los enfermos*

Por una persona enferma

Padre de misericordias y Dios de todo consuelo, nuestra
única ayuda en tiempos de necesidad: Te suplicamos
humildemente que contemples, visites y alivies a tu *siervo
N.,* por quien se nos has pedido orar. *Míralo* con los ojos
de tu misericordia; *consuélalo* con un sentido de tu bondad;
protégelo de las tentaciones del enemigo; y dale paciencia
en su aflicción. Y cuando lo decidas, devuélvele la salud y
permítele vivir el resto de su vida respetando y alabándote.
y concede que, finalmente, pueda morar contigo en la vida
eterna; por Jesucristo nuestro Señor. **Amén.**

For Recovery from Sickness

O God, the strength of the weak and the comfort of sufferers:
Mercifully accept our prayers, and grant to your servant N. the
help of your power, that *his* sickness may be turned into health,
and our sorrow into joy; through Jesus Christ our Lord. *Amen.*

or this

O God of heavenly powers, by the might of your command
you drive away from our bodies all sickness and all infirmity:
Be present in your goodness with your servant N., that *his*
weakness may be banished and *his* strength restored; and
that, *his* health being renewed, *he* may bless your holy Name;
through Jesus Christ our Lord. *Amen.*

For a Sick Child

Heavenly Father, watch with us over your child N., and
grant that *he* may be restored to that perfect health which it
is yours alone to give; through Jesus Christ our Lord. *Amen.*

or this

Lord Jesus Christ, Good Shepherd of the sheep, you gather
the lambs in your arms and carry them in your bosom: We
commend to your loving care this child N. Relieve *his* pain,
guard *him* from all danger, restore to *him* your gifts of
gladness and strength, and raise *him* up to a life of service to
you. Hear us, we pray, for your dear Name's sake. *Amen.*

Before an Operation

Almighty God our heavenly Father, graciously comfort your
servant N. in *his* suffering, and bless the means made use

Para recuperarse de una enfermedad

Dios, fortaleza de débiles y consuelo de quienes sufren:
Acepta misericordiosamente nuestras oraciones
y concede a tu *siervo N.* la ayuda de tu poder,
para que su enfermedad se convierta en salud
y nuestro dolor en alegría;
por Jesucristo nuestro Señor. **Amén.**

O esto:

Dios de poder celestial: Con el poder de tu mandato
ahuyentas de nuestros cuerpos
toda enfermedad y toda dolencia;
visita en tu bondad a tu *siervo N.,*
para que su debilidad desaparezca
y sus fuerzas se restauren;
para que con renovada salud,
bendiga tu santo nombre;
por Jesucristo nuestro Señor. **Amén.**

Por un niño enfermo

Padre Celestial, cuida con *nosotros* a tu *hijo N.,*
y concede que pueda ser *restaurado*
a esa perfecta salud que solo tú puedes dar;
por Jesucristo nuestro Señor. **Amén.**

O esto:

Señor Jesucristo, Buen Pastor de las ovejas,
que tomas a tus corderos en tus brazos
y los llevas en tu regazo:
Encomendamos a tu amoroso cuidado este *niño N.*
Alivia su dolor, *protégelo* de todo peligro,
devuélvele gozo y fortaleza
y levántalo a una vida en tu servicio.
Te rogamos que nos oigas por amor de tu nombre. **Amén.**

Antes de una operación

Dios Todopoderoso, nuestro Padre celestial:
Consuela con tu gracia a tu *siervo N.* en su sufrimiento

of for *his* cure. Fill *his* heart with confidence that, though at times *he* may be afraid, *he* yet may put *his* trust in you; through Jesus Christ our Lord. *Amen.*

or this

Strengthen your servant N., O God, to do what *he* has to do and bear what *he* has to bear; that, accepting your healing gifts through the skill of surgeons and nurses, *he* may be restored to usefulness in your world with a thankful heart; through Jesus Christ our Lord. *Amen.*

For Strength and Confidence

Heavenly Father, giver of life and health: Comfort and relieve your sick servant N., and give your power of healing to those who minister to *his* needs, that *he* may be strengthened in *his* weakness and have confidence in your loving care; through Jesus Christ our Lord. *Amen.*

For the Sanctification of Illness

Sanctify, O Lord, the sickness of your servant N., that the sense of *his* weakness may add strength to *his* faith and seriousness to *his* repentance; and grant that *he* may live with you in everlasting life; through Jesus Christ our Lord. *Amen.*

For Health of Body and Soul

May God the Father bless you, God the Son heal you, God the Holy Spirit give you strength. May God the holy and undivided Trinity guard your body, save your soul, and bring you safely to his heavenly country; where he lives and reigns for ever and ever. *Amen.*

y bendice los medios utilizados para su curación.
Llena su corazón de confianza para que,
aunque a veces tema, pueda confiar en ti;
por Jesucristo nuestro Señor. **Amén.**

O esto:

Fortalece, Dios, a tu *siervo N.*,
en hacer y soportar lo que le toque;
que, aceptando tu sanación
a través de la habilidad de *cirujanos* y *enfermeros*,
pueda volver a sus tareas diarias con corazón agradecido;
por Jesucristo nuestro Señor. **Amén.**

Por la fuerza y confianza

Padre celestial, dador de vida y salud:
Consuela y alivia a tu *siervo N.;*
y dales tu poder de curación a quienes *lo* cuidan,
para que se fortalezca en su debilidad
y tenga confianza en tu amoroso cuidado;
por Jesucristo nuestro Señor. **Amén.**

Por la santificación de la enfermedad

Santifica, oh Señor, la enfermedad de tu *siervo N.,*
para que, consciente de su debilidad,
fortalezca la fe y se arrepienta;
y concédele que viva contigo en vida eterna;
mediante Jesucristo nuestro Señor. **Amén.**

Por la salud del cuerpo y el alma

Dios Padre te bendiga, Dios Hijo te sane,
Dios Espíritu Santo te fortalezca.
Que Dios, la Santísima e indivisa Trinidad,
guarde tu cuerpo, salve tu alma
y te lleve *sano y salvo* a su patria celestial;
donde vive y reina por los siglos de los siglos. **Amén.**

For Doctors and Nurses

Sanctify, O Lord, those whom you have called to the study
and practice of the arts of healing, and to the prevention of
disease and pain. Strengthen them by your life-giving Spirit,
that by their ministries the health of the community may be
promoted and your creation glorified; through Jesus Christ
our Lord. *Amen.*

Thanksgiving for a Beginning of Recovery

O Lord, your compassions never fail and your mercies
are new every morning: We give you thanks for giving
our brother (sister) N. both relief from pain and hope
of health renewed. Continue in *him*, we pray, the good
work you have begun; that *he*, daily increasing in bodily
strength, and rejoicing in your goodness, may so order
his life and conduct that *he* may always think and do
those things that please you; through Jesus Christ our
Lord. *Amen.*

Prayers for use by a Sick Person

For Trust in God

O God, the source of all health: So fill my heart with faith
in your love, that with calm expectancy I may make room
for your power to possess me, and gracefully accept your
healing; through Jesus Christ our Lord. Amen.

In Pain

Lord Jesus Christ, by your patience in suffering
you hallowed earthly pain and gave us the example
of obedience to your Father's will: Be near me in
my time of weakness and pain; sustain me by your grace,
that my strength and courage may not fail;
heal me according to your will; and help me always
to believe that what happens to me here is of

Por médicos y enfermeros

Santifica, Señor, a quienes has llamado
a prevenir y curar enfermedades y dolencias.
Fortalécelos con tu Espíritu vivificante,
para que por sus ministerios
se promueva la salud de la comunidad
y se glorifique tu creación;
por Jesucristo nuestro Señor. **Amén.**

Acción de gracias por una convalecencia

Señor, tu compasión nunca falla
y tus misericordias se renuevan cada mañana;
te damos gracias por darle a *nuestro hermano N.*
alivio del dolor y esperanza de salud renovada.
Continúa en *él* la buena obra que has comenzado
para que cada día aumente su fuerza corporal
y se alegre en tu bondad, ordenando su vida
de manera que siempre considere y cumpla tus deseos;
por Jesucristo nuestro Señor. **Amén.**

Oraciones para uso de una persona enferma

Por la confianza en Dios

Dios, fuente de toda salud:
Llena mi corazón con fe en tu amor
para que, con calma y esperanza,
yo me abra a tu poder y sanación;
por Jesucristo nuestro Señor. Amén.

En momentos de dolor

Señor Jesucristo, que en tu sufrimiento
santificaste el dolor del mundo
y nos mostraste obediencia a los deseos de tu Padre:
Acércate en mi hora de dolor;
sostenme con tu gracia
para que no me falte la fuerza y el valor;
sáname según tu voluntad;

little account if you hold me in eternal life,
my Lord and my God. Amen.

For Sleep

O heavenly Father, you give your children sleep
for the refreshing of soul and body: Grant me this gift,
I pray; keep me in that perfect peace which you have
promised to those whose minds are fixed on you;
and give me such a sense of your presence,
that in the hours of silence I may enjoy the blessed
assurance of your love; through Jesus Christ our Savior.
Amen.

In the Morning

This is another day, O Lord. I know not what it
will bring forth, but make me ready, Lord, for whatever
it may be. If I am to stand up, help me to stand bravely.
If I am to sit still, help me to sit quietly. If I am to lie low,
help me to do it patiently. And if I am to do nothing,
let me do it gallantly. Make these words more than words,
and give me the Spirit of Jesus. Amen.

y hazme entender qué poca cosa es todo esto
si tú me sostienes en la vida eterna. Amén.

Para conseguir el sueño

Padre celestial, que nos diste el sueño
para descansar el cuerpo y el alma:
Te ruego que me des ese regalo;
guárdame en la paz perfecta
que les prometiste a quienes se centran en ti;
haz que yo sienta tan viva tu presencia
que, en las horas de quietud, disfrute
de la certeza bendita de tu amor;
por Jesucristo nuestro Salvador. Amén.

En la mañana

Señor: ya empieza un nuevo día.
Aunque no sepa lo que me depare,
prepárame para lo que sea.
Si me levanto, ayúdame a hacerlo con valor.
Si me siento, haz que me siente en calma.
Si sigo *acostado*, haz que lo haga con paciencia.
Si no he de hacer nada, haz que lo acepte con nobleza.
Haz que estas palabras se hagan realidad
y dame el Espíritu de Jesucristo. Amén.

The Burial of the Dead: Rite Two

All stand while one or more of the following anthems are sung or said. A hymn, psalm, or some other suitable anthem may be sung instead.

I am Resurrection and I am Life, says the Lord.
Whoever has faith in me shall have life,
even though he die.
And everyone who has life,
and has committed himself to me in faith,
shall not die for ever.

As for me, I know that my Redeemer lives
and that at the last he will stand upon the earth.
After my awaking, he will raise me up;
and in my body I shall see God.
I myself shall see, and my eyes behold him
who is my friend and not a stranger.

For none of us has life in himself,
and none becomes his own master when he dies.
For if we have life, we are alive in the Lord,
and if we die, we die in the Lord.
So, then, whether we live or die,
we are the Lord's possession.

Happy from now on
are those who die in the Lord!

Exequias

El pueblo, de pie. Se canta o dice una o más de las siguientes antífonas. O, en su lugar, se puede cantar un himno, salmo u otro canto.

Yo soy la resurrección y la vida, dice el Señor.
Quien cree en mí, aunque muera, vivirá.
Y *todo* aquel que tiene vida y en fe se
ha consagrado a mí nunca morirá.

Yo sé que mi Redentor vive
y que al final se levantará sobre la tierra.
Me despertaré y él me levantará;
y en mi cuerpo veré a Dios.
Sí, yo *mismo* lo veré, y mis ojos lo contemplarán
no como un extraño, sino mi amigo.

Porque ninguno de *nosotros*
tiene vida en sí *mismo*,
y nadie al morir se vuelve
su *propio dueño*.
Si vivimos, en el Señor vivimos;
y si morimos, en el Señor morimos.
Así que, *vivos* o *muertos*, somos del Señor.

¡*Dichosos* desde hoy
quienes mueren en el Señor!

So it is, says the Spirit,
for they rest from their labors.

Or else this anthem

In the midst of life we are in death;
from whom can we seek help?
From you alone, O Lord,
who by our sins are justly angered.

Holy God, Holy and Mighty,
Holy and merciful Savior,
deliver us not into the bitterness of eternal death.

Lord, you know the secrets of our hearts;
shut not your ears to our prayers,
but spare us, O Lord.

Holy God, Holy and Mighty,
Holy and merciful Savior,
deliver us not into the bitterness of eternal death.

O worthy and eternal Judge,
do not let the pains of death
turn us away from you at our last hour.

Holy God, Holy and Mighty,
Holy and merciful Savior,
deliver us not into the bitterness of eternal death.

When all are in place, the Celebrant may address the congregation,
acknowledging briefly the purpose of their gathering, and bidding their
prayers for the deceased and the bereaved.

The Celebrant then says

The Lord be with you.

People   And also with you.
Celebrant   Let us pray.

Silence may be kept; after which the Celebrant says one of the
following Collects

Así es, dice el Espíritu,
porque descansan de sus labores.

O bien esta antífona:

En medio de la vida, la muerte nos rodea;
¿A quién podemos acudir?
A ti, Señor, que nos juzgas con justicia.

Santo Dios, santo y poderoso,
santo y piadoso Salvador,
líbranos de la amargura de la muerte eterna.

Tú conoces, Señor, nuestros secretos;
no tapes tus oídos a nuestra oración;
líbranos, Señor y Salvador.

Dios santo, santo y poderoso,
santo y piadoso Salvador,
líbranos de la amargura de la muerte eterna.

Juez digno y eterno:
No permitas que la angustia de la muerte
nos separe de ti a la última hora.

Dios santo, santo y poderoso,
santo y piadoso Salvador,
líbranos de la amargura de la muerte eterna.

Cuando todos *están en su lugar, quien preside, si lo desea, puede dirigirse*
a la congregación explicando brevemente el propósito de la reunión y
pidiendo plegarias por la persona que murió y sus deudos.

Entonces quien oficia dice una de las siguientes colectas, pero primero
dice:

El Señor esté con ustedes.
Y también contigo.
Oremos.

Se puede guardar silencio.

At the Burial of an Adult

O God, who by the glorious resurrection of your
Son Jesus Christ destroyed death, and brought life
and immortality to light: Grant that your servant N.,
being raised with him, may know the strength of his
presence, and rejoice in his eternal glory;
who with you and the Holy Spirit lives and reigns,
one God, for ever and ever. *Amen.*

or this

O God, whose mercies cannot be numbered:
Accept our prayers on behalf of your servant N.,
and grant *him* an entrance into the land of light
and joy, in the fellowship of your saints;
through Jesus Christ our Lord, who lives and
reigns with you and the Holy Spirit, one God,
now and for ever. *Amen.*

or this

O God of grace and glory,
we remember before you this day our brother (sister) N.
We thank you for giving *him* to us,
his family and friends, to know and to love as
a companion on our earthly pilgrimage.
In your boundless compassion, console us who mourn.
Give us faith to see in death the gate of eternal life,
so that in quiet confidence we may continue our course
on earth, until, by your call, we are reunited
with those who have gone before; through Jesus Christ
our Lord. *Amen.*

At the Burial of a Child

O God, whose beloved Son took children into his arms and
blessed them: Give us grace to entrust N., to your never-

En las exequias de una persona adulta

Dios de todo poder:
Por la gloriosa resurrección de Jesucristo,
destruiste la muerte y revelaste la vida y la inmortalidad.
Concede que tu *siervo N.*, levantándose con Cristo,
conozca el poder de su presencia
y goce de la gloria eterna del Señor;
quien contigo y el Espíritu Santo vive y reina,
un solo Dios, ahora y siempre. **Amén.**

O bien:

Señor de bondades incontables:
Acepta las plegarias que elevamos a favor de tu *siervo N.*
y *recíbelo* en el lugar de luz y alegría
en la comunidad de tus santos y santas;
por Cristo Jesús nuestro Señor,
quien contigo y el Espíritu Santo vive y reina,
un solo Dios, ahora y siempre. **Amén.**

O bien:

Señor de gracia y gloria:
Recordamos ante ti a *nuestro hermano N.*
Te agradecemos que, con su familia y amistades,
pudimos conoce*rlo,* ama*rlo*
y peregrinar con *él* sobre la tierra.
En tu infinita compasión,
consuélanos en nuestro dolor.
Danos la fe de hallar en la muerte
la puerta a la vida eterna
para que, con confianza y calma,
podamos seguir andando por la tierra hasta que,
a tu llamado, nos reunamos con quienes nos precedieron;
por Cristo Jesús nuestro Señor. **Amén.**

En las exequias de un niño

Tu Hijo amado, Señor, abrazó y bendijo a niños y niñas;
danos fortaleza para entregar *este niño*

failing care and love, and bring us all to your heavenly kingdom; through Jesus Christ our Lord, who lives and reigns with you and the Holy Spirit, one God, now and for ever. *Amen.*

The Celebrant may add the following prayer

Most merciful God, whose wisdom is beyond our understanding, deal graciously with *NN.* in *their* grief. Surround *them* with your love, that *they* may not be overwhelmed by *their* loss, but have confidence in your goodness, and strength to meet the days to come; through Jesus Christ our Lord. *Amen.*

The people sit.

One or more of the following passages from Holy Scripture is read. If there is to be a Communion, a passage from the Gospel always concludes the Readings.

The Liturgy of the Word

From the Old Testament

Isaiah 25:6-9 (He will swallow up death for ever)
Isaiah 61:1-3 (To comfort those who mourn)
Lamentations 3:22-26, 31-33 (The Lord is good to those who wait for him)
Wisdom 3:1-5, 9 (The souls of the righteous are in the hands of God)
Job 19:21-27a (I know that my Redeemer lives)

A suitable psalm, hymn, or canticle may follow. The following Psalms are appropriate: 42:1-7, 46, 90:1-12, 121, 130, 139:1-11.

From the New Testament

Romans 8:14-19, 34-35, 37-39 (The glory that shall be revealed)
1 Corinthians 15:20-26, 35-38, 42-44, 53-58

a tu amor atento e infinito
y llévanos *todos* a tu reino celestial;
por Cristo Jesús nuestro Señor
que vive y reina contigo y el Espíritu Santo,
un solo Dios, ahora y siempre. **Amén.**

Quien oficia puede agregar la siguiente oración:

Piadoso Señor:
Tu sabiduría sobrepasa nuestro entendimiento;
ten misericordia de *NN.* en su dolor;
cobíjalos con tu amor;
que esta pérdida no *los* abrume,
sino que *confíen* en tu bondad
y enfrenten con fortaleza los días venideros;
por Cristo Jesús nuestro Señor. **Amén.**

El pueblo se sienta.

Se lee uno o más de los siguientes pasajes de las Escrituras. Si se celebra la comunión, siempre se concluyen las lecturas con un pasaje del evangelio.

Liturgia de la palabra

Del antiguo testamento

Isaías 25:6-9 (Él destruirá la muerte para siempre)
Isaías 61:1-3 (Consolar a quien está de duelo)
Lamentaciones 3:22-26, 31-33 (El Señor es bueno con quienes lo esperan)
Sabiduría 3:1-5, 9 (La vida de la gente justa está en las manos del Señor)
Job 19:21-27a (Yo sé que mi Redentor vive)

Después de la lectura, se puede continuar con un salmo, himno o cántico apropiado. Los siguientes salmos son apropiados: 42:1-7, 46, 90:1-12. 121, 130, 139:1-11.

Del nuevo testamento

Romanos 8:14-19, 34-35, 37-39 (La gloria que pronto nos ha de ser revelada)
1 Corintios 15:20-26, 35-38, 42-44, 53-58

(The imperishable body)
2 Corinthians 4:16—5:9 (Things that are unseen are eternal)
1 John 3:1-2 (We shall be like him)
Revelation 7:9-17 (God will wipe away every tear)
Revelation 21:2-7 (Behold, I make all things new)

A suitable psalm, hymn, or canticle may follow. The following Psalms are appropriate: 23, 27, 106:1-5, 116.

The Gospel

Then, all standing, the Deacon or Minister appointed reads the Gospel, first saying

> The Holy Gospel of our Lord Jesus Christ
> according to John.

People   Glory to you, Lord Christ.

John 5:24-27 (He who believes has everlasting life)
John 6:37-40 (All that the Father gives me will come to me)
John 10:11-16 (I am the good shepherd)
John 11:21-27 (I am the resurrection and the life)
John 14:1-6 (In my Father's house are many rooms)

At the end of the Gospel, the Reader says

> The Gospel of the Lord.

People   Praise to you, Lord Christ.

Here there may be a homily by the Celebrant, or a member of the family, or a friend.

The Apostles' Creed may then be said, all standing. The Celebrant may introduce the Creed with these or similar words

In the assurance of eternal life given at Baptism, let us proclaim our faith and say,

Celebrant and People

I believe in God, the Father almighty,
    creator of heaven and earth.

(Se resucita en incorrupción)
2 Corintios 4:16—5:9 (Las cosas que no se ven son eternas)
1 Juan 3:1-2 (Seremos semejantes a él)
Apocalipsis 7:9-17 (Dios enjugará toda lágrima)
Apocalipsis 21:2-7 (He aquí yo hago nuevas todas las cosas)

Después de la lectura, se puede continuar con un salmo, himno o cántico apropiado. Los siguientes salmos son apropiados: 23, 27, 106:1-5, 116.

El evangelio

El pueblo de pie. Un diácono, *o en su ausencia, quien oficia, lee el evangelio, diciendo primero:*

Santo evangelio de nuestro Señor [y Salvador] Jesucristo según.
Gloria a ti, Cristo Señor.

Juan 5:24-27 (El que cree tiene vida eterna)
Juan 6:37-40 (Todo lo que el Padre me da vendrá a mí)
Juan 10:11-16 (Yo soy el buen pastor)
Juan 11:21-27 (Yo soy la resurrección y la vida)
Juan 14:1-6 (En la casa de mi Padre hay muchas moradas)

Después del evangelio, la persona que leyó dice:

El evangelio del Señor.
Te alabamos, Cristo Señor.

Quien oficia puede predicar y/o una persona designada puede compartir unas palabras breves.

El pueblo, de pie. Se puede decir el Credo de los Apóstoles. Quien oficia puede presentarlo con estas palabras, u otras similares:

Con la certeza de la vida eterna que recibimos en el bautismo, proclamemos nuestra fe con estas palabras:

**Creo en Dios, Padre todopoderoso,
creador del cielo y de la tierra.**

I believe in Jesus Christ, his only Son, our Lord.
He was conceived by the power of the Holy Spirit
and born of the Virgin Mary.
He suffered under Pontius Pilate,
was crucified, died, and was buried.
He descended to the dead.
On the third day he rose again.
He ascended into heaven,
and is seated at the right hand of the Father.
He will come again to judge the living and the dead.

I believe in the Holy Spirit,
the holy catholic Church,
the communion of saints,
the forgiveness of sins,
the resurrection of the body,
and the life everlasting. Amen.

*If there is not to be a Communion, the Lord's Prayer is said here, and
the service continues with the Prayers of the People, or with one or
more suitable prayers (see pages 290-295).*

*When there is a Communion, the following form of the Prayers of the
People is used.*

For our brother (sister) N., let us pray to our Lord Jesus
Christ who said," I am Resurrection and I am Life."

Lord, you consoled Martha and Mary in their distress; draw near
to us who mourn for N., and dry the tears of those who weep.
Hear us, Lord.

You wept at the grave of Lazarus, your friend; comfort us in
our sorrow.
Hear us, Lord.

You raised the dead to life; give to our brother (sister)
eternal life.
Hear us, Lord.

Creo en Jesucristo, su único Hijo, nuestro Señor,
  que fue concebido por obra y gracia del Espíritu Santo,
    nació de la santa María Virgen,
  padeció bajo el poder de Poncio Pilato,
    fue crucificado, muerto y sepultado,
  descendió a los infiernos,
  al tercer día resucitó de entre los muertos,
  subió a los cielos
    y está sentado a la derecha de Dios, Padre todopoderoso.
  Desde allí ha de venir a juzgar a vivos y muertos.

Creo en el Espíritu Santo,
  la santa iglesia católica,
  la comunión de *los santos,*
  el perdón de los pecados,
  la resurrección de los muertos
  y la vida eterna. Amén.

Si no hay comunión, las exequias continúan con el Padrenuestro;

Cuando hay comunión, se continúa con una de las fórmulas de las Oraciones del pueblo que aparecen a continuación.

Nuestro Señor Jesucristo dijo:
«Yo soy la resurrección y la vida».
Oremos a Cristo por *nuestro hermano N.*

Señor: Tú consolaste a Marta y a María en su aflicción;
acompáñanos también en nuestra tristeza
mientras estamos de duelo por *N.,*
y seca las lágrimas de quienes lloran.
Escúchanos, Señor.

Tú lloraste en la tumba de Lázaro, tu amigo.
Danos consuelo en nuestro dolor.
Escúchanos, Señor.

Tú levantaste a los muertos a la vida;
dale a *nuestro hermano* la vida eterna.
Escúchanos, Señor.

You promised paradise to the thief who repented; bring our brother (sister) to the joys of heaven.
Hear us, Lord.

Our brother (sister) was washed in Baptism and anointed with the Holy Spirit; give *him* fellowship with all your saints.
Hear us, Lord.

He was nourished with your Body and Blood; grant *him* a place at the table in your heavenly kingdom.
Hear us, Lord.

Comfort us in our sorrows at the death of our brother (sister); let our faith be our consolation, and eternal life our hope.

Silence may be kept.

The Celebrant concludes with one of the following or some other prayer

Lord Jesus Christ, we commend to you our brother (sister) N., who was reborn by water and the Spirit in Holy Baptism. Grant that *his* death may recall to us your victory over death, and be an occasion for us to renew our trust in your Father's love. Give us, we pray, the faith to follow where you have led the way; and where you live and reign with the Father and the Holy Spirit, to the ages of ages.
Amen.

or this

Father of all, we pray to you for N., and for all those whom we love but see no longer. Grant to them eternal rest. Let light perpetual shine upon them. May *his* soul and the souls of all the departed, through the mercy of God, rest in peace.
Amen.

Tú le prometiste el paraíso al ladrón arrepentido;
conduce a *nuestro hermano N.* a la alegría celestial.
Escúchanos, Señor.

Nuestro hermano fue *lavado* en el bautismo
y *ungido* por el Espíritu Santo;
dale lugar entre tus santos y tus santas.
Escúchanos, Señor.

Él se alimentó con tu cuerpo y sangre;
hazle sitio a la mesa en tu reino celestial.
Escúchanos, Señor.

Alívianos en nuestro dolor por la muerte de *este hermano*;
que nuestra fe nos sirva como consuelo
y la vida eterna sea nuestra esperanza.

Se puede observar un periodo de silencio.

Quien preside concluye con la siguiente oración, o alguna otra:

Señor Jesucristo:
Te encomendamos a *nuestro hermano N.*,
quien renació del agua y del Espíritu
mediante el santo bautismo.
Concede que su muerte
nos recuerde tu triunfo sobre la muerte
y nos lleve a renovar nuestra confianza
en tu amor de Padre.
Danos, te rogamos la fe de seguir el camino que abriste
y que nos lleva a donde reinas
con el Padre y el Espíritu Santo, por los siglos de los siglos.
Amén.

O esta:

Padre de todo ser humano: Te rogamos por *N.*
y por todos nuestros seres queridos que ya no vemos.
Otórgales descanso eterno y que les brille la luz perpetua.
Que su alma y las de *todos los* que han muerto
descansen en paz, por tu gran misericordia. **Amén.**

When there is no Communion, the service continues with the
Commendation, or with the Committal.

At the Eucharist

The service continues with the Peace and the Offertory.

Preface of the Commemoration of the Dead

In place of the usual postcommunion prayer, the following is said

Almighty God, we thank you that in your great love you
have fed us with the spiritual food and drink of the Body
and Blood of your Son Jesus Christ, and have given us
a foretaste of your heavenly banquet. Grant that this
Sacrament may be to us a comfort in affliction, and a
pledge of our inheritance in that kingdom where there is
no death, neither sorrow nor crying, but the fullness of joy
with all your saints; through Jesus Christ our Savior. *Amen.*

If the body is not present, the service continues with the (blessing and)
dismissal.

Unless the Committal follows immediately in the church, the following
Commendation is used.

The Commendation

The Celebrant and other ministers take their places at the body.

This anthem, or some other suitable anthem, or a hymn, may be sung or said

Give rest, O Christ, to your servant(s) with your saints,
where sorrow and pain are no more,
neither sighing, but life everlasting.

You only are immortal, the creator and maker of mankind;
and we are mortal, formed of the earth, and to earth shall we
return. For so did you ordain when you created me, saying,
"You are dust, and to dust you shall return." All of us go
down to the dust; yet even at the grave we make our song:
Alleluia, alleluia, alleluia.

Si no hay comunión, el rito continúa con la encomendación o con la sepultura.

En la eucaristía

El rito continúa con la paz y presentación de ofrendas.

Prefacio de conmemoración de difuntos y difuntas.

En vez de la oración de poscomunión usual, se dice la siguiente:

Dios de poder:
Te damos gracias porque en tu gran amor,
nos alimentas con esta comida y bebida espiritual
del cuerpo y sangre de tu Hijo Jesucristo,
nos haces ya participar de tu banquete celestial.
Haz que este sacramento nos consuele en el dolor;
y nos recuerde la promesa de nuestra herencia:
Aquel reino sin muerte, llanto, ni pesar,
sino la plenitud de gozo con todos tus santos y santas;
por Jesucristo nuestro Salvador. **Amén.**

En ausencia de los restos mortales, el rito continúa con [la bendición y] la despedida. A menos que la sepultura siga de inmediato en la iglesia, se usa la siguiente encomendación:

La encomendación

Quien preside, junto con otros ministros, se acerca al cuerpo o a las cenizas. Se puede cantar o decir esta antífona u otra apropiada:

Dale descanso, Señor, a tu *siervo N.*
entre tus santos y santas,
donde no hay penas ni dolor,
sino vida eterna.

Solo tú eres inmortal, Señor, creador de la humanidad;
nosotros somos mortales, *formados* de la tierra,
y a la tierra volveremos.
Porque así ordenaste cuando me creaste y dijiste:
«Polvo eres y al polvo volverás».
Al polvo regresamos *todos,*
pero aún en la tumba alzamos nuestro canto:
«¡Aleluya, aleluya, aleluya!».

Give rest, O Christ, to your servant(s) with your saints,
where sorrow and pain are no more,
neither sighing, but life everlasting.

The Celebrant, facing the body, says

Into your hands, O merciful Savior, we commend your
servant N. Acknowledge, we humbly beseech you, a sheep
of your own fold, a lamb of your own flock, a sinner of
your own redeeming. Receive *him* into the arms of your
mercy, into the blessed rest of everlasting peace, and into the
glorious company of the saints in light. *Amen.*

*The Celebrant, or the Bishop if present, may then bless the people, and
a Deacon or other Minister may dismiss them, saying*

Let us go forth in the name of Christ.
Thanks be to God.

*As the body is borne from the church, a hymn, or one or more of these
anthems may be sung or said*

Christ is risen from the dead, trampling down death by
death, and giving life to those in the tomb.

The Sun of Righteousness is gloriously risen, giving light to
those who sat in darkness and in the shadow of death.

The Lord will guide our feet into the way of peace, having
taken away the sin of the world.

Christ will open the kingdom of heaven to all who believe in
his Name, saying, Come, O blessed of my Father; inherit the
kingdom prepared for you.

Dale descanso, Señor, a tu *siervo N.*
entre tus santos y santas,
donde no hay penas ni dolor,
sino vida eterna.

Quien preside, de cara al ataúd o a la urna con las cenizas, dice:

En tus manos, misericordioso Salvador,
encomendamos a tu *siervo N.*
Te rogamos que *lo* reconozcas
como oveja de tu rebaño, como cordero de tu corral,
como *pecador* que has redimido.
Abrázalo en tu amor
en el bendito descanso de la paz eterna
y en la compañía gloriosa de tus santos y santas en la luz.
Amén.

Quien preside puede bendecir al pueblo.
Un diácono o *en su ausencia, quien preside, despide al pueblo:*

Salgamos en el nombre de Cristo.
Demos gracias a Dios.

Mientras se lleva el cuerpo o las cenizas de la iglesia, se puede cantar o decir un himno o una o más de estas antífonas:

Cristo ha resucitado de los muertos
pisoteando la muerte con la muerte
y dando vida a quienes yacen en la tumba.

El Sol de Justicia se ha levantado en esplendor
dándole luz a quienes moraban en tinieblas
y en la sombra de muerte.

El Señor, que ha quitado el pecado del mundo,
guiará nuestros pasos por la senda de la paz.

Cristo abrirá el reino de los cielos
a quienes confían en su nombre
y dirá: «¡Vengan, *benditos* de mi Padre!
Hereden el reino preparado para ustedes».

Into paradise may the angels lead you. At your coming may the martyrs receive you, and bring you into the holy city Jerusalem.

or one of these Canticles,

The Song of Zechariah, *Benedictus*
The Song of Simeon, *Nunc dimittis*
Christ our Passover, *Pascha nostrum*

The Committal

The following anthem or one of those on pages 268-271 is sung or said

Everyone the Father gives to me will come to me;
I will never turn away anyone who believes in me.

He who raised Jesus Christ from the dead
will also give new life to our mortal bodies
through his indwelling Spirit.

My heart, therefore, is glad, and my spirit rejoices;
my body also shall rest in hope.

You will show me the path of life;
in your presence there is fullness of joy,
and in your right hand are pleasures for evermore.

Then, while earth is cast upon the coffin, the Celebrant says these words

In sure and certain hope of the resurrection to eternal life through our Lord Jesus Christ, we commend to Almighty God our *brother N.*, and we commit *his* body to the ground; * earth to earth, ashes to ashes, dust to dust. The Lord bless *him* and keep *him*, the Lord make his face to shine upon *him* and be gracious to *him*, the Lord lift up his countenance upon *him* and give *him* peace. *Amen.*

Que los ángeles te guíen al paraíso;
que, al llegar, mártires te den la bienvenida,
y te lleven a la ciudad santa de Jerusalén.

O bien uno de los siguientes cánticos:

El Cántico de Zacarías, *Benedictus*
El Cántico de Simeón, *Nunc dimittis*
Cristo nuestra Pascua, *Pascha nostrum*

La sepultura

*Se canta o dice una de las siguientes antífonas, o una de las que
aparecen en las páginas 268-271.*

Quienes el Padre me da vendrán a mí;
y a quien a mí viene no rechazaré jamás.

Dios, que levantó a Jesús de entre los muertos
les dará nueva vida a nuestros cuerpos mortales
mediante su Espíritu que mora en *nosotros.*

Mi corazón, pues, goza y mi alma se alegra;
mi cuerpo descansa en esperanza.

Me mostrarás el camino de la vida;
en tu presencia hay plenitud de gozo
y a tu diestra, deleites infinitos.

*Mientras se echa tierra sobre el ataúd, se cierra el nicho o cripta, se
guardan las cenizas en el columbario, o se entierran o esparcen las
cenizas, quien preside dice:*

Con esperanza firme en la vida eterna mediante la resurrección
de Jesucristo, encomendamos a Dios Todopoderoso *nuestro
hermano N.* y entregamos sus restos a la tierra*; tierra a la
tierra, cenizas a cenizas, polvo al polvo. El Señor *lo* bendiga
y *lo* guarde. El Señor haga resplandecer su rostro sobre *él* y le
tenga misericordia. El Señor le muestre su rostro y lo abrigue
en su paz. **Amén.**

* Or the deep, or the elements, or its resting place.

The Celebrant says

	The Lord be with you.
People	And also with you.
Celebrant	Let us pray.

Celebrant and People

Our Father, who art in heaven,
    hallowed be thy Name,
    thy kingdom come,
    thy will be done,
       on earth as it is in heaven.
Give us this day our daily bread.
And forgive us our trespasses,
    as we forgive those
      who trespass against us.
And lead us not into temptation,
    but deliver us from evil.
For thine is the kingdom,
    and the power, and the glory,
    for ever and ever. Amen.

Our Father in heaven,
    hallowed be your Name,
    your kingdom come,
    your will be done,
       on earth as in heaven.
Give us today our daily bread.
Forgive us our sins
    as we forgive those
      who sin against us.
Save us from the time of trial,
    and deliver us from evil.
For the kingdom, the power,
    and the glory are yours,
    now and for ever. Amen.

Other prayers may be added.

Then may be said

Rest eternal grant to *him*, O Lord;
And let light perpetual shine upon him.

May *his* soul, and the souls of all the departed,
through the mercy of God, rest in peace. *Amen.*

The Celebrant dismisses the people with these words

	Alleluia. Christ is risen.
People	The Lord is risen indeed. Alleluia.
Celebrant	Let us go forth in the name of Christ.
People	Thanks be to God.

[* *O bien*, a las profundidades, *o* a la naturaleza, *o* a este sitio de descanso.]

Quien preside dice:

El Señor esté con ustedes.
Y también contigo
Oremos.

Padre nuestro que estás en el cielo,
    santificado sea tu nombre;
    venga tu reino;
    hágase tu voluntad
        en la tierra como en el cielo.
Danos hoy nuestro pan de cada día.
Perdona nuestras ofensas,
    como también *nosotros* perdonamos
        a los que nos ofenden.
No nos dejes caer en la tentación
    y líbranos del mal.
Porque tuyo es el reino, el poder y la gloria,
    ahora y por siempre. Amén.

Se pueden agregar otras oraciones.

Entonces se puede decir:

Concédele, Señor, descanso eterno:
Que brille sobre *él* la luz perpetua

Que su alma, y las de *todos los difuntos,*
por la piedad de Dios descanse en paz. **Amén.**

Quien preside despide al pueblo con estas palabras:

¡Aleluya! Cristo ha resucitado.
Es verdad: El Señor ha resucitado. ¡Aleluya!
Salgamos en el nombre de Cristo.
Demos gracias a Dios.

or with the following

The God of peace, who brought again from the dead our Lord Jesus Christ, the great Shepherd of the sheep, through the blood of the everlasting covenant: Make you perfect in every good work to do his will, working in you that which is well-pleasing in his sight; through Jesus Christ, to whom be glory for ever and ever. *Amen.*

The Consecration of a Grave

If the grave is in a place that has not previously been set apart for Christian burial, the Priest may use the following prayer, either before the service of Committal or at some other convenient time

O God, whose blessed Son was laid in a sepulcher in the garden: Bless, we pray, this grave, and grant that *he* whose body is (is to be) buried here may dwell with Christ in paradise, and may come to your heavenly kingdom; through your Son Jesus Christ our Lord. *Amen.*

Additional Prayers

Almighty God, with whom still live the spirits of those who die in the Lord, and with whom the souls of the faithful are in joy and felicity: We give you heartfelt thanks for the good examples of all your servants, who, having finished their course in faith, now find rest and refreshment. May we, with all who have died in the true faith of your holy Name, have perfect fulfillment and bliss in your eternal and everlasting glory, through Jesus Christ our Lord. *Amen.*

O God, whose days are without end, and whose mercies cannot be numbered: Make us, we pray, deeply aware of the shortness and uncertainty of human life; and let your Holy Spirit lead us in holiness and righteousness all our days; that, when we shall have served you in our generation, we may

O bien:

El Dios de paz, que mediante la sangre de la alianza eterna
levantó de nuevo a Jesús, el Gran Pastor de las ovejas,
los perfeccione en toda buena obra,
logrando en ustedes todo lo que lo complace;
por Jesucristo, a quien sea la gloria
por los siglos de los siglos. **Amén.**

Consagración del sitio de sepultura

*Si la tumba o sitio de sepultura no ha sido apartado previamente
para una sepultura cristiana, quien preside puede usar la siguiente
oración, ya sea antes del rito de sepultura o en otro momento que sea
conveniente.*

Dios Padre, cuyo bendito Hijo
fue sepultado en un jardín:
Bendice este lugar de sepultura.
Concede que *el difunto* que aquí dejamos
more con Cristo en el paraíso
y participe en tu reino celestial;
por tu Hijo Cristo Jesús nuestro Señor. **Amén.**

Oraciones adicionales

Dios de poder: Contigo viven y gozan en felicidad
todos los que mueren en el Señor.
Te damos gracias por el buen ejemplo
de quienes completaron fielmente su carrera
y ahora descansan en buen recreo;
concédenos la dicha y perfección de tu gloria eterna
con quienes han muerto confiando en tu santo nombre.
por Cristo Jesús nuestro Señor. **Amén.**

Señor Dios, Rey del pueblo fiel:
Alabamos la gloria de tu nombre
por toda persona que te sirvió con devoción
y terminó con fe la carrera de la vida;
por la bienaventurada Virgen María;
por santos patriarcas y matriarcas,

be gathered to our ancestors, having the testimony of a good conscience, in the communion of the Catholic Church, in the confidence of a certain faith, in the comfort of a religious and holy hope, in favor with you, our God, and in perfect charity with the world. All this we ask through Jesus Christ our Lord. *Amen.*

O God, the King of saints, we praise and glorify your holy Name for all your servants who have finished their course in your faith and fear: for the blessed Virgin Mary; for the holy patriarchs, prophets, apostles, and martyrs; and for all your other righteous servants, known to us and unknown; and we pray that, encouraged by their examples, aided by their prayers, and strengthened by their fellowship, we also may be partakers of the inheritance of the saints in light; through the merits of your Son Jesus Christ our Lord. *Amen.*

Lord Jesus Christ, by your death you took away the sting of death: Grant to us your servants so to follow in faith where you have led the way, that we may at length fall asleep peacefully in you and wake up in your likeness; for your tender mercies' sake. *Amen.*

Father of all, we pray to you for those we love, but see no longer: Grant them your peace; let light perpetual shine upon them; and, in your loving wisdom and almighty power, work in them the good purpose of your perfect will; through Jesus Christ our Lord. *Amen.*

Merciful God, Father of our Lord Jesus Christ who is the Resurrection and the Life: Raise us, we humbly pray, from the death of sin to the life of righteousness; that when we depart this life we may rest in him, and at the resurrection receive that blessing which your well-beloved Son shall then pronounce: "Come, you blessed of my Father, receive the kingdom prepared for you from the beginning of the world." Grant this, O merciful Father, through Jesus Christ, our Mediator and Redeemer. *Amen.*

por profetas, apóstoles y mártires;
y por toda persona que, aunque tal vez no conozcamos,
te ha servido en rectitud;
y te rogamos que, bajo la inspiración de sus ejemplos,
ayudados por sus oraciones
y *fortalecidos* por su comunidad
también *nosotros* compartamos la herencia
de los santos y santas en la luz;
por Jesucristo, tu Hijo único, nuestro Señor. **Amén.**

Señor Jesucristo: Con tu muerte
has arrancado el aguijón de la muerte;
haz que sigamos con fe el camino que lideras
y así podamos, llegado el día,
dormirnos en tu paz y despertarnos en tu semejanza;
por tu ternura y tu misericordia. **Amén.**

Padre de todo ser, te rogamos por *N.*
y por todos los seres queridos
que han partido de este mundo;
concédeles tu paz; que les brille la luz perpetua;
en tu sabiduría, tu amor y tu poder,
cumple en *ellos* tu intención y voluntad;
por Cristo Jesús nuestro Señor. **Amén.**

Dios de piedad, Padre de aquel Cristo
que es la resurrección y la vida:
Te rogamos con humildad
que nos levantes de la muerte del pecado
a la vida de la justicia;
que cuando partamos de esta vida descansemos con él,
y recibamos, en la resurrección,
la bendición que tu Hijo amado pronunciará;
«¡Vengan, *benditos* de mi Padre!
Hereden el reino que les ha sido preparado
desde la fundación del mundo».
Esto concédenos, Padre piadoso,
por Jesucristo, nuestro Mediador y Redentor. **Amén.**

Grant, O Lord, to all who are bereaved the spirit
of faith and courage, that they may have strength
to meet the days to come with steadfastness and patience;
not sorrowing as those without hope, but in thankful
remembrance of your great goodness, and in the joyful
expectation of eternal life with those they love.
And this we ask in the Name of Jesus Christ our Savior.
Amen.

Almighty God, Father of mercies and giver of comfort:
Deal graciously, we pray, with all who mourn; that,
casting all their care on you, they may know the
consolation of your love; through Jesus Christ our Lord.
Amen.

Concede, Señor, a quienes están de duelo
un espíritu de fe y de valentía
para que enfrenten los días venideros
con firmeza, paciencia y fortaleza;
que brille, en su luto, una esperanza,
que en gratitud recuerden que eres bueno
y que esperen el gozoso día
en que vivirán por siempre con los seres que aman.
Esto te pedimos
en el nombre de Jesucristo nuestro Salvador. **Amén.**

Padre de misericordia y fuente de consuelo:
Te rogamos que visites con tu gracia
a toda persona que hoy está de duelo
para que, dejando en ti toda inquietud,
conozcan el abrazo de tu amor;
por Cristo Jesús nuestro Señor. **Amén.**

Prayers and Thanksgivings

Prayers

For use after the Collects of Morning or Evening Prayer or separately.

Prayers for the World

1. For Joy in God's Creation

O heavenly Father, who *hast filled* the world with beauty:
Open our eyes to behold *thy* gracious hand in all *thy* works;
that, rejoicing in *thy* whole creation, we may learn to serve
thee with gladness; for the sake of him through whom all
things were made, *thy* Son Jesus Christ our Lord. *Amen.*

2. For All Sorts and Conditions of Men

O God, the creator and preserver of all mankind,
we humbly beseech thee for all sorts and conditions
of men; that thou wouldest be pleased to make thy
ways known unto them, thy saving health unto
all nations. More especially we pray for thy holy
Church universal; that it may be so guided and

Oraciones y acciones de gracias

Oraciones

Para usarse ya sea después de las colectas de la Oración de la Mañana o del Atardecer, o bien por separado.

Oraciones por el mundo

1. Por gozo en la creación de Dios

Padre celestial, que has colmado el mundo de belleza:
Ábrenos los ojos para reconocer
tu mano bondadosa en todas tus obras,
para que, deleitándonos en toda tu creación,
aprendamos a servirte con gozo;
por amor de aquel
por quien todas las cosas fueron hechas,
tu Hijo Jesucristo nuestro Señor. **Amén.**

2. Por personas de toda clase y condición

Dios creador y preservador de vida:
Con humildad te rogamos
por personas de toda clase y condición;
muéstrales tus sendas
y otorga tu gracia a todas las naciones.
En especial te rogamos
por tu santa iglesia universal;

governed by thy good Spirit, that all who profess and call themselves Christians may be led into the way of truth, and hold the faith in unity of spirit, in the bond of peace, and in righteousness of life. Finally, we commend to thy fatherly goodness all those who are in any ways afflicted or distressed, in mind, body, or estate; [especially those for whom our prayers are desired]; that it may please thee to comfort and relieve them according to their several necessities, giving them patience under their sufferings, and a happy issue out of all their afflictions. And this we beg for Jesus Christ's sake. *Amen.*

3. *For the Human Family*

O God, you made us in your own image and redeemed us through Jesus your Son: Look with compassion on the whole human family; take away the arrogance and hatred which infect our hearts; break down the walls that separate us; unite us in bonds of love; and work through our struggle and confusion to accomplish your purposes on earth; that, in your good time, all nations and races may serve you in harmony around your heavenly throne; through Jesus Christ our Lord. *Amen.*

4. *For Peace*

Eternal God, in whose perfect kingdom no sword is drawn but the sword of righteousness, no strength known but the strength of love: So mightily spread abroad your Spirit, that all peoples may be gathered under the banner of the Prince of Peace, as children of one Father; to whom be dominion and glory, now and for ever. *Amen.*

que sea dirigida y gobernada por tu buen Espíritu;
que así, quienes profesan ser de Cristo
sean *guiados* a la verdad
y guarden la fe en unidad de espíritu,
en vínculo de paz y en rectitud de vida.
Como un padre, derrama tu bondad
sobre toda persona afligida o angustiada
de cuerpo, mente, o condición
[especialmente a quienes hoy recordamos];
y como una madre, dales consuelo y alivio
según sus necesidades,
para que tengan paciencia en su sufrimiento
y sus penas resulten en su bienestar;
por nuestro Señor Cristo Jesús te lo rogamos. **Amén.**

3. *Por la familia humana*

Señor, que nos has creado a tu propia imagen
y nos has redimido mediante tu Hijo Jesús:
Mira con compasión a la familia humana entera;
quita el odio y la arrogancia que nos infectan el corazón;
derrumba las barreras que nos separan;
únenos en vínculos de amor;
y, a pesar del conflicto y confusión de nuestras vidas,
lleva a cabo tus propósitos en la tierra,
para que así, a su debido tiempo,
todas las naciones y pueblos te adoren en armonía
alrededor de tu trono celestial;
por Jesucristo nuestro Señor. **Amén.**

4. *Por la paz*

Eterno Dios, en cuyo reino perfecto
la única espada es la justicia
y la única fuerza es el amor:
Derrama con poder a tu Espíritu sobre todo pueblo,
a fin de que, *unidos* como hijos e hijas de un mismo Padre,
bajo el estandarte del Príncipe de Paz,
tuyos sean el dominio y la gloria,
por los siglos de los siglos. **Amén.**

5. For Peace Among the Nations

Almighty God our heavenly Father, guide the nations of the world into the way of justice and truth, and establish among them that peace which is the fruit of righteousness, that they may become the kingdom of our Lord and Savior Jesus Christ. *Amen.*

6. For our Enemies

O God, the Father of all, whose Son commanded us to love our enemies: Lead them and us from prejudice to truth; deliver them and us from hatred, cruelty, and revenge; and in your good time enable us all to stand reconciled before you; through Jesus Christ our Lord. *Amen.*

Prayers for the Church

7. For the Church

Gracious Father, we pray for thy holy Catholic Church. Fill it with all truth, in all truth with all peace. Where it is corrupt, purify it; where it is in error, direct it; where in any thing it is amiss, reform it. Where it is right, strengthen it; where it is in want, provide for it; where it is divided, reunite it; for the sake of Jesus Christ thy Son our Savior. *Amen.*

8. For the Mission of the Church

Everliving God, whose will it is that all should come to you through your Son Jesus Christ: Inspire our witness to him, that all may know the power of his forgiveness and the hope of his resurrection; who lives and reigns with you and the Holy Spirit, one God, now and for ever. *Amen.*

5. *Por la paz entre las naciones*

Dios de poder, nuestro Padre celestial:
Guía a todas las naciones del mundo
por la senda de justicia y de verdad,
y establece entre ellas esa paz que es fruto de la rectitud,
a fin de que lleguen a ser
el reino de nuestro Señor y Salvador Jesucristo. **Amén.**

6. *Por nuestros enemigos*

Dios y Padre de la humanidad,
cuyo Hijo nos mandó amar a *nuestros enemigos;*
guíalos a *ellos* y a *nosotros* del prejuicio a la verdad;
líbranos a *ellos* y a *nosotros*
del odio, la crueldad y la venganza;
y, a tu debido tiempo,
prepáranos para comparecer, *reconciliados,*
ante tu presencia;
por Jesucristo nuestro Señor. **Amén.**

Oraciones por la iglesia

7. *Por la iglesia*

Padre de bondad:
Te rogamos por tu santa iglesia católica;
cólmala de toda verdad, en toda verdad y con toda paz.
En lo que esté corrompida, purifícala;
cuando esté en error, corrígela;
donde haya fallado, refórmala.
En lo que sea justa, fortalécela;
cuanto carezca, otórgale;
y donde esté dividida, únela;
por amor de Jesucristo tu Hijo nuestro Salvador. **Amén.**

8. *Por la misión de la iglesia*

Dios de eternidad, cuya voluntad es que *todos* vengan a ti
por medio de tu Hijo Jesucristo: Inspira nuestro testimonio
de él, para que *todos* conozcan el poder de su perdón y la
esperanza de su resurrección; quien vive y reina contigo y el
Espíritu Santo, un solo Dios, ahora y por siempre. **Amén.**

9. For Clergy and People

Almighty and everlasting God, from whom cometh every good and perfect gift: Send down upon our bishops, and other clergy, and upon the congregations committed to their charge, the healthful Spirit of thy grace; and, that they may truly please thee, pour upon them the continual dew of thy blessing. Grant this, O Lord, for the honor of our Advocate and Mediator, Jesus Christ. *Amen.*

10. For the Diocese

O God, by your grace you have called us in this Diocese to a goodly fellowship of faith. Bless our Bishop(s) N. [and N.], and other clergy, and all our people. Grant that your Word may be truly preached and truly heard, your Sacraments faithfully administered and faithfully received. By your Spirit, fashion our lives according to the example of your Son, and grant that we may show the power of your love to all among whom we live; through Jesus Christ our Lord. *Amen.*

11. For the Parish

Almighty and everliving God, ruler of all things in heaven and earth, hear our prayers for this parish family. Strengthen the faithful, arouse the careless, and restore the penitent. Grant us all things necessary for our common life, and bring us all to be of one heart and mind within your holy Church; through Jesus Christ our Lord. *Amen.*

9. Por el clero y el pueblo

Dios de poder y eternidad,
de quien procede toda buena dádiva y perfecto don:
Envíales el Espíritu saludable de tu gracia
a tus *obispos*, al clero y a las congregaciones a su cargo;
y, para que en verdad te sirvan,
rocíalos sin pausa con tu bendición;
concédenos esto, Señor, por honor de Jesucristo,
nuestro Abogado y Mediador. **Amén.**

10. Por la diócesis

Señor, que nos has llamado por tu gracia
a que, en esta diócesis,
formemos una bendita comunión de fe:
Bendice a *nuestro obispo* N. [y N.],
al resto del clero y a todo nuestro pueblo.
Concede que tu Palabra
se predique y se escuche de verdad,
y que tus sacramentos
se administren y reciban fielmente.
Modela nuestras vidas con tu Espíritu,
conforme al ejemplo de tu Hijo,
y concede que le mostremos a nuestro prójimo
el poder de tu amor;
por Jesucristo nuestro Señor. **Amén.**

11. Por una parroquia

Dios de poder y eternidad, que riges en cielo y tierra:
Escucha nuestras oraciones por esta familia parroquial;
fortalece *al* fiel, despierta *al* indiferente
y restaura *al* penitente;
concédenos lo necesario para nuestra vida en común,
y únenos en mente y corazón en tu santa iglesia;
por Jesucristo nuestro Señor. **Amén.**

12. For a Church Convention or Meeting

Almighty and everliving God, source of all wisdom and understanding, be present with those who take counsel [in_____] for the renewal and mission of your Church. Teach us in all things to seek first your honor and glory. Guide us to perceive what is right, and grant us both the courage to pursue it and the grace to accomplish it; through Jesus Christ our Lord. *Amen.*

13. For the Election of a Bishop or other Minister

Almighty God, giver of every good gift: Look graciously on your Church, and so guide the minds of those who shall choose a bishop for this Diocese (*or*, rector for this parish), that we may receive a faithful pastor, who will care for your people and equip us for our ministries; through Jesus Christ our Lord. *Amen.*

14. For the Unity of the Church

O God the Father of our Lord Jesus Christ, our only Savior, the Prince of Peace: Give us grace seriously to lay to heart the great dangers we are in by our unhappy divisions; take away all hatred and prejudice, and whatever else may hinder us from godly union and concord; that, as there is but one Body and one Spirit, one hope of our calling, one Lord, one Faith, one Baptism, one God and Father of us all, so we may be all of one heart and of one soul, united in one holy bond of truth and peace, of faith and charity, and may with one mind and one mouth glorify *thee*; through Jesus Christ our Lord. *Amen.*

12. Por una convención o reunión de la Iglesia

Dios de poder y eternidad,
fuente de saber y entendimiento,
acompaña a quienes deliberan [en_____]
para la renovación y misión de tu Iglesia.
Enséñanos a que, en todas las cosas,
busquemos primero tu honor y tu gloria.
Guíanos para percibir lo que es justo;
concédenos valentía para buscarlo
y gracia para lograrlo;
por Jesucristo nuestro Señor. **Amén.**

13. Por la elección de un obispo u otra persona en el ministerio

Dios de todo poder, de quien toda dádiva procede:
Mira con bondad a tu Iglesia
e inspira a quienes elegirán *obispo* para esta diócesis
(o: *rector* para esta parroquia)
a fin de que recibamos *un pastor* fiel
que cuide a tu pueblo
y nos capacite en nuestros ministerios;
por Jesucristo nuestro Señor. **Amén.**

14. Por la unidad de la iglesia

Dios, Padre de nuestro Señor Jesucristo,
nuestro único Salvador, Príncipe de Paz:
Danos gracia para tener en cuenta
cuánto nos hacen peligrar
nuestras amargas divisiones;
aparta de *nosotros* todo odio, prejuicio,
y cuanto estorbe la santa unión y la concordia;
y, ya que no hay más que un Cuerpo y un Espíritu,
una esperanza en nuestra vocación,
un Dios y Padre de *todos*,
haz que seamos unánimes de alma y corazón,
unidos en vínculo sagrado
de verdad y paz, de fe y caridad,
y que te glorifiquemos con una sola mente y voz;
por Jesucristo nuestro Señor. **Amén.**

15. For those about to be Baptized or to renew their Baptismal Covenant

O God, you prepared your disciples for the coming of the Spirit through the teaching of your Son Jesus Christ: Make the hearts and minds of your servants ready to receive the blessing of the Holy Spirit, that they may be filled with the strength of his presence; through Jesus Christ our Lord. *Amen.*

16. For Monastic Orders and Vocations

O Lord Jesus Christ, you became poor for our sake, that we might be made rich through your poverty: Guide and sanctify, we pray, those whom you call to follow you under the vows of poverty, chastity, and obedience, that by their prayer and service they may enrich your Church, and by their life and worship may glorify your Name; for you reign with the Father and the Holy Spirit, one God, now and for ever. *Amen.*

17. For Church Musicians and Artists

O God, whom saints and angels delight to worship in heaven: Be ever present with your servants who seek through art and music to perfect the praises offered by your people on earth; and grant to them even now glimpses of your beauty, and make them worthy at length to behold it unveiled for evermore; through Jesus Christ our Lord. *Amen.*

15. *Por quienes van a ser bautizados o van a renovar su pacto bautismal*

Dios Uno y Trino,
que preparaste a tus *discípulos*,
a través de las enseñanzas de tu Hijo Jesucristo,
para la venida del Espíritu:
Dispone la mente y corazón de quienes te sirven
para recibir la bendición del Espíritu Santo
y llenarse del poder de su presencia;
por Jesucristo nuestro Señor. **Amén.**

16. *Por las órdenes religiosas y las vocaciones*

Señor Jesucristo,
que por *nosotros* te hiciste pobre
para enriquecernos mediante tu pobreza:
Guía y santifica a quienes has llamado
a seguirte bajo los votos de pobreza,
castidad y obediencia,
a fin de que en su orar y servir enriquezcan tu iglesia
y en su vivir y adorar glorifiquen tu nombre;
tú que reinas con el Padre y el Espíritu Santo,
un solo Dios, ahora y por siempre. **Amén.**

17. *Por músicos y artistas de la iglesia*

Santo Dios,
a quien los coros celestiales adoran con deleite:
Acompaña a quienes perfeccionan,
a través del arte y de la música,
las alabanzas de tu pueblo aquí en la tierra;
concede que vislumbren tu belleza
y *hazlos dignos* de que algún día la contemplen
con toda claridad y para siempre;
por Jesucristo nuestro Señor. **Amén.**

Prayers for National Life

18. *For our Country*

Almighty God, who hast given us this good land for our heritage: We humbly beseech thee that we may always prove ourselves a people mindful of thy favor and glad to do thy will. Bless our land with honorable industry, sound learning, and pure manners. Save us from violence, discord, and confusion; from pride and arrogance, and from every evil way. Defend our liberties, and fashion into one united people the multitudes brought hither out of many kindreds and tongues. Endue with the spirit of wisdom those to whom in thy Name we entrust the authority of government, that there may be justice and peace at home, and that, through obedience to thy law, we may show forth thy praise among the nations of the earth. In the time of prosperity, fill our hearts with thankfulness, and in the day of trouble, suffer not our trust in thee to fail; all which we ask through Jesus Christ our Lord. *Amen.*

19. *For the President of the United States and all in Civil Authority*

O Lord our Governor, whose glory is in all the world: We commend this nation to *thy* merciful care, that, being guided by *thy* Providence, we may dwell secure in *thy* peace. Grant to the President of the United States, the Governor of this State (*or* Commonwealth), and to all in authority, wisdom and strength to know and to do *thy* will. Fill them with the love of truth and

Oraciones por la vida nacional

18. *Por nuestra patria*

Dios de gran poder,
que nos has dado esta buena tierra por herencia:
Con humildad te suplicamos
que siempre recordemos tus bondades
y nos alegre cumplir tu voluntad.
Bendice nuestro país con trabajo honrado,
conocimiento íntegro y costumbres virtuosas.
Guárdanos de toda violencia, discordia y confusión;
de orgullo, de arrogancia y de toda maldad.
Defiende nuestras libertades;
de las diversas lenguas y naciones
que aquí se dan encuentro,
haznos un pueblo unido.
Dales el espíritu de sabiduría
a quienes les confiamos el poder de gobernar,
para que haya justicia y paz en el país
que, al obedecer tu ley, demos prueba de alabarte
ante las naciones de la tierra.
En tiempo de prosperidad,
llena nuestros corazones de gratitud;
y en el día de la angustia,
no permitas que nos falle la fe en ti;
todo esto te lo pedimos por Jesucristo nuestro Señor.
Amén.

19. *Por* el presidente *de la nación y todas las autoridades civiles*

Señor, que gobiernas
y cubres todo el mundo con tu gloria:
Encomendamos esta nación a tu cuidado
para que, *guiados* por tu Providencia,
vivamos sin peligros en tu paz.
Concede *al Presidente* de este país,
al Gobernador de este estado
y a todas las autoridades
sabiduría y fortaleza para conocer y hacer tu voluntad.

righteousness, and make them ever mindful of their calling to serve this people in *thy* fear; through Jesus Christ our Lord, who *liveth* and *reigneth* with *thee* and the Holy Spirit, one God, world without end. *Amen.*

20. *For Congress or a State Legislature*

O God, the fountain of wisdom, whose will is good and gracious, and whose law is truth: We beseech *thee* so to guide and bless our Senators and Representatives in Congress assembled (*or* in the Legislature of this State, *or* Commonwealth), that they may enact such laws as shall please *thee*, to the glory of *thy* Name and the welfare of this people; through Jesus Christ our Lord. *Amen.*

21. *For Courts of Justice*

Almighty God, *who sittest* in the throne judging right: We humbly beseech *thee* to bless the courts of justice and the magistrates in all this land; and give *unto* them the spirit of wisdom and understanding, that they may discern the truth, and impartially administer the law in the fear of *thee* alone; through him who shall come to be our Judge, *thy* Son our Savior Jesus Christ. *Amen.*

22. *For Sound Government*

The responses in italics may be omitted.

O Lord our Governor, bless the leaders of our land,
that we may be a people at peace among ourselves
and a blessing to other nations of the earth.
Lord, keep this nation under your care.

To the President and members of the Cabinet,
to Governors of States, Mayors of Cities, and to all in

Llénalos de amor a la verdad y a la justicia
y haz que jamás olviden su vocación
de servir a este pueblo en obediencia a ti;
por Jesucristo nuestro Señor,
que vive y reina contigo y el Espíritu Santo,
un solo Dios, por los siglos de los siglos. **Amén.**

20. *Por el Congreso o La Asamblea Legislativa*

Señor, fuente de sabiduría:
Tu voluntad es buena y bondadosa, y tu ley es verdadera;
te suplicamos que guíes y bendigas
a *nuestros* representantes *reunidos* para legislar
de modo que promulguen leyes que te agraden,
para la gloria de ti y el bienestar de este pueblo;
por Jesucristo nuestro Señor. **Amén.**

21. *Por las cortes y los tribunales de justicia*

Dios de todo poder,
que desde tu trono juzgas con equidad:
Con humildad te suplicamos que bendigas
a los tribunales de justicia
y a *los magistrados* de esta tierra;
dales sabiduría y entendimiento
para que disciernan la verdad
y, en sumisión a ti, emitan juicios imparciales;
por aquel que vendrá para juzgarnos,
tu Hijo nuestro Salvador Jesucristo. **Amén.**

22. *Por un gobierno justo*

Las respuestas en letra negrita pueden omitirse.

Señor, gobernante nuestro
bendice a quienes dirigen nuestra patria,
para que tengamos paz entre *nosotros*
y seamos una bendición
para las demás naciones de la tierra.
Señor, cuida esta nación.

Otorga sabiduría y bondad *al Presidente*,
a *gobernadores* y a *alcaldes*

administrative authority, grant wisdom and grace
in the exercise of their duties.
Give grace to your servants, O Lord.

To Senators and Representatives,
and those who make our laws in States, Cities,
and Towns, give courage, wisdom, and foresight
to provide for the needs of all our people,
and to fulfill our obligations in the community of nations.
Give grace to your servants, O Lord.

To the Judges and officers of our Courts give understanding
and integrity, that human rights may be safeguarded and
justice served.
Give grace to your servants, O Lord.

And finally, teach our people to rely on
your strength and to accept their responsibilities
to their fellow citizens, that they may elect trustworthy
leaders and make wise decisions for the well-being
of our society; that we may serve you faithfully
in our generation and honor your holy Name.

*For yours is the kingdom, O Lord, and you are exalted as head above
all. Amen.*

23. For Local Government

Almighty God our heavenly Father, send down upon those
who hold office in this State (Commonwealth, City, County,
Town,_____) the spirit of wisdom, charity, and justice;
that with steadfast purpose they may faithfully serve in their
offices to promote the well-being of all people; through Jesus
Christ our Lord. *Amen.*

y a toda autoridad del gobierno,
[especialmente a_____,]
en el cumplimiento fiel de sus deberes.
Señor, dales tu gracia.

Otorga valentía, sabiduría y visión
a *senadores* y *legisladores*
en *estados*, *provincias* y ciudades,
para que respondan
a las necesidades de nuestro pueblo
y cumplan con nuestras obligaciones
ante la comunidad de naciones.
Señor, dales tu gracia.

Otorga integridad y entendimiento
a *jueces* y *funcionarios* de los tribunales
para que los derechos humanos se protejan
y se haga justicia.
Señor, dales tu gracia.

Finalmente, enseña a nuestro pueblo
a confiar en tu poder
y tener consciencia de sus obligaciones al prójimo
para que elijan líderes *fidedignos*
y tomen decisiones sabias
por el bienestar de nuestra sociedad;
a fin de que, siendo fieles en servirte,
nuestra generación honre tu santo nombre.
Porque tuyo, Señor, es el reino
y tú eres el más alto Soberano. Amén.

23. *Por el gobierno local*

Dios de poder, nuestro Padre celestial,
derrama sobre los que ejercen cargos públicos
en este *estado (provincia, municipio, ciudad, pueblo)*
el espíritu de sabiduría, caridad y justicia;
para que desempeñen su tarea fiel y firmemente
y así promuevan el bienestar de todo el pueblo;
por Jesucristo nuestro Señor. **Amén.**

24. For an Election

Almighty God, to whom we must account for all our powers and privileges: Guide the people of the United States (*or* of this community) in the election of officials and representatives; that, by faithful administration and wise laws, the rights of all may be protected and our nation be enabled to fulfill your purposes; through Jesus Christ our Lord. *Amen.*

25. For those in the Armed Forces of our Country

Almighty God, we commend to your gracious care and keeping all the men and women of our armed forces at home and abroad. Defend them day by day with your heavenly grace; strengthen them in their trials and temptations; give them courage to face the perils which beset them; and grant them a sense of your abiding presence wherever they may be; through Jesus Christ our Lord. *Amen.*

26. For those who suffer for the sake of Conscience

O God our Father, whose Son forgave his enemies while he was suffering shame and death: Strengthen those who suffer for the sake of conscience; when they are accused, save them from speaking in hate; when they are rejected, save them from bitterness; when they are imprisoned, save them from despair; and to us your servants, give grace to respect their witness and to discern the truth, that our society may be cleansed and strengthened. This we ask for the sake of Jesus Christ, our merciful and righteous Judge. *Amen.*

24. Por las elecciones

Dios de poder, a quien debemos rendir cuentas
de todos nuestros poderes y privilegios:
Guía al pueblo de este país (o *de esta comunidad*)
en la elección de gobernantes y representantes
para que, con fiel mayordomía y leyes sabias,
los derechos de *todos* se protejan
y nuestro país cumpla tus propósitos;
por Jesucristo nuestro Señor. **Amén.**

25. Por quienes sirven en las fuerzas armadas del país

Dios de gran poder,
encomendamos a tu cuidado y protección
a quienes sirven en nuestras fuerzas armadas,
donde quiera que estén.
Con tu gracia celestial, acude día a día a su defensa;
dales fuerza en sus pruebas y tentaciones;
dales valor para enfrentar todo peligro
y concede que, donde se encuentren,
sientan tu presencia segura;
por Jesucristo nuestro Señor. **Amén.**

26. Por quienes sufren a causa de su conciencia

Dios y Padre nuestro,
cuyo Hijo perdonó a sus enemigos
a la hora de su agonía y muerte:
Fortalece a *los* que sufren a causa de su conciencia;
cuando sean acusados, líbralos de responder con odio;
cuando sean rechazadas, líbralas de la amargura;
cuando sean encarcelados, líbralos de la desesperanza;
y a *nosotros* danos la gracia
de respetar su testimonio y discernir la verdad,
para que así nuestra sociedad se purifique y fortalezca.
Te lo pedimos por amor de Jesucristo,
nuestro Juez misericordioso y justo. **Amén.**

Prayers for the Social Order

27. For Social Justice

Grant, O God, that your holy and life-giving Spirit may so move every human heart [and especially the hearts of the people of this land], that barriers which divide us may crumble, suspicions disappear, and hatreds cease; that our divisions being healed, we may live in justice and peace; through Jesus Christ our Lord. *Amen.*

28. In Times of Conflict

O God, you have bound us together in a common life. Help us, in the midst of our struggles for justice and truth, to confront one another without hatred or bitterness, and to work together with mutual forbearance and respect; through Jesus Christ our Lord. *Amen.*

29. For Agriculture

Almighty God, we thank you for making the earth fruitful, so that it might produce what is needed for life: Bless those who work in the fields; give us seasonable weather; and grant that we may all share the fruits of the earth, rejoicing in your goodness; through Jesus Christ our Lord. *Amen.*

30. For the Unemployed

Heavenly Father, we remember before you those who suffer want and anxiety from lack of work. Guide the people of this land so to use our public and private wealth that all may find suitable and fulfilling employment, and receive just payment for their labor; through Jesus Christ our Lord. *Amen.*

Oraciones por el orden social

27. Por la justicia social

Dios de justicia,
concédenos que tu Santo Espíritu vivificador
inspire a toda persona [especialmente a las de este país]
hasta que se derrumben las barreras que nos dividen,
desaparezcan las sospechas y cesen los odios;
para que, sanadas nuestras divisiones,
podamos vivir en justicia y paz;
por Jesucristo nuestro Señor. **Amén.**

28. En tiempos de conflicto

Dios de concordia, que nos has ligado *unos a otros*
en una vida común:
Ayúdanos en medio de nuestras luchas
por la justicia y la verdad,
para que nos confrontemos sin odio ni rencor
y trabajemos *juntos* con paciencia y respeto mutuo;
por Jesucristo nuestro Señor. **Amén.**

29. Por la agricultura

Dios creador, te damos gracias por haber hecho la tierra
tan fructífera que produce lo necesario para la vida;
danos un clima apacible,
bendice a quienes trabajan en los campos,
y enséñanos a compartir sus frutos,
alegrándonos en tu bondad;
por Jesucristo nuestro Señor. **Amén.**

30. Por los desempleados

Dios trabajador, recordamos ante ti
a quienes sufren la privación y angustia del desempleo.
Dirige al pueblo de esta tierra
para que usemos los recursos públicos y privados
de tal manera que *todos* tengan
trabajo adecuado y gratificador,
y reciban pago justo por su labor;
mediante Jesucristo nuestro Señor. **Amén.**

31. For Schools and Colleges

O Eternal God, bless all schools, colleges, and universities [and especially_____], that they may be lively centers for sound learning, new discovery, and the pursuit of wisdom; and grant that those who teach and those who learn may find you to be the source of all truth; through Jesus Christ our Lord. *Amen.*

32. For the Good Use of Leisure

O God, in the course of this busy life, give us times of refreshment and peace; and grant that we may so use our leisure to rebuild our bodies and renew our minds, that our spirits may be opened to the goodness of your creation; through Jesus Christ our Lord. *Amen.*

33. For Cities

Heavenly Father, in your Word you have given us a vision of that holy City to which the nations of the world bring their glory: Behold and visit, we pray, the cities of the earth. Renew the ties of mutual regard which form our civic life. Send us honest and able leaders. Enable us to eliminate poverty, prejudice, and oppression, that peace may prevail with righteousness, and justice with order, and that men and women from different cultures and with differing talents may find with one another the fulfillment of their humanity; through Jesus Christ our Lord. *Amen.*

34. For Towns and Rural Areas

Lord Christ, when you came among us, you proclaimed the kingdom of God in villages, towns, and lonely places: Grant

31. Por escuelas, colegios y universidades

Dios de sabiduría, mira con tu favor
a todas las escuelas, colegios y universidades
[especialmente a_____),
y haz que sean centros dinámicos de aprendizaje,
de nuevos descubrimientos y de amor a la sabiduría;
y otorga a quienes enseñan y a quienes aprenden
que te reconozcan como fuente de toda verdad;
por Jesucristo nuestro Señor. **Amén.**

32. Por el buen uso del descanso

Buen Dios, danos en esta vida atareada,
momentos de tranquilidad y paz;
que usemos nuestro descanso
para reanimar el cuerpo y renovar la mente,
y apreciar la bondad de tu creación;
por Jesucristo nuestro Señor. **Amén.**

33. Por las ciudades

Padre celestial, en tu Palabra nos has dado una visión
de aquella ciudad santa
a la que todas las naciones del mundo
contribuyen su gloria;
considera y visita, te pedimos, a las ciudades de la tierra.
Renueva los lazos de respeto mutuo
que forjan nuestra vida cívica;
envíanos líderes *honestos* y competentes,
y capacítanos para eliminar la pobreza,
el prejuicio y la opresión,
para que predomine la paz con rectitud,
y la justicia con el orden;
y las mujeres y hombres de diversas culturas y talentos,
descubran juntos la plenitud de su humanidad;
por Jesucristo nuestro Señor. **Amén.**

34. Por pueblos y áreas rurales

Señor Jesucristo, cuando viniste a *nosotros*,
proclamaste el reino de Dios en pueblos,

that your presence and power may be known throughout this land. Have mercy upon all of us who live and work in rural areas [especially_____]; and grant that all the people of our nation may give thanks to you for food and drink and all other bodily necessities of life, respect those who labor to produce them, and honor the land and the water from which these good things come. All this we ask in your holy Name. *Amen.*

35. *For the Poor and the Neglected*

Almighty and most merciful God, we remember before you all poor and neglected persons whom it would be easy for us to forget: the homeless and the destitute, the old and the sick, and all who have none to care for them. Help us to heal those who are broken in body or spirit, and to turn their sorrow into joy. Grant this, Father, for the love of your Son, who for our sake became poor, Jesus Christ our Lord. *Amen.*

36. *For the Oppressed*

Look with pity, O heavenly Father, upon the people in this land who live with injustice, terror, disease, and death as their constant companions. Have mercy upon us. Help us to eliminate our cruelty to these our neighbors. Strengthen those who spend their lives establishing equal protection of the law and equal opportunities for all. And grant that every one of us may enjoy a fair portion of the riches of this land; through Jesus Christ our Lord. *Amen.*

aldeas y lugares aislados;
da a conocer tu presencia y poder en toda esta nación.
Ten piedad de quienes viven y trabajan en áreas rurales
[especialmente_____];
y concede que,
en todas las necesidades corporales de la vida,
la gente te agradezca su alimento,
respete a quienes trabajan para producirlo
y honren la tierra y las aguas
de donde proviene toda cosa buena;
esto te lo pedimos por tu santo nombre. **Amén.**

35. *Por personas pobres y desamparadas*

Dios de todo poder y misericordia,
en tu presencia recordamos
a toda persona pobre y desamparada
que tan fácilmente relegamos al olvido:
indigentes, sin hogar, *ancianas* o *enfermos*,
que no cuentan con nadie;
ayúdanos a sanar su sufrimiento de cuerpo y alma,
y así, convertir su tristeza en alegría.
Concede esto, Padre, por amor a tu Hijo,
que por *nosotros* se hizo pobre, Jesucristo nuestro Señor.
Amén.

36. *Por personas oprimidas*

Dios celestial, mira en tu compasión
a quienes en este país sufren a diario
injusticia, terror, enfermedad y muerte.
Ten piedad de *nosotros.*
Ayúdanos a eliminar nuestra crueldad
hacia nuestros semejantes.
Fortalece a quienes dedican sus vidas
a garantizar igualdad de oportunidades
y la protección imparcial de la ley;
y concede que cada *uno* de *nosotros* disfrute
de la justa distribución de los bienes de este país;
por Jesucristo nuestro Señor. **Amén.**

37. For Prisons and Correctional Institutions

Lord Jesus, for our sake you were condemned as a criminal:
Visit our jails and prisons with your pity and judgment.
Remember all prisoners, and bring the guilty to repentance
and amendment of life according to your will, and give them
hope for their future. When any are held unjustly, bring
them release; forgive us, and teach us to improve our justice.
Remember those who work in these institutions; keep them
humane and compassionate; and save them from becoming
brutal or callous. And since what we do for those in prison,
O Lord, we do for you, constrain us to improve their lot. All
this we ask for your mercy's sake. *Amen.*

38. For the Right Use of God's Gifts

Almighty God, whose loving hand *hath* given us all that we
possess: Grant us grace that we may honor *thee* with our
substance, and, remembering the account which we must one
day give, may be faithful stewards of *thy* bounty, through
Jesus Christ our Lord. *Amen.*

39. For those who Influence Public Opinion

Almighty God, you proclaim your truth in every age by many
voices: Direct, in our time, we pray, those who speak where
many listen and write what many read; that they may do
their part in making the heart of this people wise, its mind
sound, and its will righteous; to the honor of Jesus Christ our
Lord. *Amen.*

37. *Por las cárceles e instituciones correccionales*

Señor Jesucristo, que por nuestra causa,
fuiste condenado como un criminal:
Visita nuestras cárceles y prisiones
con tu juicio misericordioso.
No te olvides de las personas presas:
a *los* culpables, otórgales arrepentimiento,
renovación de vida, y esperanza en su futuro;
a *los* injustamente *presos*, libertad.
Acuérdate de quienes trabajan en estas instituciones;
hazlos más *humanos* y *compasivos*
y menos crueles e insensibles.
A *nosotros*, perdónanos y enséñanos
a mejorar nuestro sistema judicial.
Y ya que todo lo que hacemos
por las personas encarceladas, lo hacemos por ti,
comprométenos a mejorar sus vidas.
Todo esto te lo pedimos por tu misericordia. **Amén.**

38. *Por el uso justo de los dones de Dios*

Dios generoso,
tu mano amorosa nos ha dado todo lo que tenemos;
danos gracia para honrarte con nuestros bienes
y recordando la cuenta que un día te rendiremos,
ser fieles mayordomos de tu generosidad;
por Jesucristo nuestro Señor. **Amén.**

39. *Por quienes influyen en la opinión pública*

Dios verdadero, en cada generación
proclamas tu verdad por medio de muchas voces;
te pedimos que dirijas, en nuestros días,
a quienes hablan donde muchos escuchan
y quienes escriben lo que muchos leen;
para que participen en la creación de un pueblo
de corazón sabio, mente sana y voluntad justa;
para honra de Jesucristo nuestro Señor. **Amén.**

Prayers for the Natural Order

40. *For Knowledge of God's Creation*

Almighty and everlasting God, you made the universe with
all its marvelous order, its atoms, worlds, and galaxies, and
the infinite complexity of living creatures: Grant that, as
we probe the mysteries of your creation, we may come to
know you more truly, and more surely fulfill our role in your
eternal purpose; in the name of Jesus Christ our Lord. *Amen.*

41. *For the Conservation of Natural Resources*

Almighty God, in giving us dominion over things on earth,
you made us fellow workers in your creation: Give us
wisdom and reverence so to use the resources of nature,
that no one may suffer from our abuse of them, and that
generations yet to come may continue to praise you for your
bounty; through Jesus Christ our Lord. *Amen.*

42. *For the Harvest of Lands and Waters*

O gracious Father, *who openest thine* hand and *fillest* all things
living with plenteousness: Bless the lands and waters, and
multiply the harvests of the world; let *thy* Spirit go forth, that
it may renew the face of the earth; show *thy* loving-kindness,
that our land may give her increase; and save us from selfish
use of what *thou givest*, that men and women everywhere may
give *thee* thanks; through Christ our Lord. *Amen.*

Oraciones por la naturaleza

40. *Por el conocimiento de la creación de Dios*

Dios, poderoso y eterno, que creaste el universo
con su maravilloso orden,
sus átomos, mundos y galaxias,
y una complejidad infinita de seres vivientes:
Concede que,
según vamos explorado los misterios de tu creación,
lleguemos a conocerte mejor,
y cumplamos más fielmente nuestro papel
en tu propósito eterno;
en nombre de Jesucristo nuestro Señor. **Amén.**

41. *Por la conservación de los recursos naturales*

Dios todopoderoso,
nos has dado mayordomía sobre la tierra
y nos has hecho *colaboradores* en tu creación:
Danos también sabiduría y reverencia
en el uso de sus recursos naturales,
para que nadie sufra por nuestro abuso de ellos
y generaciones venideras
continúen alabando tu generosidad;
mediante Jesucristo nuestro Señor. **Amén.**

42. *Por los frutos de la tierra y de las aguas*

Padre bueno, que abres tu mano
y colmas de bendición a todo ser viviente:
Bendice la tierra y las aguas;
multiplica las cosechas del mundo;
envía tu Espíritu a renovar la faz de la tierra;
manifiesta tu bondad en la fertilidad de nuestros campos,
y líbranos del abuso egoísta de tus dones;
para que toda persona en todo lugar te dé gracias;
por Jesucristo nuestro Señor. **Amén.**

43. For Rain

O God, heavenly Father, who by *thy* Son Jesus Christ
hast promised to all those who seek *thy* kingdom and its
righteousness all things necessary to sustain their life: Send
us, we entreat *thee*, in this time of need, such moderate rain
and showers, that we may receive the fruits of the earth,
to our comfort and to *thy* honor; through Jesus Christ our
Lord. *Amen.*

44. For the Future of the Human Race

O God our heavenly Father, you have blessed us and given us
dominion over all the earth: Increase our reverence before the
mystery of life; and give us new insight into your purposes
for the human race, and new wisdom and determination in
making provision for its future in accordance with your will;
through Jesus Christ our Lord. *Amen.*

Prayers for Family and Personal Life

45. For Families

Almighty God, our heavenly Father, who settest the solitary
in families: We commend to thy continual care the homes
in which thy people dwell. Put far from them, we beseech
thee, every root of bitterness, the desire of vainglory, and
the pride of life. Fill them with faith, virtue, knowledge,
temperance, patience, godliness. Knit together in constant
affection those who, in holy wedlock, have been made one
flesh. Turn the hearts of the parents to the children, and the
hearts of the children to the parents; and so enkindle fervent
charity among us all, that we may evermore be kindly
affectioned one to another; through Jesus Christ our Lord.
Amen.

43. *Por la lluvia*

Dios, Padre celestial, por tu Hijo Jesucristo has prometido
a los que buscan tu reino y su justicia
todo lo necesario para sus vidas;
en este tiempo de necesidad,
envíanos lluvias moderadas y aguaceros
para obtener los frutos de la tierra,
para nuestro provecho y tu honra;
por Jesucristo nuestro Señor. **Amén.**

44. *Por el futuro de la humanidad*

Dios, Padre celestial,
nos has bendecido con la mayordomía de la tierra;
aumenta nuestra reverencia ante el misterio de la vida;
danos una nueva comprensión
de tus designios para el género humano,
y una nueva sabiduría y valentía
para proveer por nuestro futuro
de acuerdo con tu voluntad;
por Jesucristo nuestro Señor. **Amén.**

Oraciones por la vida familiar y personal

45. *Por las familias*

Dios, amoroso, Padre celestial,
que estableces en familias *al solitario*:
Encomendamos a tu cuidado continuo
los hogares en que vive tu pueblo.
Aparta de ellos toda raíz de amargura,
deseo de vanagloria y orgullo de vida.
Llénalos de fe, virtud, conocimiento,
moderación, paciencia y santidad.
Enlaza en amor constante
a quienes se han unido en santo matrimonio.
Une los corazones de toda esta familia,
y enciende tanto amor entre *nosotros*,
que estemos siempre *unidos* en cariño familiar;
mediante Jesucristo nuestro Señor. **Amén.**

46. *For the Care of Children*

Almighty God, heavenly Father, you have blessed us with the joy and care of children: Give us calm strength and patient wisdom as we bring them up, that we may teach them to love whatever is just and true and good, following the example of our Savior Jesus Christ. *Amen.*

47. *For Young Persons*

God our Father, you see your children growing up in an unsteady and confusing world: Show them that your ways give more life than the ways of the world, and that following you is better than chasing after selfish goals. Help them to take failure, not as a measure of their worth, but as a chance for a new start. Give them strength to hold their faith in you, and to keep alive their joy in your creation; through Jesus Christ our Lord. *Amen.*

48. *For Those Who Live Alone*

Almighty God, whose Son had nowhere to lay his head: Grant that those who live alone may not be lonely in their solitude, but that, following in his steps, they may find fulfillment in loving you and their neighbors; through Jesus Christ our Lord. *Amen.*

49. *For the Aged*

Look with mercy, O God our Father, on all whose increasing years bring them weakness, distress, or isolation. Provide for them homes of dignity and peace; give them understanding helpers, and the willingness to accept help; and, as their strength diminishes, increase their faith and their assurance of your love. This we ask in the name of Jesus Christ our Lord. *Amen.*

46. Por el cuidado de hijos e hijas

Señor, como padre y madre de *todos*
nos has bendecido
con la alegría y el cuidado de hijos e hijas;
danos, en su crianza, fortaleza serena y sabiduría paciente,
enseñándoles a amar todo lo justo, verdadero y bueno,
siguiendo el ejemplo de nuestro Salvador Jesucristo. **Amén.**

47. Por jóvenes

Dios Padre, tú te fijas en tus *hijos*
que se enfrentan a un mundo inestable y confuso;
enséñales que tus caminos
dan más vida que los del mundo,
y que seguirte es mejor que perseguir metas egoístas.
Ayúdalos a aceptar que fracasar no es valer menos,
sino la oportunidad para empezar de nuevo.
Dales fortaleza para mantenerse firmes en la fe
y seguir viviendo con confianza en tu bondad;
por Jesucristo nuestro Señor. **Amén.**

48. Por personas solas

Dios todopoderoso,
tu Hijo no tuvo ni donde recostar la cabeza;
haz que toda persona sola
no se sienta abandonada en su soledad,
sino que, siguiendo las huellas de Jesús,
encuentre plenitud de vida amándote a ti y al prójimo;
por Jesucristo nuestro Señor. **Amén.**

49. Por la gente mayor

Dios Padre, mira con misericordia
a quienes, por su edad avanzada,
sufren debilidad, aflicción o aislamiento.
Provéeles hogares dignos y apacibles;
concédeles la ayuda de personas comprensivas
y la disposición para aceptarla;
y, a medida que sus fuerzas disminuyan,
aumenta su fe y la certeza de tu amor.
Te lo pedimos en nombre de Jesucristo nuestro Señor.
Amén.

50. *For a Birthday*

O God, our times are in your hand: Look with favor, we
pray, on your servant N. as *he* begins another year. Grant
that *he* may grow in wisdom and grace, and strengthen *his*
trust in your goodness all the days of *his* life; through Jesus
Christ our Lord. *Amen.*

51. *For a Birthday*

Watch over thy child, O Lord, as *his* days increase; bless
and guide *him* wherever *he* may be. Strengthen *him* when
he stands; comfort *him* when discouraged or sorrowful;
raise *him* up if *he* fall; and in *his* heart may thy peace which
passeth understanding abide all the days of *his* life; through
Jesus Christ our Lord. *Amen.*

52. *For the Absent*

O God, whose fatherly care *reacheth* to the uttermost parts
of the earth: We humbly beseech *thee* graciously to behold
and bless those whom we love, now absent from us. Defend
them from all dangers of soul and body; and grant that both
they and we, drawing nearer to *thee*, may be bound together
by *thy* love in the communion of *thy* Holy Spirit, and in
the fellowship of *thy* saints; through Jesus Christ our Lord.
Amen.

53. *For Travelers*

O God, our heavenly Father, whose glory fills the whole
creation, and whose presence we find wherever we go:
Preserve those who travel [in particular_____]; surround
them with your loving care; protect them from every danger;
and bring them in safety to their journey's end; through Jesus
Christ our Lord. *Amen.*

50. En un cumpleaños

Amado Dios, nuestros días están en tus manos;
mira con favor, te pedimos, a tu *siervo N.*
que comienza un nuevo año.
Concede que siga creciendo en sabiduría y gracia
y fortalece su confianza en tu bondad
todos los días de su vida;
por Jesucristo nuestro Señor. **Amén.**

51. En un cumpleaños

Dios bueno, vela por tu *hijo N.,*
según van aumentando sus días;
bendícelo y *guíalo* donde se encuentre.
Fortalécelo cuando se mantenga en pie;
consuélalo al sentirse *desanimado* o triste;
levántalo si cae;
y que la paz que sobrepasa todo entendimiento
permanezca en su corazón todos los días de su vida;
por Jesucristo nuestro Señor. **Amén.**

52. Por personas ausentes

Señor, tu amor materno
alcanza hasta los confines de la tierra;
humildemente te pedimos
que consideres y bendigas con tu bondad
a *nuestros queridos* ausentes.
Defiéndelos de todo peligro de cuerpo y alma
y concede que *todos,* acercándonos más a ti,
estemos *unidos* por tu amor con tus santos y santas
en la comunión de tu Santo Espíritu,
por Jesucristo nuestro Señor. **Amén.**

53. Por quienes viajan

Dios, Padre celestial, cuya gloria llena toda la creación y te
encuentras dondequiera que vamos: Protege a quienes viajan
[especialmente a_____]: *abrázalos* con tu cuidado y amor;
protégelos de todo peligro y haz que lleguen *sanos* y *salvos* a
su destino; por Jesucristo nuestro Señor. **Amén.**

54. *For those we Love*

Almighty God, we entrust all who are dear to us to *thy* never-failing care and love, for this life and the life to come, knowing that *thou art* doing for them better things than we can desire or pray for; through Jesus Christ our Lord. *Amen.*

55. *For a Person in Trouble or Bereavement*

O merciful Father, who hast taught us in thy holy Word that thou dost not willingly afflict or grieve the children of men: Look with pity upon the sorrows of thy servant for whom our prayers are offered. Remember *him*, O Lord, in mercy, nourish *his* soul with patience, comfort *him* with a sense of thy goodness, lift up thy countenance upon *him*, and give *him* peace; through Jesus Christ our Lord. *Amen.*

56. *For the Victims of Addiction*

O blessed Lord, you ministered to all who came to you: Look with compassion upon all who through addiction have lost their health and freedom. Restore to them the assurance of your unfailing mercy; remove from them the fears that beset them; strengthen them in the work of their recovery; and to those who care for them, give patient understanding and persevering love. *Amen.*

57. *For Guidance*

Direct us, O Lord, in all our doings with *thy* most gracious favor, and further us with *thy* continual help; that in all our works begun, continued, and ended in *thee*, we may glorify *thy* holy Name, and finally, by *thy* mercy, obtain everlasting life; through Jesus Christ our Lord. *Amen.*

54. Por nuestros seres queridos

Dios providente, encomendamos a nuestros seres queridos
a tu fiel cuidado y amor durante esta vida y la venidera,
sabiendo que haces por ellos mejores cosas
que lo que podamos desear o pedirte;
por Jesucristo nuestro Señor. **Amén**

55. Por una persona afligida

Padre misericordioso,
en tu santa Palabra nos has enseñado
que no afliges ni entristeces voluntariamente
a tus criaturas:
Atiende el sufrimiento de tu *siervo*
por quien oramos.
Acuérdate de *él*, Señor, en tu amor;
colma su alma de paciencia;
consuélalo con el sentido de tu bondad;
alza tu rostro hacia *él* y concédele paz;
mediante Jesucristo nuestro Señor. **Amén.**

56. Por las víctimas de la adicción

Bendito Señor Jesucristo,
que ministraste a toda persona que acudía a ti:
Mira en tu compasión a quienes han perdido
su salud y libertad a causa de su adicción.
Restáurales la confianza en tu infinito amor;
aparta los temores que *los* acechan;
fortalécelos en su labor de recuperación;
y dales comprensión paciente y amor perseverante
a quienes *los* cuidan. **Amén.**

57. Por la dirección divina

Dirígenos, Dios, en todo lo que hacemos, con tu gracia,
y llévanos adelante con tu constante ayuda;
para que, en todo lo que comencemos,
continuemos y terminemos en ti,
glorifiquemos tu santo nombre
y finalmente, por tu misericordia,
obtengamos la vida eterna;
por Jesucristo nuestro Señor. **Amén.**

58. For Guidance

O God, by whom the meek are guided in judgment, and light *riseth* up in darkness for the godly: Grant us, in all our doubts and uncertainties, the grace to ask what *thou wouldest* have us to do, that the Spirit of wisdom may save us from all false choices, and that in *thy* light we may see light, and in *thy* straight path may not stumble; through Jesus Christ our Lord. *Amen.*

59. For Quiet Confidence

O God of peace, *who hast* taught us that in returning and rest we shall be saved, in quietness and in confidence shall be our strength: By the might of *thy* Spirit lift us, we pray *thee*, to *thy* presence, where we may be still and know that *thou art* God; through Jesus Christ our Lord. *Amen.*

60. For Protection

Assist us mercifully, O Lord, in these our supplications and prayers, and dispose the way of *thy* servants towards the attainment of everlasting salvation; that, among all the changes and chances of this mortal life, they may ever be defended by *thy* gracious and ready help; through Jesus Christ our Lord. *Amen.*

61. A Prayer of Self-Dedication

Almighty and eternal God, so draw our hearts to *thee*, so guide our minds, so fill our imaginations, so control our wills, that we may be wholly *thine*, utterly dedicated *unto thee*; and then use us, we pray *thee*, as *thou wilt*, and always to *thy* glory and the welfare of *thy* people; through our Lord and Savior Jesus Christ. *Amen.*

58. *Por la dirección divina*

Señor, que guías a *los* inocentes en su entendimiento
e iluminas a *los* fieles en la oscuridad:
Concédenos, en todas nuestras dudas e incertidumbres,
la gracia de buscar tu voluntad,
para que el Espíritu de sabiduría
nos proteja de malas decisiones,
y, en tu luz, veamos luz
para no tropezar en tu camino recto;
por Jesucristo nuestro Señor. **Amén.**

59. *Por la confianza y la tranquilidad*

Dios de paz, nos has enseñado
que en nuestra conversión y entrega a ti seremos *salvos,*
y en la tranquilidad y confianza estará nuestra fortaleza;
por el poder de tu Espíritu, llévanos a tu presencia,
donde podamos estar *tranquilos* y saber que tú eres Dios;
por Jesucristo nuestro Señor. **Amén.**

60. *Por la protección divina*

Asístenos, Dios de misericordia,
en nuestras súplicas y oraciones,
y prepara el camino de tus *servidores*
hacia la salvación eterna;
que, en los cambios y riesgos
de esta vida mortal,
seamos siempre *defendidos*
por tu bondadosa y pronta ayuda;
por Jesucristo nuestro Señor. **Amén.**

61. *Acto de dedicación personal*

Dios todopoderoso y eterno,
atrae a ti nuestro corazón, guía nuestra mente,
inspira nuestra imaginación y gobierna nuestra voluntad,
para que seamos totalmente *tuyos,*
dedicados por completo a ti.
Úsanos según tu voluntad,
y siempre para tu gloria y el bienestar de tu pueblo;
por Jesucristo nuestro Señor y Salvador. **Amén.**

62. A Prayer attributed to St. Francis

Lord, make us instruments of your peace. Where there is hatred, let us sow love; where there is injury, pardon; where there is discord, union; where there is doubt, faith; where there is despair, hope; where there is darkness, light; where there is sadness, joy. Grant that we may not so much seek to be consoled as to console; to be understood as to understand; to be loved as to love. For it is in giving that we receive; it is in pardoning that we are pardoned; and it is in dying that we are born to eternal life. *Amen.*

Other Prayers

63. In the Evening

O Lord, support us all the day long, until the shadows lengthen, and the evening comes, and the busy world is hushed, and the fever of life is over, and our work is done. Then in *thy* mercy, grant us a safe lodging, and a holy rest, and peace at the last. *Amen.*

64. Before Worship

O Almighty God, *who pourest* out on all who desire it the spirit of grace and of supplication: Deliver us, when we draw near to *thee*, from coldness of heart and wanderings of mind, that with steadfast thoughts and kindled affections we may worship *thee* in spirit and in truth; through Jesus Christ our Lord. *Amen.*

62. *Oración atribuida a San Francisco de Asís*

Señor, haznos instrumentos de tu paz,
que donde haya odio, sembremos amor;
donde haya ofensa, perdón;
donde haya discordia, unión; donde haya duda, fe;
donde haya desesperación, esperanza;
donde haya tinieblas, luz;
donde haya tristeza, gozo.
Concede que no busquemos ser *consolados*, sino consolar;
ser *comprendidos*, sino comprender;
ser *amados*, sino amar.
Porque dando es como recibimos;
perdonando es como somos *perdonados*;
y muriendo, es como nacemos a la vida eterna. **Amén.**

Otras oraciones

63. *Al anochecer*

Dios eterno, nuestro apoyo durante el día:
Ahora que las sombras se extienden y cae la noche,
el mundo atareado se calma,
la fiebre de la vida pasa
y nuestro trabajo termina,
concédenos, en tu misericordia, tu seguro albergue,
santo descanso, y finalmente, paz. **Amén.**

64. *Antes de la liturgia*

Dios omnipotente, que derramas sobre quienes lo desean,
el espíritu de gracia y oración:
Cuando nos acercamos a ti,
líbranos de tibieza de corazón y distracciones de la mente,
para que, con pensamientos claros y caluroso afecto,
te adoremos en espíritu y en verdad;
por Jesucristo nuestro Señor. **Amén.**

65. For the Answering of Prayer

Almighty God, who hast promised to hear the petitions
of those who ask in thy Son's Name: We beseech thee
mercifully to incline thine ear to us who have now made our
prayers and supplications unto thee; and grant that those
things which we have faithfully asked according to thy will,
may effectually be obtained, to the relief of our necessity,
and to the setting forth of thy glory; through Jesus Christ
our Lord. *Amen.*

66. Before Receiving Communion

Be present, be present, O Jesus, our great High Priest, as you
were present with your disciples, and be known to us in the
breaking of bread; who live and reign with the Father and
the Holy Spirit, now and for ever. *Amen.*

67. After Receiving Communion

O Lord Jesus Christ, who in a wonderful Sacrament hast
left unto us a memorial of thy passion: Grant us, we beseech
thee, so to venerate the sacred mysteries of thy Body and
Blood, that we may ever perceive within ourselves the fruit of
thy redemption; who livest and reignest with the Father and
the Holy Spirit, one God, for ever and ever. *Amen.*

68. After Worship

Grant, we beseech *thee*, Almighty God, that the words
which we have heard this day with our outward ears, may,
through *thy* grace, be so grafted inwardly in our hearts,
that they may bring forth in us the fruit of good living, to
the honor and praise of *thy* Name; through Jesus Christ our
Lord. *Amen.*

65. Por respuesta a la oración

Dios todopoderoso, has prometido
escuchar las peticiones en nombre de tu Hijo;
te suplicamos que, en tu misericordia,
escuches nuestras oraciones;
concede que obtengamos efectivamente
lo que con fe te pedimos según tu voluntad,
para aliviar nuestras necesidades
y manifestar tu gloria;
por Jesucristo nuestro Señor. **Amén.**

66. Antes de comulgar

Hazte presente, hazte presente, Señor Jesús,
nuestro gran Sumo Sacerdote,
tal como estuviste presente con tus *discípulos,*
y muéstrate a *nosotros* al partir el pan;
tú que vives y reinas con el Padre y el Espíritu Santo,
ahora y siempre. **Amén.**

67. Después de comulgar

Señor Jesucristo, en un maravilloso sacramento
nos dejaste el memorial de tu pasión;
concédenos que veneremos
los sagrados misterios de tu Cuerpo y Sangre,
y que en nuestro ser reconozcamos siempre
el fruto de tu liberación;
tú que vives y reinas con el Padre y el Espíritu Santo,
un solo Dios, por los siglos de los siglos. **Amén.**

68. Después de la liturgia

Concede Dios todopoderoso, por tu gracia,
que lo que hemos oído hoy nos llegue al corazón
y produzca en *nosotros* los frutos de una buena vida,
para honor y gloria de tu nombre;
por Jesucristo nuestro Señor. **Amén.**

69. *On Sunday*

O God our King, by the resurrection of your Son Jesus
Christ on the first day of the week, you conquered sin, put
death to flight, and gave us the hope of everlasting life:
Redeem all our days by this victory; forgive our sins, banish
our fears, make us bold to praise you and to do your will;
and steel us to wait for the consummation of your kingdom
on the last great Day; through the same Jesus Christ our
Lord. *Amen.*

70. *Grace at Meals*

Give us grateful hearts, our Father, for all *thy* mercies, and
make us mindful of the needs of others; through Jesus Christ
our Lord. *Amen.*

or this

Bless, O Lord, *thy* gifts to our use and us to *thy* service; for
Christ's sake. *Amen.*

or this

Blessed are you, O Lord God, King of the Universe, for you
give us food to sustain our lives and make our hearts glad;
through Jesus Christ our Lord. *Amen.*

or this

For these and all his mercies, God's holy Name be blessed
and praised; through Jesus Christ our Lord. *Amen.*

69. *En domingo*

Dios, Soberano nuestro,
por la resurrección de tu Hijo Jesucristo
el primer día de la semana,
venciste al pecado, ahuyentaste la muerte
y nos diste la esperanza de vida eterna;
por esta victoria, redime todos nuestros días;
perdona nuestros pecados, destierra nuestros temores,
danos valor para alabarte y hacer tu voluntad,
y fortalécenos para esperar la consumación
de tu reino en el gran día final;
por el mismo Jesucristo nuestro Señor. **Amén.**

70. *Bendición de la comida*

Padre nuestro, danos corazones agradecidos,
por todas tus bondades, y haznos conscientes
de las necesidades de los demás;
por Jesucristo nuestro Señor. **Amén.**

O bien:

Bendice, Señor, estos tus dones para nuestro uso,
y a *nosotros* para tu servicio; por amor de Cristo. **Amén.**

O bien:

Bendito eres Señor Dios, Rey del universo,
que nos alimentas para mantener nuestras vidas
y alegrar nuestros corazones; por Jesucristo nuestro Señor.
Amén.

O bien:

Bendito y alabado sea el santo nombre de Dios,
por estas y todas sus bondades;
mediante Jesucristo nuestro Señor. **Amén.**

:

Thanksgivings

General Thanksgivings

1. A General Thanksgiving

Accept, O Lord, our thanks and praise for all that you have done for us. We thank you for the splendor of the whole creation, for the beauty of this world, for the wonder of life, and for the mystery of love.

We thank you for the blessing of family and friends, and for the loving care which surrounds us on every side.

We thank you for setting us at tasks which demand our best efforts, and for leading us to accomplishments which satisfy and delight us.

We thank you also for those disappointments and failures that lead us to acknowledge our dependence on you alone.

Above all, we thank you for your Son Jesus Christ; for the truth of his Word and the example of his life; for his steadfast obedience, by which he overcame temptation; for his dying, through which he overcame death; and for his rising to life again, in which we are raised to the life of your kingdom.

Grant us the gift of your Spirit, that we may know Christ and make him known; and through him, at all times and in all places, may give thanks to you in all things. *Amen.*

2. A Litany of Thanksgiving

For optional use on Thanksgiving Day, in place of the Prayers of the People at the Eucharist, or at any time after the Collects at Morning or Evening Prayer, or separately.

Acciones de Gracias

Acciones de gracias de uso general

1. Acción de gracias de uso general

Acepta, Señor, nuestras gracias y alabanza
por todo lo que has hecho por *nosotros*.
Por el esplendor de toda la creación,
por la belleza de este mundo,
el milagro de la vida y el misterio del amor.

Te damos gracias por la bendición
de familiares y amistades,
y por el tierno cuidado que siempre nos rodea.

Te damos gracias porque nos das tareas
que requieren nuestros mejores esfuerzos,
y nos guías hacia logros que nos satisfacen y deleitan.

Te damos gracias también por las desilusiones y fracasos
que nos enseñan a reconocer que dependemos solo de ti.

Sobre todo, te damos gracias por tu Hijo Jesucristo;
por la verdad de su Palabra y el ejemplo de su vida;
por su fiel obediencia, con la cual venció a la tentación;
por su muerte, con la que venció a la muerte;
y por su resurrección,
en la que somos *resucitados* a la vida de tu reino.

Danos el don de tu Espíritu,
para reconocer a Cristo y manifestarlo;
y que, por medio de él, te demos gracias en todo tiempo,
y todo lugar, y en todas las cosas. **Amén.**

2. Letanía de acción de gracias

*Para uso opcional en el Día de Acción de Gracias, en lugar de
las oraciones del pueblo en la Eucaristía, o en cualquier ocasión
después de las colectas de la Oración de la Mañana o del Atardecer o
separadamente.*

Let us give thanks to God our Father for all his gifts so freely bestowed upon us.

For the beauty and wonder of your creation, in earth and sky and sea,

We thank you, Lord.

For all that is gracious in the lives of men and women, revealing the image of Christ,

We thank you, Lord.

For our daily food and drink, our homes and families, and our friends,

We thank you, Lord.

For minds to think, and hearts to love, and hands to serve,

We thank you, Lord.

For health and strength to work, and leisure to rest and play,

We thank you, Lord.

For the brave and courageous, who are patient in suffering and faithful in adversity,

We thank you, Lord.

For all valiant seekers after truth, liberty, and justice,

We thank you, Lord.

For the communion of saints, in all times and places,

We thank you, Lord.

Above all, we give you thanks for the great mercies and promises given to us in Christ Jesus our Lord;

Demos gracias a Dios, nuestro Padre, por todos los dones que libremente nos ha dado.

Por la belleza y maravilla de tu creación, en tierra, cielo y mar,
Te damos gracias, Señor.

Por toda gracia presente en la vida de hombres y mujeres, que revela la imagen de Cristo,
Te damos gracias, Señor.

Por nuestro sustento diario, nuestros hogares, familias y amistades,
Te damos gracias, Señor.

Por mente para pensar, corazón para amar y manos para servir,
Te damos gracias, Señor.

Por la salud y el vigor para trabajar y el tiempo libre para descansar y jugar,
Te damos gracias, Señor.

Por personas esforzadas y valientes, pacientes en el sufrimiento y fieles en la adversidad,
Te damos gracias, Señor.

Por personas que trabajan por la verdad, la libertad y la justicia,
Te damos gracias, Señor.

Por la comunión de los santos y santas en todo tiempo y lugar,
Te damos gracias, Señor.

Sobre todo, te damos gracias por las grandes promesas y misericordias que nos has dado en Cristo Jesús nuestro Señor;

To him be praise and glory, with you, O Father, and the Holy Spirit, now and for ever. Amen.

Thanksgivings for the Church

3. For the Mission of the Church

Almighty God, you sent your Son Jesus Christ to reconcile the world to yourself: We praise and bless you for those whom you have sent in the power of the Spirit to preach the Gospel to all nations. We thank you that in all parts of the earth a community of love has been gathered together by their prayers and labors, and that in every place your servants call upon your Name; for the kingdom and the power and the glory are yours for ever. *Amen.*

4. For the Saints and Faithful Departed

We give thanks to you, O Lord our God, for all your servants and witnesses of time past: for Abraham, the father of believers, and Sarah his wife; for Moses, the lawgiver, and Aaron, the priest; for Miriam and Joshua, Deborah and Gideon, and Samuel with Hannah his mother; for Isaiah and all the prophets; for Mary, the mother of our Lord; for Peter and Paul and all the apostles; for Mary and Martha, and Mary Magdalene; for Stephen, the first martyr, and all the martyrs and saints in every age and in every land. In your mercy, O Lord our God, give us, as you gave to them, the hope of salvation and the promise of eternal life; through Jesus Christ our Lord, the first-born of many from the dead. *Amen.*

A él sea la alabanza y la gloria contigo, Padre, y el Espíritu Santo, ahora y siempre. Amén.

Acciones de gracias por la iglesia

3. *Por la misión de la iglesia*

Dios todopoderoso, que enviaste a tu Hijo Jesucristo
a reconciliar al mundo contigo:
Te alabamos y te bendecimos
por quienes has enviado en el poder del Espíritu
a proclamar el evangelio a todas las naciones.
Y te damos gracias porque en todas partes del mundo
se han reunido comunidades de amor
y por doquier tus *servidores*, mediante palabra y obra,
invocan tu santo nombre.
Tuyo es el reino, el poder y la gloria por siempre jamás.
Amén.

4. *Por* los santos *y fieles* difuntos

Te damos gracias, Dios nuestro,
por tus *servidores* y testigos de antaño:
por Abrahán, padre de los creyentes, y Sara su esposa;
por Moisés, dador de la ley, y Aarón, sacerdote;
por Miriam, profetisa, y Josué, Débora y Gedeón;
por Samuel y Ana, su madre;
por Isaías y *todos los* profetas;
por María, madre de nuestro Señor;
por Pedro y Pablo y *todos los* apóstoles;
por María y Marta, y María Magdalena;
por Esteban, el primer mártir,
y por mártires, santos y santas de todo tiempo y lugar.
Señor Dios nuestro, en tu piedad,
danos la misma esperanza de liberación
y la promesa de vida eterna;
por Jesucristo nuestro Señor,
el primogénito de entre los muertos. **Amén.**

Thanksgivings for National Life

5. *For the Nation*

Almighty God, giver of all good things:

We thank you for the natural majesty and beauty of this land. They restore us, though we often destroy them.

Heal us.

We thank you for the great resources of this nation. They make us rich, though we often exploit them.

Forgive us.

We thank you for the men and women who have made this country strong. They are models for us, though we often fall short of them.

Inspire us.

We thank you for the torch of liberty which has been lit in this land. It has drawn people from every nation, though we have often hidden from its light.

Enlighten us.

We thank you for the faith we have inherited in all its rich variety. It sustains our life, though we have been faithless again and again.

Renew us.

Help us, O Lord, to finish the good work here begun. Strengthen our efforts to blot out ignorance and prejudice, and to abolish poverty and crime. And hasten the day when all our people, with many voices in one united chorus, will glorify your holy Name. *Amen.*

Acciones de gracias por la vida nacional

5. *Por la nación*

Dios todopoderoso, dador de todo buen don: Te damos gracias por la majestad de la naturaleza y la belleza de esta tierra que nos restauran, aunque muchas veces las destruimos.

Sánanos.

Te damos gracias por los grandes recursos de esta nación que nos enriquecen, aunque muchas veces los abusamos.

Perdónanos.

Te damos gracias por hombres y mujeres que han hecho de este, un país fuerte, y que son nuestro ejemplo, aunque muchas veces no alcancemos su estatura.

Inspíranos.

Te damos gracias por la antorcha de la libertad encendida en esta tierra, que ha atraído personas de todas las naciones, aunque muchas veces nos escondemos de su luz.

Ilumínanos.

Te damos gracias por la fe que hemos heredado en toda su rica variedad y que sustenta nuestra vida, aunque hemos sido infieles una y otra vez.

Renuévanos.

Ayúdanos, Señor, a terminar la buena obra aquí comenzada; fortalece nuestros esfuerzos para extirpar la ignorancia y el prejuicio, y abolir la pobreza y el crimen; y apresura el día en que todo nuestro pueblo, unido en un coro de muchas voces, glorifique tu santo nombre. **Amén.**

6. *For Heroic Service*

O Judge of the nations, we remember before you with grateful hearts the men and women of our country who in the day of decision ventured much for the liberties we now enjoy. Grant that we may not rest until all the people of this land share the benefits of true freedom and gladly accept its disciplines. This we ask in the Name of Jesus Christ our Lord. *Amen.*

Thanksgiving for the Social Order

7. *For the Diversity of Races and Cultures*

O God, who created all peoples in your image, we thank you for the wonderful diversity of races and cultures in this world. Enrich our lives by ever-widening circles of fellowship, and show us your presence in those who differ most from us, until our knowledge of your love is made perfect in our love for all your children; through Jesus Christ our Lord. *Amen.*

Thanksgivings for the Natural Order

8. *For the Beauty of the Earth*

We give you thanks, most gracious God, for the beauty of earth and sky and sea; for the richness of mountains, plains, and rivers; for the songs of birds and the loveliness of flowers. We praise you for these good gifts, and pray that we may safeguard them for our posterity. Grant that we may continue to grow in our grateful enjoyment of your abundant creation, to the honor and glory of your Name, now and for ever. *Amen.*

6. Por los héroes *de la patria*

Juez de las naciones,
recordamos ante ti con agradecimiento
a hombres y mujeres de nuestra patria,
que en el día decisivo arriesgaron mucho
por las libertades que ahora gozamos.
No nos dejes descansar hasta que todo este país
comparta los beneficios de la auténtica libertad
y gozosamente acepte sus obligaciones.
Te lo pedimos en nombre de Jesucristo nuestro Señor.
Amén.

Acción de gracias por el orden social

7. Por la diversidad de pueblos y culturas

Dios, tú creaste a todos los pueblos a tu imagen: te damos
gracias por la maravillosa diversidad de culturas de este
mundo. Enriquece nuestras vidas con abundantes lazos de
comunidad, y muéstranos tu presencia en quienes parecen
más diferentes a *nosotros*, hasta que nuestro conocimiento de
tu amor se perfeccione en nuestro amor por todos tus hijos e
hijas; por Jesucristo nuestro Señor. **Amén.**

Acciones de gracias por la naturaleza

8. Por la belleza del planeta tierra

Padre bondadoso, te damos gracias
por la belleza de cielo, tierra y mar;
por la riqueza de las montañas, las llanuras y los ríos;
por el canto de los pájaros y la hermosura de las flores.
Te alabamos por todas estas buenas dádivas,
y te pedimos que las conservemos para nuestra posteridad.
Concede que continuemos creciendo
en el gozo agradecido de tu abundante creación,
para honra y gloria de tu nombre, ahora y siempre. **Amén.**

9. For the Harvest

Most gracious God, by whose knowledge the depths are broken up and the clouds drop down the dew: We yield thee hearty thanks and praise for the return of seedtime and harvest, for the increase of the ground and the gathering in of its fruits, and for all the other blessings of thy merciful providence bestowed upon this nation and people. And, we beseech thee, give us a just sense of these great mercies, such as may appear in our lives by a humble, holy, and obedient walking before thee all our days; through Jesus Christ our Lord, to whom, with thee and the Holy Ghost be all glory and honor, world without end. *Amen.*

Thanksgivings for Family and Personal Life

10. For the Gift of a Child

Heavenly Father, you sent your own Son into this world. We thank you for the life of this child, N., entrusted to our care. Help us to remember that we are all your children, and so to love and nurture *him*, that *he* may attain to that full stature intended for *him* in your eternal kingdom; for the sake of your dear Son, Jesus Christ our Lord. *Amen.*

11. For the Restoration of Health

Almighty God and heavenly Father, we give *thee* humble thanks because *thou hast* been graciously pleased to deliver from *his* sickness *thy* servant N., in whose behalf we bless and praise *thy* Name. Grant, O gracious Father, that *he*, through *thy* help, may live in this world according to *thy* will, and also be partaker of everlasting glory in the life to come; through Jesus Christ our Lord. *Amen.*

9. *Por las cosechas*

Dios bondadoso, por tu sabiduría
se abren los cielos y las nubes derraman el rocío;
te damos sinceras gracias y alabanza
por el retorno de la siembra,
la abundancia de la tierra, las cosechas
y toda bendición que tu bondadosa providencia
ha derramado sobre este pueblo y nación.
Otórganos que, al reconocer estos grandes favores,
se manifieste siempre en *nosotros*
una conducta humilde, santa y obediente ante ti;
por Jesucristo nuestro Señor,
a quien contigo y el Espíritu Santo
sea todo honor y gloria, por los siglos de los siglos. **Amén.**

Acciones de gracias por la vida familiar y personal

10. *Por la dádiva de un niño o niña*

Padre amoroso,
que enviaste a tu propio Hijo a este mundo:
Te damos gracias por la vida de *este niño N.,*
que ha sido confiado a nuestro cuidado.
Ayúdanos a recordar que *todos* somos hijos e hijas tuyos,
y a *amarlo* y *criarlo* de modo que llegue a la plena estatura
que quieres para *él* en tu reino celestial;
por amor de tu amado Hijo, Jesucristo nuestro Señor.
Amén.

11. *Por la restauración de la salud*

Omnipotente Dios y Padre celestial,
te rendimos humildes gracias, bendiciones y alabanzas,
porque en tu bondad te has dignado
librar de su enfermedad a tu *siervo N.;*
concede, Padre generoso, que con tu ayuda
viva en este mundo según tu voluntad,
y en la vida venidera participe de la gloria eterna;
por Jesucristo nuestro Señor. **Amén.**

CPSIA information can be obtained
at www.ICGtesting.com
Printed in the USA
JSHW010808150523
41517JS00004B/4

9 781640 656116